DISCOVERING THE AMERICAN PAST

DISCOVERING THE AMERICAN PAST

A LOOK AT THE EVIDENCE

FOURTH EDITION

∽ VOLUME II: SINCE 1865 ∽

William Bruce Wheeler
University of Tennessee

Susan D. Becker
University of Tennessee

HOUGHTON MIFFLIN COMPANY   Boston   New York

Executive Editor: Patricia A. Coryell
Assistant Editor: Keith Mahoney
Senior Project Editor: Christina M. Horn
Senior Production/Design Coordinator: Jennifer Waddell
Manufacturing Manager: Florence Cadran
Marketing Manager: Sandra McGuire

Cover Design: Len Massiglia
Cover Image: *Brooklyn Bridge,* by Leigh Behnke, from the Collection of
Deloitte and Touche, N.Y.

CONTENTS

∽ CHAPTER ELEVEN ∽

Democracy and Diversity: Affirmative Action in California

PREFACE

Of all the books published on American history in 1997, one of the most interesting and controversial was Annette Gordon-Reed's *Thomas Jefferson and Sally Hemings: An American Controversy* (Charlottesville: University Press of Virginia, 1997). In the book, Gordon-Reed did not really attempt to answer the long-debated question of whether Thomas Jefferson did or did not have an extended, intimate relationship with Sally Hemings, one of his slaves. Instead, Gordon-Reed concentrated her attention on how a number of earlier historians who had examined this issue had—intentionally or unintentionally—distorted, misused, or occasionally even ignored key pieces of evidence. Gordon-Reed is an attorney and associate professor of law at New York University Law School. How, she asked, can we trust historians' accounts of the past unless we can see how they are using—or misusing—evidence?

Similarly, in the complex world in which we live, how can we rely on statements made by a president of the United States, any other world leader, the chairman of the Federal Reserve Board, a member of Congress, a radio talk show host, or a professor unless we are able to examine and analyze the available evidence to understand how it is being used? How can we ourselves learn to use evidence intelligently when we write a report, make a public address, or participate in a debate? The subject of this volume is American history, but the important skills of examination, analysis, and proper use of evidence are important to every person in every vocation.

In *Discovering the American Past: A Look at the Evidence,* we show students the importance of acquiring and sharpening these skills. Moreover, as they acquire or hone these skills, students generally discover that they enjoy "doing history," welcome the opportunity to become active learners, retain more historical knowledge, and are eager to solve a series of historical problems themselves rather than simply being told about the past. Unlike a source reader, this book prompts students actually to *analyze* a wide variety of authentic primary-source material, make inferences, and draw conclusions based on the available evidence, much in the same way that historians do.

As in previous editions, we try to expose students to the broad scope of the American experience by providing a mixture of types of historical problems and a balance among political, social, diplomatic, economic, intellectual, and cultural history. This wide variety of historical topics and events engages students' interest and rounds out their view of American history.

∽ FORMAT OF THE BOOK ∽

Historians are fully aware that everything that is preserved from the past can be used as evidence to solve historical problems. In that spirit, we have included as many different *types* of historical evidence as we could. Almost every chapter gives students the opportunity to work with a different type of evidence: works of art, first-person accounts, trial transcripts, statistics, maps, letters, charts, biographical sketches, court decisions, music lyrics, prescriptive literature, newspaper accounts, congressional debates, speeches, diaries, proclamations and laws, political cartoons, photographs, architectural plans, advertisements, posters, film reviews, fiction, memoirs, and oral interviews. In this book, then, we have created a kind of historical sampler that we believe will help students learn the methods and skills historians use, as well as help them learn historical content.

Each type of historical evidence is combined with an introduction to the appropriate methodology in an effort to teach students a wide variety of research skills. As much as possible, we have tried to let the evidence speak for itself and have avoided leading students to one particular interpretation or another. This approach is effective in many different classroom situations, including seminars, small classes, discussion sections, and large lecture classes. Indeed, we have found that the previous editions of *Discovering the American Past* have proven themselves equally stimulating and effective in very large classes as well as very small ones. An Instructor's Resource Manual that accompanies the book offers numerous suggestions on how *Discovering the American Past* can be used effectively in large classroom situations.

Each chapter is divided into six parts: The Problem, Background, The Method, The Evidence, Questions to Consider, and Epilogue. Each of the parts relates to or builds upon the others, creating a uniquely integrated chapter structure that helps guide the reader through the analytical process. "The Problem" section begins with a brief discussion of the central issues of the chapter and then states the questions students will explore. A "Background" section follows, designed to help students understand the historical context of the problem. The section called "The Method" gives students suggestions for studying and analyzing the evidence. "The Evidence" section is the heart of the chapter, providing a variety of primary source material on the particular historical event or issue described in the chapter's "Problem" section. The section called "Questions to Consider" focuses students' attention on specific evidence and on linkages among different evidence material. The "Epilogue" section gives the aftermath or the historical outcome of the evidence—what happened to the people involved, who won the election, the results of a debate, and so on.

❧ CHANGES IN THE FOURTH EDITION ❧

In response to student and faculty reactions, we have made significant alterations in the content of this edition. There are six new chapters, three in Volume I and three in Volume II.

In Volume I, Chapter 6 focuses on the removal of the Cherokees, using contemporary letters, speeches, essays, a message to Congress, and a petition to assess the historical alternatives that were available to President Andrew Jackson. Chapter 9 examines the rhetoric of the slavery question through a close analysis of excerpts from the U.S. Senate debates on the Compromise of 1850. The final new chapter in the first volume, Chapter 11, considers the difficult question of why President Andrew Johnson allowed so many former Confederates to vote while at the same time opposing suffrage for freedmen. A variety of sources, including letters, proclamations, and interviews, helps students to explain why Johnson acted in the way he did.

The three new chapters in Volume II begin with Chapter 8 and the controversial events surrounding the USS *Greer* and the coming of World War II. In this chapter, students are asked to determine what actually happened in the North Atlantic on that day and then to analyze President Franklin Roosevelt's actions in relation to public opinion. To answer these questions, students need to sort through and arrange evidence consisting of public opinion polls, news reports, and speeches. Our new focus in the postwar period is on African American civil rights and *Brown v. Board of Education of Topeka, Kansas* (1954). Through *amicus curiae* briefs, oral arguments of attorneys for both sides, and excerpts from the U.S. Supreme Court decision, students are asked to explain the reasoning that led to the reversal of the "separate but equal" doctrine in education. Lastly, Chapter 11 requires students to understand recent major demographic trends and to consider the changing meanings of the American ideal of equality as illustrated in a variety of evidence. Because of its diverse population and recent referendum on state affirmative action legislation, California provides a kind of "test case" that students can use to analyze current events.

∽ INSTRUCTOR'S RESOURCE MANUAL ∽

An Instructor's Resource Manual suggests ways that might be useful in guiding students through the evidence, provides answers to questions students often ask, and offers a variety of methods in which the students' learning may be evaluated. The manual also clarifies our teaching and learning objectives for each chapter. Indeed, many useful ideas have come from instructors who have used the first three editions of this book. For this edition, we have also updated the bibliographic suggestions for further reading in each chapter.

∽ ACKNOWLEDGMENTS ∽

We would like to thank all the students and instructors who have helped us in developing and refining our ideas. In addition to our colleagues across the United States, we would like to thank especially our colleagues at the University of Tennessee who offered suggestions and read chapter drafts. Stephen Ash, John R. Finger, Charles W. Johnson, and Jonathan G. Utley were particularly helpful. Jennifer Breeden, Penny Hamilton, and Kim Harrison helped in preparing the manuscript. At Houghton Mifflin, we are indebted to Keith Mahoney and Christina Horn for their editorial assistance. Finally, colleagues at other institutions who reviewed chapter drafts made significant contributions to this edition, and we would like to thank them for their generosity, both in time and in helpful ideas and specific suggestions:

Harriet Hyman Alonso, *Fitchburg State College*
Elizabeth Ansnes, *San Jose State University*
Regina Lee Blaszczyk, *Boston University*
Bill Cecil-Fronsman, *Washburn University*
Jonathan M. Chu, *University of Massachusetts—Boston*

Claudia Clark, *Central Michigan University*
Bruce Cohen, *Worcester State College*
Kari Frederickson, *University of Central Florida*
Connie Jones, *Tidewater Community College*
Gaylen Lewis, *Bakersfield College*
Dane Morrison, *Salem State College*
Robert C. Pierce, *Foothill College*
Kim Risedorph, *Nebraska Wesleyan University*
Susan Sessions Rugh, *Brigham Young University*
Margaret A. Spratt, *California University of Pennsylvania*
Lillian Taiz, *California State University, Los Angeles*
William Tanner, *Humboldt State University*
Tom Taylor, *Wittenberg University*
Bruce Way, *Tiffin University*
Lynn Y. Weiner, *Roosevelt University*

As with our three previous editions, we dedicate these volumes to all our colleagues who seek to offer a challenging and stimulating academic experience to their students, and to those students themselves, who make all our work worthwhile.

W. B. W.
S. D. B.

DISCOVERING THE
AMERICAN PAST

CHAPTER 1

THE PROBLEMS OF RECONSTRUCTION: ANDREW JOHNSON, CONGRESS, AND SOUTHERN SUFFRAGE

∽ THE PROBLEM ∽

After four years of bloody warfare, the end came quickly. On April 2, 1865, General Ulysses Grant's Army of the Potomac crashed through Confederate lines at Petersburg, Virginia, leaving the Confederate capital, Richmond, vulnerable. Confederate president Jefferson Davis's government scattered, while General Robert E. Lee, commander of the Army of Northern Virginia, tried to escape westward. But Lee was stopped near Appomattox Court House and on April 9 surrendered to his adversary in a modest farmhouse.[1] After accepting Lee's surrender, Grant told his troops, "The war is over. The rebels are our countrymen again."[2]

And yet Grant's promises were not so easily kept. With the end of the fighting, the North had to decide how it would deal with the South. On what terms would the southern states be allowed to take up their proper places in the Union? How should former Confederates be treated? And, most important, who should be allowed to vote in setting up state governments and electing people to state and national offices?

Five days after Lee's surrender at Appomattox, President Abraham Lincoln was shot while attending the theater (he died at 7:22 A.M. the next day, on April 15). The new president,

1. Confederate general Joseph E. Johnston's troops were still in the field, but they surrendered to Union general William Tecumseh Sherman at Durham Station, North Carolina, on April 26.

2. Bruce Catton, *Grant Takes Command* (Boston: Little, Brown, 1969), p. 468.

CHAPTER 1

THE PROBLEMS OF
RECONSTRUCTION:
ANDREW JOHNSON,
CONGRESS, AND
SOUTHERN
SUFFRAGE

Andrew Johnson of Tennessee, was faced with these crucially important questions. Earlier, he had said, "Treason must be made odious, and the traitors must be punished and impoverished," a sentence that he had used in many speeches, including his 1864 acceptance of the vice presidency.

Yet almost immediately after his assumption of the presidency, President Andrew Johnson changed course. At first appearing to side with Radical Republicans[3] in Congress, Johnson soon took a different path, granting numerous pardons to ex-Confederates (thus allowing them to reclaim their former property, hold office, and vote) and not supporting the right to vote for the freedmen. In his last public speech (April 11, 1865), Lincoln had endorsed a limited suffrage for African Americans, so Johnson could not claim to be merely following the policies of his predecessor.[4]

Your task in this chapter will not be an easy one. By examining and analyzing the evidence, determine why President Johnson chose the path he did with regard to who would vote in the postwar South. Why did he pardon so many former Confederates? Why did he oppose African American suffrage? Who should be allowed to vote in a free society, and who should determine the requirements for voting (residency, citizenship, property, literacy, etc.)? Most important, how would the United States secure its victory in the American Civil War?

∞ BACKGROUND ∞

From the outset of the Civil War, President Abraham Lincoln pursued a dual policy. On one hand, he attempted to crush the rebellion with armed might; on the other, he almost ceaselessly tried to get the South to give up its rebellion voluntarily and return to the Union.[5] Thus on September 22, 1862, he issued a Preliminary Emancipation Proclamation, promising that any southern states that gave up the struggle prior to January 1, 1863, would be allowed to take up their normal places in the Union with slavery intact. After that date, Lincoln warned, he would act to free the slaves in those states still in rebellion. It was an invitation that no Confederate state accepted. Thus, keeping his promise, Lincoln issued the Emanci-

3. The Radical Republicans were the left wing of the Republican party. They favored the abolition of slavery, a harsher policy against the defeated South, and full equality for African Americans.

4. On Lincoln's endorsement of limited African American suffrage, see Roy P. Basler, ed., *The Collected Works of Abraham Lincoln* (New Brunswick, N.J.: Rutgers University Press, 1953), Vol. VIII, pp. 399–405, esp. p. 403.

5. Lincoln continuously maintained that the southern states had not left the Union and had no right to secede, although he did admit that their normal relations with the rest of the states had been "suspended" or "disturbed"—hence the name "civil" war.

pation Proclamation on January 1, 1863.[6]

In a similar vein, on December 8, 1863, President Lincoln issued his Proclamation of Amnesty and Reconstruction. In it he set forth the way in which a state could resume normal relations within the Union. A lenient plan, it offered full pardon and restoration of all rights ("except as to slaves") to all persons who took an oath of loyalty to the Union and promised to accept emancipation, the lone exceptions being high-ranking civil and military officers of the Confederate government. When 10 percent of the number of people who had cast votes in the state in 1860 had taken the oath, a new state government could be established and the state was permitted to take its regular place in the Union. Nothing was said about black suffrage.[7] In July 1864, Radical Republicans in Congress passed a considerably harsher plan (the Wade-Davis bill), but Lincoln pocket-vetoed it.

All of these proclamations as well as other efforts were wartime measures designed to sap the Confederacy of white support by offering the mildest of surrender, amnesty, and reconstruction terms. Since President Lincoln was trying to lure white southerners away from their loyalty to the Confederacy while at the same time pursuing the war vigorously on the field, one would have been surprised had his terms been more stringent.

What the president's plans actually were, especially with regard to who would be able to vote in the postwar South, will never be known, for he died less than a week after Lee's surrender. His last public speech nevertheless hinted that he was moving toward embracing limited African American suffrage.

Although they outdid each other in oratorical eulogies to the fallen president, secretly Radical Republicans were not altogether displeased by Lincoln's death. For one thing, Lincoln could be used as a martyr for their own cause, which included building a Republican party in the South by disfranchising pro-Confederate whites and instituting African American suffrage. Surely this was the reason they tried to concoct the notion that Lincoln's assassination had been part of a pro-southern plot, behind which were former Confederate president Jefferson Davis and other leading "rebels." More important, however, was the Radical Republicans' belief that Andrew Johnson would be more sympathetic to their cause, which included a thorough reconstruction of the southern economy, society, and life. After all, hadn't Johnson been a harsh military governor of Tennessee (1862–1864) and hadn't he said many times that treason "must be made odious, and the traitors must be punished and impoverished"?[8] Black abolitionist Frederick Douglass had said that slavery "is not abolished until the black man has the ballot," and the American

6. For the Preliminary Emancipation Proclamation, see Basler, *Lincoln Works,* Vol. V, pp. 433–436. For the Emancipation Proclamation, see ibid., Vol. VI, pp. 28–30.
7. For the Proclamation of Amnesty and Reconstruction, see ibid., Vol. VII, pp. 53–56.

8. Johnson had included this phrase in many of his speeches, including his acceptance of the Union party's vice-presidential nomination in 1864.

CHAPTER 1

THE PROBLEMS OF
RECONSTRUCTION:
ANDREW JOHNSON,
CONGRESS, AND
SOUTHERN
SUFFRAGE

Anti-Slavery Society (with its new president, Wendell Phillips) took up the motto, "No Reconstruction Without Negro Suffrage."[9] Radical Republicans believed Johnson was more sympathetic to these entreaties than Lincoln had been.

And yet the Radical Republicans seriously misjudged President Andrew Johnson. Although many of his initial statements and speeches as president had given Radicals the impression that he supported a more thoroughgoing reconstruction of the South than Lincoln had (on the issue of African American suffrage, he told Radical Republican senator Charles Sumner that there was "no difference between us"),[10] by the end of May 1865, Radicals were increasingly alarmed that the president either had misled them or had changed his mind with regard to the reconstruction of the South.

Andrew Johnson was an exceedingly complex individual—virtually a bundle of contradictions. Born to a very poor family in Raleigh, North Carolina, in 1808 (his father was a janitor, and his mother worked as a servant in a local inn), young Andrew was bound out as an apprentice to learn the tailor's trade. Moving to Greeneville, Tennessee, in 1826, Johnson married the daughter of a shoemaker, became comparatively well off by speculating in real estate, and discovered a taste for politics. Elected as a Greeneville

alderman in 1829, he worked his way up the Democratic party political ladder: mayor, state representative, state senator, U.S. congressman, governor of Tennessee, and U.S. senator. His political power base was the white yeoman farmer, and for years he fought against Tennessee's planter aristocracy, which on one occasion he had called an "illegitimate, swaggering, bastard, scrub aristocracy."[11] Yet at the same time he defended the institution of slavery and in the 1840s delivered a speech in Congress in which he stated that the "black race of Africa were inferior to the white man in point of intellect—better calculated in physical structure to undergo drudgery and hardship."[12]

Johnson had harbored presidential ambitions as early as 1852. When the Democratic convention met in Charleston in 1860, he hoped that he would emerge as a compromise candidate and secure the party's nomination. The convention, however, broke up without nominating a candidate; delegates from the lower South walked out when a platform guaranteeing federal protection of slavery in the territories was rejected. When the convention reconvened in Baltimore, Johnson hoped he would secure the vice-presidential nomination behind Illinois senator Stephen Douglas, but he withdrew his name when that prospect appeared unlikely. During the 1860 campaign, Johnson supported

9. William Lloyd Garrison had resigned the presidency of the society at the end of the Civil War.
10. See Sumner to Wendell Phillips, May 1, 1865, in Beverly Wilson Palmer, ed., *The Selected Letters of Charles Sumner* (Boston: Northeastern University Press, 1990), Vol. II, p. 298.

11. See Hans L. Trefousse, *Andrew Johnson, A Biography* (New York: W. W. Norton, 1989), p. 64.
12. *Congressional Globe,* 28th Cong., 1st sess., 1843–1844, appendix 95–98.

southern Democrat John C. Breckinridge.

When senators from the seceding states walked out of Congress in 1861, Johnson was the only southern senator who refused to leave; he continued to occupy a seat until Lincoln appointed him military governor of Tennessee on March 3, 1862. By late August 1863, he had reversed his position on emancipation, energetically aided in the recruitment of twenty thousand African American soldiers for the Union army, and later promised blacks, "I will indeed be your Moses, and lead you through the Red Sea of war and bondage to a fairer future of liberty and peace."[13] Thus, when Lincoln was looking for a "War Democrat" to balance the Union party's ticket in 1864 (to replace Vice President Hannibal Hamlin, who wanted to return to the Senate), his eyes almost naturally fell on Andrew Johnson.[14]

As noted earlier, Andrew Johnson was a bundle of contradictions. A man who never joined any religious denomination and was referred to by some of his enemies as an "infidel," in 1855 he defended Roman Catholics against the Know-Nothings and in 1858 opposed the use of federal troops against the Mormons in Utah. An opponent of government spending, he tried to get the federal government to take over and maintain the Hermitage, Andrew Jackson's home. A defender of slavery (until mid-1863), he opposed, at the same time, the Constitution's three-fifths clause.[15] A man who made a large amount of money in real estate, he pioneered a bill that would have given federal land to prospective farmers decades before its ultimate passage (the Homestead Act of 1862). It is little wonder that Radical Republicans had misgauged the new president. Not only was Johnson a wily politician who often told people what they wanted to hear, but he also was as erratic, unpredictable, and inconsistent as almost any other political figure in modern American history.

Your task in this chapter will be to explain the behavior of this immensely complex man with regard to suffrage in the postwar South. If Johnson had made a political career battling against the South's plantation aristocracy and had fought so viciously against the Confederacy, why did he pardon so many former rebels, thus allowing them to vote and hold office? Of the approximately fifteen thousand white southerners who applied for pardons, over seven thousand had been granted by 1866. If Johnson had promised to be a "Moses" to African Americans and had told Massachusetts senator Charles Sumner that "there is no difference between us," why did he not press the states of the former Confederacy—or even states in the North—to approve suffrage for blacks? Who should be allowed to vote in a free society? Who should set voting requirements? How would the United States secure its victory in the American Civil War?

13. For Johnson's 1864 "Moses" speech, see LeRoy P. Graf, ed., *The Papers of Andrew Johnson* (Knoxville: University of Tennessee Press, 1986), Vol. VII, pp. 251–253.
14. For the 1864 election, the Republicans renamed themselves the Union party.

15. See U.S. Constitution, Article I, Section 3.

CHAPTER 1

THE PROBLEMS OF
RECONSTRUCTION:
ANDREW JOHNSON,
CONGRESS, AND
SOUTHERN
SUFFRAGE

⚭ THE METHOD ⚭

Unlike other presidents (James K. Polk, for example), Andrew Johnson did not keep a diary, nor did he write many letters to his friends.[16] Therefore, we have no private letters that can answer the question of Johnson's motivation. Thus, we will have to infer, from Johnson's speeches, interviews, and letters to him, what caused him to take the path that he did.

Begin by reviewing the situation when Johnson became president on April 15, 1865. Union armies occupied parts of the South; principal Confederate officeholders and military leaders were being rounded up and imprisoned; African Americans had been freed and in many cases were abandoning the plantations and heading for southern cities and towns in search of employment. Southern cities like Petersburg, Richmond, Atlanta, and Columbia had been totally or partially destroyed, and the vast majority of white southerners agreed with Georgian Herschel V. Walker when he wrote that the "people are soul-sick and heartily tired of the hateful, hopeless strife" and wanted only to resume their former lives in peace. Indeed, the South was crushed and prostrate; it would have to accept almost any plan for its reconstruction that the federal government demanded.

16. For example, the Thomas Jefferson papers (being published by Princeton University), when finished, may exceed seventy-five volumes. Johnson's papers (published by the University of Tennessee Press) will be completed in sixteen to seventeen volumes. And in Volume VIII of the *Johnson Papers* (which ʋvers May–August 1865), of the 815 items, ly 87 are by Johnson, the rest being letters, morials, petitions, and other items to him.

Recall also, however, that Johnson was a Democrat who was now at the head of a Republican administration. Did his political future lie with the Republicans or the Democrats? Too, Republicans must have realized that a quick restoration of the South (whose white voters were mostly Democrats) to its normal place in the Union could jeopardize their own political position. Could enfranchised blacks provide the foundation of a Republican party in the South? In addition, it was still not clear that Lincoln's assassination had not been part of a massive southern conspiracy. Would northerners want the South to "pay" for Lincoln's death?

Finally, Congress was not in session when Lincoln was assassinated and would not convene in regular session until December 1865. If Johnson wanted to restore all the southern states to their proper places in the Union and if he knew that his own terms were dramatically different from those of Congress, then he would have to hurry. Believing, as did Lincoln, that the president had the authority to do this (under Article IV, Section 4 of the Constitution, guaranteeing each state a republican form of government), Johnson had no time to waste. State governments would have to be reorganized, new state constitutions written, requirements for voting decided on, and state and federal elections held using those suffrage requirements.

As you examine each piece of evidence, make a note of what that piece might be telling you about why Johnson chose to adopt a lenient policy of reconstruction—pardoning numerous former Confederates and not insisting (when he certainly had the opportunity) that southern states enfranchise the freedmen. Very few pieces of evidence explicitly state a possible motivation that would explain Johnson's actions. Instead, you will have to use your historical imagination to infer what that motivation might have been.

Very quickly you will see that the evidence points you in many different directions, offering the possibility of not one single motive but several. Use your knowledge of Johnson's background, the man himself, and the situation he faced to conclude which motive was the *most likely,* the most plausible. Determining why certain individuals in the past behaved in the ways they did is the most difficult and hazardous task that historians do. And yet it is something they must do nearly every day in order to make the past understandable to themselves and to others.

In the evidence, spelling and punctuation have been left unaltered from the original text.

∞ THE EVIDENCE ∞

Sources 1–7 and 9–14 from Paul H. Bergeron, ed., *The Papers of Andrew Johnson* (Knoxville: University of Tennessee Press, 1989–1992), Vol. VIII, pp. 62–63, 119, 129–130, 136–137, 188, 282, 289–290, 365, 378, 516–523, 599–600; Vol. IX, pp. 179–180; Vol. X, pp. 43–47.

1. Johnson's Reply to a Delegation of African American Clergymen, May 11, 1865.

I was the first that stood in a slave community and announced the great fact that the slaves of Tennessee were free upon the same principle as those were who assumed to own them.

I know it is easy to talk and proclaim sentiments upon paper, but it is one thing to have theories and another to reduce them to practice; and I must say here, what I have no doubt is permanently fixed in your minds, and the impression deep, that there is one thing you ought to teach, and they should understand, that in a transition state, passing from bond to free, when the tyrant's rod has been bent and the yoke broken, we find too many—it is best to talk plain—there are, I say, too many in this transition state, passing from bondage to freedom, who feel as if they should have nothing to do, and fall back upon the Government for support; too many incline to become loafers and depend upon the Government to take care of them. They seem to think that with freedom every thing they need is to come like manna from heaven.

CHAPTER 1

THE PROBLEMS OF
RECONSTRUCTION:
ANDREW JOHNSON,
CONGRESS, AND
SOUTHERN
SUFFRAGE

Now, I want to impress this upon your minds, that freedom simply means liberty to work and enjoy the product of your own hands. This is the correct definition of freedom, in the most extensive sense of the term. . . .

[*Johnson then told the ministers that they must quickly perform marriage ceremonies for ex-slaves who had not been formally married.*]

It is not necessary for me to give you any assurance of what my future course will be in reference to your condition. Now, when the ordeal is passed, there can be no reason to think that I shall turn back in the great cause in which I have sacrificed much, and perilled all.

I can give you no assurance worth more than my course heretofore, and I shall continue to do all that I can for the elevation and amelioration of your condition; and I trust in God the time may soon come when you shall be gathered together, in a clime and country suited to you, should it be found that the two races cannot get along together.

I trust God will continue to conduct us till the great end shall be accomplished, and the work reach its great consummation. . . .

2. Joseph Noxon[17] to Johnson, May 27, 1865.

Andrew Johnson Prest.

You say you believe in democratic government, or *consent* of loyal people. Yet you *dare not* avow with practical effect the right of the colord man to vote. Are you honest?

You profess to protect loyal men & to punish traitors; yet you *refuse* the franchise to loyal colord people, the *only* means effectual for their protection or advancement. Are you honest?

You know rebels disappointed will wreak revenge on loyal blacks, & yet you refuse the franchise for their protection.

You say you have no right to grant it. You know in the first elections to be held to reorganize a seceded state *you* have the *power,* the *right,* & the *duty* to say who shall vote. Otherwise rebels will re-elect rebels, as witness Virginia.

You know by *prompt* & vigorous action *now,* the question of negro suffrage can be *settled* & *accepted* by the people as an *accomplished fact.* Why not settle it & take it *out* of political controversy.

17. Joseph Noxon was a Tennessee Unionist who was driven out of the state by Confederates for being a scout for the Union army. He was an ally of Johnson.

Do you believe the *loyal* Union party's success essential to the peace & prosperity of this country? Then dont refuse 850,000 *loyal votes* that are *always sure* for liberty & the Republic.

3. Amnesty Proclamation, May 29, 1865.

To the end, therefore, that the authority of the government of the United States may be restored, and that peace, order, and freedom may be established, I, ANDREW JOHNSON, President of the United States, do proclaim and declare that I hereby grant to all persons who have, directly or indirectly, participated in the existing rebellion, except as hereinafter excepted, amnesty and pardon, with restoration of all rights of property, except as to slaves, and except in cases where legal proceedings, under the laws of the United States providing for the confiscation of property of persons engaged in rebellion, have been instituted; but upon the condition, nevertheless, that every such person shall take and subscribe the following oath, (or affirmation,) and thenceforward keep and maintain said oath inviolate; and which oath shall be registered for permanent preservation, and shall be of the tenor and effect following, to wit:

I, _____ _____, do solemnly swear, (or affirm,) in presence of Almighty God, that I will henceforth faithfully support, protect, and defend the Constitution of the United States, and the union of the States thereunder; and that I will, in like manner, abide by, and faithfully support all laws and proclamations which have been made during the existing rebellion with reference to the emancipation of slaves. So help me God.

The following classes of persons are excepted from the benefits of this proclamation: 1st, all who are or shall have been pretended civil or diplomatic officers or otherwise domestic or foreign agents of the pretended Confederate government; 2d, all who left judicial stations under the United States to aid the rebellion; 3d, all who shall have been military or naval officers of said pretended Confederate government above the rank of colonel in the army or lieutenant in the navy; 4th, all who left seats in the Congress of the United States to aid the rebellion; 5th, all who resigned or tendered resignations of their commissions in the army or navy of the United States to evade duty in resisting the rebellion; 6th, all who have engaged in any way in treating otherwise than lawfully as prisoners of war persons found in the United States service, as officers, soldiers, seamen, or in other capacities; 7th, all persons who have been, or are absentees from the United

CHAPTER 1

THE PROBLEMS OF
RECONSTRUCTION:
ANDREW JOHNSON,
CONGRESS, AND
SOUTHERN
SUFFRAGE

States for the purpose of aiding the rebellion; 8th, all military and naval officers in the rebel service, who were educated by the government in the Military Academy at West Point or the United States Naval Academy; 9th, all persons who held the pretended offices of governors of States in insurrection against the United States; 10th, all persons who left their homes within the jurisdiction and protection of the United States, and passed beyond the Federal military lines into the pretended Confederate States for the purpose of aiding the rebellion; 11th, all persons who have been engaged in the destruction of the commerce of the United States upon the high seas, and all persons who have made raids into the United States from Canada, or been engaged in destroying the commerce of the United States upon the lakes and rivers that separate the British Provinces from the United States; 12th, all persons who, at the time when they seek to obtain the benefits hereof by taking the oath herein prescribed, are in military, naval, or civil confinement, or custody, or under bonds of the civil, military, or naval authorities, or agents of the United States as prisoners of war, or persons detained for offences of any kind, either before or after conviction; 13th, all persons who have voluntarily participated in said rebellion, and the estimated value of whose taxable property is over twenty thousand dollars; 14th, all persons who have taken the oath of amnesty as prescribed in the President's proclamation of December 8th, A.D. 1863, or an oath of allegiance to the government of the United States since the date of said proclamation, and who have not thenceforward kept and maintained the same inviolate. . . .

4. Proclamation Establishing Government for North Carolina, May 29, 1865.

Whereas the 4th section of the 4th article of the Constitution of the United States declares that the United States shall guarantee to every State in the Union a republican form of government, and shall protect each of them against invasion and domestic violence; and whereas the President of the United States is, by the Constitution, made Commander-in-chief of the army and navy, as well as chief civil executive officer of the United States, and is bound by solemn oath faithfully to execute the office of President of the United States, and to take care that the laws be faithfully executed; and whereas the rebellion, which has been waged by a portion of the people of the United States against the properly constituted authorities of the government thereof, in the most violent and revolting form, but whose organized and armed forces have now been almost entirely overcome, has, in its revolutionary progress, deprived the people of the State of North Carolina of all civil government; and whereas it becomes necessary and proper to carry out and enforce the obligations of the United States to the people of North Carolina, in securing them in the enjoyment of a republican form of government:

Now, THEREFORE, in obedience to the high and solemn duties imposed upon me by the Constitution of the United States, and for the purpose of enabling the loyal people of said State to organize a State government, whereby justice may be established, domestic tranquillity insured, and loyal citizens protected in all their rights of life, liberty, and property, I, ANDREW JOHNSON, President of the United States, and commander-in-chief of the army and navy of the United States, do hereby appoint WILLIAM W. HOLDEN provisional governor of the State of North Carolina, whose duty it shall be, at the earliest practicable period, to prescribe such rules and regulations as may be necessary and proper for convening a convention, composed of delegates to be chosen by that portion of the people of said State who are loyal to the United States, and no others, for the purpose of altering or amending the constitution thereof; and with authority to exercise, within the limits of said State, all the powers necessary and proper to enable such loyal people of the State of North Carolina to restore said State to its constitutional relations to the Federal government, and to present such a republican form of State government as will entitle the State to the guarantee of the United States therefor, and its people to protection by the United States against invasion, insurrection, and domestic violence; *provided* that, in any election that may be hereafter held for choosing delegates to any State convention as aforesaid, no person shall be qualified as an elector, or shall be eligible as a member of such convention, unless he shall have previously taken and subscribed the oath of amnesty, as set forth in the President's proclamation of May 29, A.D. 1865, and is a voter qualified as prescribed by the constitution and laws of the State of North Carolina in force immediately before the 20th day of May, A.D. 1861, the date of the so-called ordinance of secession; and the said convention, when convened, or the legislature that may be thereafter assembled, will prescribe the qualification of electors, and the eligibility of persons to hold office under the constitution and laws of the State, a power the people of the several States composing the Federal Union have rightfully exercised from the origin of the government to the present time. . . .

CHAPTER 1

THE PROBLEMS OF
RECONSTRUCTION:
ANDREW JOHNSON,
CONGRESS, AND
SOUTHERN
SUFFRAGE

5. James B. Bingham to Johnson, June 6, 1865.

Memphis, Tenn., June 6, 1865.

Dear Governor:[18]

I have only time to congratulate you. Thus far every thing goes right. Your amnesty gives satisfaction to all fair-minded men, and you have struck the true keynote on reconstruction. Your position on the question of negro suffrage is impregnable. It belongs, under the constitution to the States. Wendell Phillips, Greeley & Chase[19] will kick against that in vain. The country will sustain you. I find a great re-action going on in your favor. Fellows who used to curse and damn you begin now to talk sweet about you, and to do you justice. Lincoln never was as popular with Tennesseans as you are to-day; and I believe what is true of Tennesseans is equally so of the people of the loyal States.

6. Interview with a Delegation of South Carolina Former Confederates, June 24, 1865.

. . . I will again say to you that slavery is gone. Its status is changed. There is no hope you can entertain of being admitted to representation either in the Senate or House of Representatives till you give evidence that you, too, have accepted and recognized that that institution is gone. That done, the policy adopted is not to restore the supremacy of the Government at the point of the bayonet, but by the action of the people. While this rebellion has emancipated a great many negroes, it has emancipated still more white men. The negro in South Carolina that belonged to a man that owned from one to five hundred slaves, thought himself better than the white man who owned none. He felt the white man's superior. I know the position of the poor white man in the South, compelled to till the barren, sandy, and—poor soil for a subsistence. You cannot deny how he was, in your eyes, of less value than the negro. Some here in the North think they can control and exercise a greater influence over the negro than you can, though his future must materially depend on you. Let us speak plainly on this subject. I, too am a Southern man, have owned slaves, bought slaves, but never sold one.

---

18. Bingham, a fellow Tennessean, was addressing Johnson as the former governor of Tennessee.
19. Phillips was the president of the American Anti-Slavery Society, Horace Greeley was the editor of the *New York Tribune* and a noted abolitionist, and Salmon P. Chase was chief justice of the United States and a prominent Radical Republican.

You and I understand this better; we know our friends are mistaken, [here the President rose up and continued emphatically,] and I tell you that I don't want you to have the control of these negro votes against the vote of this poor white man. I repeat our friends here are mistaken, as you and I know as to where the control of negro vote would fall. When they come to talk about the elective franchise, I say let each State judge for itself. I am for free government; for emancipation; and am for emancipating the white man as well as the black man. . . .

7. Duff Green to Johnson, June 25, 1865.[20]

Confidential
To His Ex Andrew Johnson
President U States

You are now in a Situation Calling for the Sympathy and Support of your friends, for no one in your position, with a proper regard for his reputation, can be indifferent to the opinion of his Country men and that opinion will be indicated by the Election in 1868.

That extraordinary efforts will be made to organise an unscrupulous opposition to your administration and to your Election in 1868 you cannot doubt. That Chase or Sherman[21] or both will be opposing Candidates is clearly indicated, and that the vote of the South will control the Election in your favor, if you act wisely is to me now manifest.

The democracy of the north look to the South to reinstate them in power. If you identify yourself with the ultra abolitionists, in thier [sic] warfare on the South, then the democracy will rally on Sherman, and, aided as he will be by his brother's influence in Ohio, he will carry the conservative Whigs and organise the North West & the South against New England. If you so act, towards the South, as to command thier [sic] Confidence and Support you will carry the democratic party and unite the North West & the South in your support and Secure an overwhelming majority.

Do you ask what the South want? They desire to be reinstated as loyal, patriotic members of the Union. They want your proclamation restoring the people of the South to thier [sic] rights as loyal citizens and to thier [sic] rights of property.

20. Duff Green (1791–1875) was a journalist, businessman, and politician. He was a member of Andrew Jackson's Kitchen Cabinet, continued to be influential throughout the antebellum period, and supported the Confederacy during the Civil War.
21. Chief Justice Salmon Chase and General William Tecumseh Sherman, both rumored to have been presidential aspirants.

CHAPTER 1

THE PROBLEMS OF
RECONSTRUCTION:
ANDREW JOHNSON,
CONGRESS, AND
SOUTHERN
SUFFRAGE

Let the fourth day of July be a day of Jubilee. Throw wide open the prison doors. Send home the Captives to thier [sic] anxious friends at the public expense. Recal the Exiles and rest assured that there will be one unanimous loyal grateful response throughout the South and that no one can compete with you for thier [sic] confidence or Support. I would make no exceptions among those who are guilty of political offences only. No not one. But if exceptions are made they should be few. I would be glad to see and converse with you but will not obtrude.

Your Sincere freind [sic] Duff Green

Source 8 from Beverly Wilson Palmer, ed., *The Selected Letters of Charles Sumner* (Boston: Northeastern University Press, 1990), Vol. II, pp. 312–313.

8. Charles Sumner[22] to Salmon P. Chase,[23] July 1, 1865.

There is madness in the Presdt.—His policy is already dividing the party & drawing the praises of the copperheads. Of course, if he perseveres he will become the temporary head of the latter, to be cast aside at the proper moment.

The people were ready to accept the true principle. Never before were they so ready. Business-men see how clearly their welfare is associated with its establishment.

The Blairs have triumphed.[24] I see their influence, not only here but in other things. When I left Washington Mr Johnson had assured me that on this question "there was no difference between us."

He has appointed Carl Schurtz [Schurz][25] to visit the rebel states & report on the reconstruction policy & has said that, if the present policy did not work well, he was ready to change it. Alas! that the country should be subjected to this uncertainty, where from the beginning our rulers ought to have been clear & positive.

22. Charles Sumner (1811–1874) was a U.S. senator from Massachusetts and a leader of the Radical Republicans in the Senate.
23. Salmon P. Chase (1808–1873) was chief justice of the United States and a Radical Republican.
24. Francis Preston Blair and his son Montgomery Blair, of Maryland, were political intimates of Johnson who believed that southern whites should decide who should vote in the southern states. See Source 14 on page 23.
25. Carl Schurz (1829–1906) was a Union veteran, a journalist, and an advocate of enfranchisement for blacks.

9. Thaddeus Stevens to Johnson, July 6, 1865.[26]

His Excellency Andrew Johnson
Sir

I am sure you will pardon me for speaking to you with a candor to which men in high places are seldom accustomed. Among all the leading Union men of the North with whom I have had intercourse I do not find one who approves of your policy. They believe that "restoration" as announced by you will destroy our party (which is of but little consequence) and will greatly injure the country. Can you not hold your hand and wait the action of Congress and in the mean time govern them by military rulers? Profuse pardoning also will greatly embarrass Congress if they should wish to make the enemy pay the expenses of the war or a part of it.

10. Francis Preston Blair[27] to Johnson, August 1, 1865.

The rebellion is crushed and with it the Slavery that animated it, but like the Hydra it puts out new heads—from the vines of the old trunk. It sprouts out with the bold front of negro equality. Negro suffrage shouts out on one side with a political aspect and on the other we have the social aspect to emerge in the shape of amalgamation. What can come of this adulturation of our Anglo-Saxon race and Anglo-Saxon Government by Africanization, but the degradation of the free spirit & lofty aspirations which our race inherited from their ancestry and brought to this continent; and turn that whole portion of it engaged as manual Operatives into that class of mongrels which cannot but spring from the unnatural blending of the blacks & whites in one common class of laborers and giving to both an assimilation through that color, which has unhappily marked servitude during all generations from the days of Ham.[28] The result would inevitably be to make a distinction in caste and put a brand on all our race associated in employment with people of color & crisped hair. It would not create equality between those thus associated and those engaged in professional & political

26. Thaddeus Stevens (1792–1868) was a U.S. senator from Pennsylvania and one of the leading Radical Republicans.
27. Francis Preston Blair (1821–1875), a native of Kentucky, was an opponent of slavery, a brigadier general in the Union army, and was opposed to the enfranchisement of the freedmen.
28. A reference to the commonly held belief at the time that Ham, the disgraced and banished son of Noah, was the father of the Negro race. See Genesis 9:21–25.

CHAPTER 1

THE PROBLEMS OF
RECONSTRUCTION:
ANDREW JOHNSON,
CONGRESS, AND
SOUTHERN
SUFFRAGE

pursuits. It would hasten the creation of a lower order—a serfdom—a foundation for an Aristocracy crowned with Royalty. . . .

The idea that suffrage will produce equality between the two races at the South is illusory. The black freedmen will find the prejudices of caste increased among the mass of white laborers by the new priviledge. They will become competitors with the superior race in that which touches their pride and it will be found more than was necessary to get under the wing of the master who hires them, for protection. They will be obliged to have white leaders at the polls as they had in the camps of both armies & those who hire them will control their ballot more absolutely than has ever been done by persons occupying similar relations because their safety will depend upon their employers in the exercise of their priviledge in the service of an increased prejudice & more powerful caste. It is absurd to suppose that the rich, educated, intelligent men will not command the suffrages of their negro hirelings if they venture to bring them to the polls to assert equality with the whites. . . .

The result of the contact of races marked by nature to be distinct has induced all the great statesmen of our country to look to colonization & segregation as the means of saving the colored race & giving to them a Government of their own & with it the equality and independence they desire & deserve. The party who oppose this scheme, (yours as well as your predecessors), have no expectation of maintaining equality for the emancipated by suffrage. They assert it for them, some with a view to drive the whites from the Gulf States—others with the design of keeping those States out of the Union. To vote their members of congress out because those States refuse to obey the behests of other States as to the regulation of the right of suffrage, committed to them by the constitution, is to vote a dissolution of the Union—a subversion of the constitution. The pretense of establishing negro equality in a country which is compelled by the fist of the central Government to submit its suffrage to its control, makes the idea of equality with the arbitrary power asserting this superiority, absolutely absurd. If the Representatives of a state in one section are expelled because it does not surrender its constitutional rights, may not a state in another section be expelled because it will not surrender some of its rights at the dictation of a majority in congress? Why not expell the representatives from California & Oregon for refusing the suffrage to the Chinese & the whole group of the North eastern States for refusing it to free negroes? This movement against the south has its motive in the ambition which prompted Mr. Chase to say at the beginning of the rebellion, "Let the Seceding States go, they are not worth fighting for." . . .

The motions of the coming elections are felt already in the great States of New York Ohio & Pennsylvania. The Democracy which gave such immense votes against Lincoln during a war that commanded even their approval at heart, are now in favor of all the objects you design to accomplish by it. You indeed make it their war by the consequences you bring from it, and those men who now seek to pervert those consequences into a defeat of the restoration of the Union, with equality among the States, deserve to forfeit the favor they gained by giving the war their countenance. The Democrats will nominate candidates pledged to support all your leading policy. Their opponents are already out in Massachusetts and other states with manifestos not only at war with your avowed policy but abhorent to the constitution & tending to make Congress a revolutionary club—a convention of northern representatives bent on subjecting the south to their will and using negro enfranchisement as the means of the disfranchisement of our white brethren of that section, of their equality as citizens and states in the Union. . . .

This is your mission at this moment on entering the new Era of our history and let me entreat you to open the process of the new elections and of the creation of new parties in the approaching Congress with a new Cabinet strongly imbued with your opinions, entirely worthy of your confidence and of a caste calculated to win the confidence of men of all parties, who are willing to embrace the scheme of restoration to which you commit your administration in the nomination of the heads of its Departments.

The Democracy, I learn, north and South will make its nominations for National & State Representatives & for other functionaries of men of the type to which I have Just referred. The Republicans will be divided in their nominations, a portion going for the scheme of the Faneuil Hall manifesto derived from the movement which took the shape of the bill passed & presented to the President at the last congress to defeat his plan of re-Union.[29] If you declare your design to the nation by the creation of a new cabinet to express & to execute it distinctly & patently, the party opposed to it who would go to the people & come into congress as the friends of the administration, but really to defeat its policy, will I believe be reduced to a faction. But if you allow them to proceed under the shadow of a great party name, & under prestige already acquired by them of swaying the Cabinet they will command in Congress as at the last session & through it may

29. On June 21, 1865, Republicans met at Faneuil Hall in Boston and endorsed African American suffrage.

CHAPTER 1

THE PROBLEMS OF
RECONSTRUCTION:
ANDREW JOHNSON,
CONGRESS, AND
SOUTHERN
SUFFRAGE

command the country unless overthrown by the Democracy which will take a stand against it and the Rump Cabinet. . . .

If however you were at once to make a new Cabinet drawn from the different sections of the country and representing the various parties in it, yet agreeing to support your plan of reconstruction, on an issue so essential, it would be no matter what party organization returned members, men who gave in this adhesion would become identified with the administration. Their election would be your success and in this epoch of reconstruction would create a new party, embracing the whole Union, adverse to that of Faneuil Hall limited to a northern latitude and exulting in a revolutionary creed. . . .

The vote of the south will be drawn almost as an unit to the side of that party which it finds in opposition to a ministry known to be hostile to its dearest rights in the Union & confederated with the scheme promulgated at Faneuil Hall, which would deprive its *States* of equality *as States,* would create a war of caste & a war of Sections a war of factions breaking up the ancient foundations of the constitution. . . .

11. Johnson to Mississippi Provisional Governor William L. Sharkey, August 15, 1865.

Governor William L. Sharkey,
Jackson, Miss.

I am gratified to see that you have organized your Convention without difficulty. I hope that without delay your Convention will amend your State Constitution abolishing slavery, and denying to all future legislatures the power to legislate that there is property in man—Also that they will adopt the Amendment to the Constitution of the United States abolishing slavery.

If you could extend the elective franchise to all persons of color who can read the constitution of the United States in English and write their names, and to all persons of color who own real estate valued at not less than two-hundred and fifty dollars and pay taxes thereon, you would completely disarm the adversary and set an example the other States will follow.

This you can do with perfect safety, and you thus place the Southern States, in reference to free persons of color, upon the same basis with the Free States. I hope and trust your convention will do this, and as a consequence the Radicals, who are wild upon negro franchise, will be completely foiled in their attempts to keep the Southern States from renewing their relations to the Union by not accepting their Senators and Representatives.

12. Johnson's Interview with George L. Stearns, October 3, 1865.

[Johnson]: We must not be in too much of a hurry; it is better to let them [white southerners] reconstruct themselves than to force them to it; for if they go wrong, the power is in our hands and we can check them at any stage, to the end, and oblige them to correct their errors; we must be patient with them. I did not expect to keep out all who were excluded from the amnesty, or even a large number of them, but I intended they should sue for pardon, and so realize the enormity of the crime they had committed.

You could not have broached the subject of equal suffrage, at the North, seven years ago, and we must remember that the changes at the South have been more rapid, and they have been obliged to accept more unpalatable truth than the North has; we must give them time to digest a part, for we cannot expect such large affairs will be comprehended and digested at once. We must give them time to understand their new position.

I have nothing to conceal in these matters, and have no desire or willingness to take indirect courses to obtain what we want.

Our government is a grand and lofty structure; in searching for its foundation we find it rests on the broad basis of popular rights. The elective franchise is not a natural right, but a political right. I am opposed to giving the States too much power, and also to a great consolidation of power in the central government.

If I interfered with the vote in the rebel States, to dictate that the negro shall vote, I might do the same thing for my own purposes in Pennsylvania. Our only safety lies in allowing each State to control the right of voting by its own laws, and we have the power to control the rebel States if they go wrong. If they rebel we have the army, and can control them by it, and, if necessary by legislation also. If the General Government controls the right to vote in the States, it may establish such rules as will restrict the vote to a small number of persons, and thus create a central despotism.

My position here is different from what it would be if I was in Tennessee.

There I should try to introduce negro suffrage gradually; first those who had served in the army; those who could read and write, and perhaps a property qualification for others, say $200 or $250.

It will not do to let the negroes have universal suffrage now. It would breed a war of races.

There was a time in the Southern States when the slaves of large owners looked down upon non-slaveowners because they did not own slaves; the larger the number of slaves their masters owned, the prouder they were, and this has produced hostility between the mass of the whites and the negroes. The outrages are mostly from non-slaveholding whites against the negro, and from the negro upon the non-slaveholding whites.

CHAPTER 1

THE PROBLEMS OF
RECONSTRUCTION:
ANDREW JOHNSON,
CONGRESS, AND
SOUTHERN
SUFFRAGE

The negro will vote with the late master whom he does not hate, rather than with the non-slaveholding white, whom he does hate. Universal suffrage would create another war, not against us, but a war of races. . . .

13. Johnson's Interview with an African American Delegation, February 7, 1866.

[THE PRESIDENT.] Now, it is always best to talk about things practically and in a common sense way. Yes, I have said, and I repeat here, that if the colored man in the United States could find no other Moses, or any Moses that would be more able and efficient than myself, I would be his Moses to lead him from bondage to freedom; that I would pass him from a land where he had lived in slavery to a land (if it were in our reach) of freedom. Yes, I would be willing to pass with him through the Red sea to the Land of Promise—to the land of liberty; but I am not willing, under either circumstance, to adopt a policy which I believe will only result in the sacrifice of his life and the shedding of his blood. I think I know what I say. I feel what I say; and I feel well assured that if the policy urged by some be persisted in, it will result in great injury to the white as well as to the colored man. There is a great deal of talk about the sword in one hand accomplishing an end, and the ballot accomplishing another at the ballot-box.

These things all do very well, and sometimes have forcible application. We talk about justice; we talk about right; we say that the white man has been in the wrong in keeping the black man in slavery as long as he has. That is all true. Again, we talk about the Declaration of Independence and equality before the law. You understand all that, and know how to appreciate it. But, now, let us look each other in the face; let us go to the great mass of colored men throughout the slave States; let us take the condition in which they are at the present time—and it is bad enough, we all know—and suppose, by some magic touch you could say to every one, "You shall vote to-morrow," how much would that ameliorate their condition at this time? . . .

[*Here Johnson stated that, in his opinion, the former slave looked down on the nonslaveholding whites and identified more closely with his former master. Frederick Douglass (1817?–1895), an important African American abolitionist editor and speaker and a member of the delegation, disagreed with Johnson. Johnson continued his statement.*]

Now, we are talking about where we are going to begin. We have got at the hate that existed between the two races. The query comes up whether these two races, situated as they were before, without preparation, without time for passion and excitement to be appeased, and without time for the slightest improvement, whether the one should be turned loose upon the other, and be thrown together at the ballot-box with this enmity and hate existing between them. The query comes up right there, whether we don't commence a war of races. I think I understand this thing, and especially is this the case when you force it upon a people without their consent.

You have spoken about government. Where is power derived from? We say it is derived from the people. Let us take it so and refer to the District of Columbia by way of illustration. Suppose, for instance, here, in this political community, which, to a certain extent must have government, must have laws, and putting it now upon the broadest basis you can put it—take into consideration the relation which the white has heretofore borne to the colored race—is it proper to force upon this community, without their consent, the elective franchise, without regard to color, making it universal?

Now, where do you begin? Government must have a controlling power; must have a lodgment. For instance, suppose Congress should pass a law authorizing an election to be held at which all over twenty-one years of age, without regard to color, should be allowed to vote, and a majority should decide at such election that the elective franchise should not be universal; what would you do about it? Who would settle it? Do you deny that first great principle of the right of the people to govern themselves? Will you resort to an arbitrary power, and say a majority of the people shall receive a state of things they are opposed to? . . .

Each community is better prepared to determine the depository of its political power than anybody else, and it is for the Legislature, for the people of Ohio to say who shall vote, and not for the Congress of the United States. I might go down here to the ballot-box to-morrow and vote directly for universal suffrage; but if a great majority of the people said no, I should consider it would be tyrannical in me to attempt to force such upon them without their will. It is a fundamental tenet in my creed that the will of the people must be obeyed. Is there anything wrong or unfair in that?

MR. DOUGLASS (smiling). A great deal that is wrong, Mr. President, with all respect.

THE PRESIDENT. It is the people of the States that must for themselves determine this thing. I do not want to be engaged in a work that will

CHAPTER 1

THE PROBLEMS OF
RECONSTRUCTION:
ANDREW JOHNSON,
CONGRESS, AND
SOUTHERN
SUFFRAGE

commence a war of races. I want to begin the work of preparation, and the States, or the people in each community, if a man demeans himself well, and shows evidence that this new state of affairs will operate, will protect him in all his rights, and give him every possible advantage when they become reconciled socially and politically to this state of things. Then will this new order of things work harmoniously; but forced upon the people before they are prepared for it, it will be resisted, and work inharmoniously. I feel a conviction that driving this matter upon the people, upon the community, will result in the injury of both races, and the ruin of one or the other. God knows I have no desire but the good of the whole human race. I would it were so that all you advocate could be done in the twinkling of an eye; but it is not in the nature of things, and I do not assume or pretend to be wiser than Providence, or stronger than the laws of nature.

Let us now seek to discover the laws governing this thing. There is a great law controlling it; let us endeavor to find out what that law is, and conform our actions to it. All the details will then properly adjust themselves and work out well in the end.

God knows that anything I can do I will do. In the mighty process by which the great end is to be reached, anything I can do to elevate the races, to soften and ameliorate their condition I will do, and to be able to do so is the sincere desire of my heart.

I am glad to have met you, and thank you for the compliment you have paid me.

MR. DOUGLASS. I have to return to you our thanks, Mr. President, for so kindly granting us this interview. We did not come here expecting to argue this question with your Excellency, but simply to state what were our views and wishes in the premises. If we were disposed to argue the question, and you would grant us permission, of course we would endeavor to controvert some of the positions you have assumed. . . .

THE PRESIDENT. I think you will find, so far as the South is concerned, that if you will all inculcate there the idea in connection with the one you urge, that the colored people can live and advance in civilization to better advantage elsewhere than crowded right down there in the South, it would be better for them.[30]

---

30. According to one of Johnson's secretaries, after the delegation left his office, Johnson erupted, "Those d----d sons of b-----s thought they had me in a trap! I know that d----d Douglass; he's just like any nigger, and he would sooner cut a white man's throat as not." See *The Papers of Andrew Johnson,* Vol. X, p. 48, n. 3.

Source 14 from Hans L. Trefousse, *Andrew Johnson, A Biography* (New York: W. W. Norton, 1989), p. 233.

14. Christopher Memminger to Carl Schurz, April 26, 1871.[31]

I think you are right in saying that if we had originally adopted a different course as to the Negroes, we would have escaped present difficulties [congressional Reconstruction]. But if you will consider for a moment, you will see that it was as impossible, as for us to have emancipated them before the war. The then President [Johnson] held up before us the hope of a "white man's government," and this led us to set aside Negro suffrage.

---

31. Memminger (1803–1888) was a former Confederate secretary of the treasury.

Source 15 from Morton Keller, *The Art and Politics of Thomas Nast* (New York: Oxford University Press, 1968), plate 55. Courtesy of the publisher.

15. Thomas Nast Cartoon Concerning Suffrage in the South, August 5, 1865.

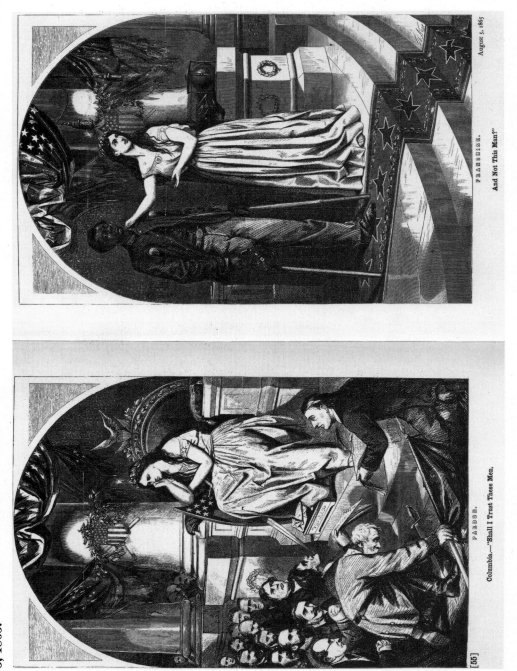

∽ QUESTIONS TO CONSIDER ∽

Remember that your task in this chapter is to determine why President Andrew Johnson chose the path he did with regard to who should vote in the postwar South—pardoning thousands of ex-Confederates whom he had specifically excepted from his general amnesty (Source 3) while simultaneously opposing African American suffrage.

Whenever historians find the central question they seek to answer too large or too complicated, they often break that question into smaller questions that they can answer. The central question in this chapter lends itself to such an approach. That question can be divided into two parts:

1. Why did President Johnson restore voting rights (through pardoning) to so many former Confederates whom he previously had excluded?
2. Why did President Johnson resist extending the suffrage to African Americans?

As you can readily see, once having answered these two smaller questions, you will be able to put the two answers together to answer the central question.

Sources 1 and 2 concern African Americans, but in decidedly different ways. Source 1 is Johnson's reply to a delegation of African American clergymen. How do the president's remarks reveal his attitude toward African Americans? What examples can you glean from his remarks that reveal this attitude? By inference, can the source be used to help explain why

Johnson resisted African Americans' voting? See also Source 13, an interview between Johnson and a delegation of African Americans. Here again Johnson reveals his attitude toward African Americans, but there are other possible motives as well. When the president refers to the "shedding of his [the black man's] blood," to what is he referring? How does he see relations between the African Americans and poor whites? Between African Americans and the South's plantation owners? Finally, what bodies did Johnson believe should establish qualifications to vote?

Source 2 also deals with African American suffrage, but again in a quite different way. Joseph Noxon, the letter writer, clearly believes that African American voters could be used to build a Republican party in the postwar South.[32] For this same argument, see also Sources 8 and 9. That Johnson did not take Noxon's advice (to enfranchise black voters to build a Republican party in the South) can be explained either by the fact that he disagreed with the political tactic or by the fact that he had other political maneuvers in mind. See the very important letters to Johnson from Duff Green (Source 7) and Francis Preston Blair (Source 10). What do you think Johnson's political ambitions were? How would his opposing African American suffrage aid those ambi-

32. Remember that the Union party Noxon referred to is the name the Republicans took for the 1864 electoral campaign.

[25]

CHAPTER 1

THE PROBLEMS OF
RECONSTRUCTION:
ANDREW JOHNSON,
CONGRESS, AND
SOUTHERN
SUFFRAGE

tions? See also Sources 5 and 9. Source 4, Johnson's "Proclamation Establishing Government for North Carolina," says nothing about requiring the states formerly in rebellion to institute African American suffrage. What signal did that send to the white South? See Source 14.

In his interview with the delegation of former Confederates from South Carolina (Source 6), Johnson hints at another possible motive for opposing African American suffrage. Remember that the president had built his political career on the support of the South's yeoman white farmers and on his almost continual political warfare with the planter elite. How did Johnson believe African Americans would vote?

In his interview with George L. Stearns (Source 12), Johnson offers what he believed was a constitutional objection to his institution of black suffrage (see also Sources 5, 9, and 13).

Thus we have not one possible motive that explains Johnson's opposition to African Americans but at least five possible motives (prejudice against blacks, political ambition, desire to avoid race war, fear of how African Americans would vote, and constitutional reservations). How are you to establish which of these was the most important? By examining the evidence more closely (including

Sources 11 and 12, two rather insincere statements in support of very limited black suffrage), try to determine when Johnson is being the most genuine and the least duplicitous. Make an effort to determine which of the letter writers (or receivers of letters from him) were closest to Johnson—people around whom he might more readily "let his hair down." Does any single motive stand out or underlie other motives?

As to the pardoning of former Confederates, begin with Source 3, Johnson's Amnesty Proclamation, in which he specifically excludes fourteen classes of people from general amnesty and pardon. What groups are excluded? Why do you suppose Johnson granted pardons to many in these excluded groups? Review the five possible motives regarding opposing African American suffrage. Do any of those possible motives help to explain why Johnson pardoned almost half of all individuals who requested that he do so? See also Sources 7 and 10.[33]

Now put the two questions back together. What motive or motives do you believe best explain President Andrew Johnson's decisions with regard to who should vote in the postwar South and, by implication, what Johnson elieved the nature of politics and race relations in the postwar South should be?

---

33. With the exception of Jefferson Davis, ultimately all former Confederates either were pardoned or died before their cases were taken up (as in the case of Robert E. Lee). Davis was "restored to the full rights of citizenship" by joint congressional resolution on October 17, 1978.

⟳ EPILOGUE ⟳

President Johnson's efforts to have all the states of the former Confederacy restored to their normal places in the Union before Congress reconvened in December 1865 turned out to be an almost complete disaster. The president's less-than-subtle signals to the South that he favored a mild reconstruction, would not insist on ratification of the Thirteenth Amendment or African American suffrage, and would oppose Radical Republicans' efforts to impose a harsher reconstruction caused the South to believe that it could act with impunity. Only North Carolina admitted that secession had been wrong; South Carolina refused to repudiate its Confederate debt; Mississippi did not ratify the Thirteenth Amendment.[34] When elections were held to send representatives back to the federal Congress, four former Confederate generals, five former colonels, and numerous former Confederate congressmen were elected. In Mississippi, the winning candidate for governor was elected before he had been pardoned. Reorganized southern state legislators passed a series of laws known as "black codes," differing little from the old slave codes. Violence against African Americans was widespread.

Northerners were appalled, sensing that the victory earned with an enormous amount of blood (approximately 360,000 Union dead) appeared to be slipping through their fingers. Union veterans running for office and editors and cartoonists such as Thomas Nast (Source 15) whipped northern voters into a frenzy of anti-South enthusiasm, and in the congressional elections of 1866 they returned a Congress in which Radical Republicans were strong enough to override Johnson's vetoes and pass a series of Reconstruction acts that were considerably harsher than Johnson's more lenient plans. The South was divided into five military districts in which commanders had power over civil governments, were instructed to register voters (especially African Americans) and to disfranchise disloyal whites, and were to organize state constitutional conventions to draft new state constitutions (which had to be acceptable to Congress). When states had written acceptable constitutions *and* had ratified the Fourteenth Amendment, then they could take their normal places in the Union.

President Johnson's futile efforts to block Radical Reconstruction, along with his attempt to remove Secretary of War Edwin Stanton from his cabinet, led to his impeachment by the House of Representatives. And although he was not removed from the presidency (the Senate failed by one vote to achieve the two-thirds necessary for removal), his effectiveness as a chief executive was completely eroded. Johnson's dream of winning the presidency in his own right in 1868 (whether through a Republican nomination or by fashioning a new political party of disaffected southerners

34. The Mississippi legislature actually did ratify the Thirteenth Amendment—on March 16, 1995.

[27]

CHAPTER 1

THE PROBLEMS OF
RECONSTRUCTION:
ANDREW JOHNSON,
CONGRESS, AND
SOUTHERN
SUFFRAGE

and conservative northerners) completely collapsed. The Democrats, viewing Johnson as a political albatross, ignored him in favor of New York politician and former governor Horatio Seymour. For their part, the Republicans nominated the popular and malleable Ulysses Grant.

Although Radical Reconstruction was never as harsh as white southerners chose to remember it, white southerners nevertheless resisted even the mildest efforts to change their economic, social, and political institutions. Reconstruction state governments accomplished some worthwhile objectives (especially in establishing state-financed systems of public education in the South), but they were opposed by a majority of white southerners. And as northern fervor diminished and general amnesty proclamations restored the suffrage to all but a few former Confederates, gradually white southerners recaptured control of their state governments and (as they put it) "redeemed" their states.[35] The disputed presidential election of 1876 finally put an end to Reconstruction in the South.

Andrew Johnson returned to Tennessee in 1869 with the hope of rebuilding his smashed political career, but the remainder of his life was filled with sadness. His wife, Eliza, had become an invalid and required almost constant care. One of his sons, an alcoholic, committed suicide. He lost his bid to return to the U.S. Senate in 1869, was the subject of some vicious rumors (including alcoholism and marital infidelity), contracted cholera in 1873, and lost well over $70,000 in the financial panic of that year. At last elected to the Senate in 1875, he died of a stroke before taking office. His wife followed him six months later.

Increasingly impatient with the South's poor record regarding African American suffrage, in 1869 Congress passed, and a year later a sufficient number of states ratified, the Fifteenth Amendment to the Constitution, which prohibited denying the vote to individuals "on account of race, color, or previous condition of servitude." Ironically, the last state to ratify the Fifteenth Amendment was Johnson's home state of Tennessee, which did so on April 2, 1997.

---

35. Virginia and Tennessee were "redeemed" in 1869, North Carolina in 1870, Georgia in 1871, Texas in 1873, Alabama and Arkansas in 1874, and Mississippi in 1875. By the election of 1876, only South Carolina, Florida, and Louisiana remained under Radical rule.

CHAPTER 2

THE ROAD TO TRUE FREEDOM: AFRICAN AMERICAN ALTERNATIVES IN THE NEW SOUTH

◅⃝ THE PROBLEM ⃝▻

By 1895, when the venerable Frederick Douglass died, African Americans in the South had been free for thirty years. Yet in many ways, their situation had barely improved from that of servitude, and in some ways, it had actually deteriorated. Economically, very few had been able to acquire land of their own, and the vast majority continued to work for white landowners under various forms of labor arrangements and sometimes under outright peonage.[1] Political and civil rights supposedly had been guaranteed under the Fourteenth and Fifteenth amendments to the Constitution (ratified in 1868 and 1870, respectively), but those rights often were violated, federal courts offered little protection, and, beginning in the early 1890s, southern states began a successful campaign to disfranchise black voters and to institute legal segregation through legislation that collectively became known as Jim Crow laws.[2] In some ways more threatening, violence against African Americans

---

1. Whatever names were given to these labor arrangements (tenancy, sharecropping, and so on), in most of the arrangements a white landowner or merchant furnished farm workers with foodstuffs and fertilizer on credit, taking a percentage of the crops grown in return. For a fascinating description of how the system worked, see Theodore Rosengarten, *All God's Dangers: The Life of Nate Shaw* (New York: Alfred A. Knopf, 1974).

2. The term "Jim Crow," generally used to refer to issues relating to African Americans, originated in the late 1820s with white minstrel singer Thomas "Daddy" Rice, who performed the song "Jump Jim Crow" in blackface makeup. By the 1840s, the term was used to refer to racially segregated facilities in the North.

CHAPTER 2

THE ROAD TO
TRUE FREEDOM:
AFRICAN
AMERICAN
ALTERNATIVES
IN THE NEW
SOUTH

was increasing and in most cases going unpunished. Between 1889 and 1900, 1,357 lynchings of African Americans were recorded in the United States, the vast majority in the states of the former Confederacy. In 1898, in New Bern, North Carolina, one white orator proposed "choking the Cape Fear River with the bodies of Negroes." In truth, by the 1890s it had become evident for all who cared to see that Lincoln's emancipation of southern slaves had been considerably less than complete.

A number of spokespersons offered significantly different strategies for improving the situation of African Americans in the South. We have chosen four such spokespersons, all of them extremely well known to blacks in the New South. Ida B. Wells (1862–1931) was a journalist, lecturer, and crusader who was well known in both the United States and Europe. Booker T. Washington (1856–1915) was a celebrated educator, author, and political figure who many believed should have inherited the mantle of Frederick Douglass as the principal spokesper-

son for African Americans. Henry McNeal Turner (1834–1915) was a bishop of the African Methodist Episcopal church and a controversial speaker and writer. W. E. B. Du Bois (pronounced Du Boys', 1868–1963) was an academician and editor and one of the founders of the National Association for the Advancement of Colored People (NAACP). Each of these spokespersons offered a contrasting alternative for African Americans.

In this chapter, you will be analyzing the situation that African Americans in the South faced in the years after Reconstruction and identifying the principal alternatives open to them. What different strategies did Wells, Washington, Turner, and Du Bois offer African Americans? Were there other options they did not mention? Finally, based on your examination of the evidence and the use of your historical imagination, which alternative do you think was the best one for African Americans at the turn of the twentieth century? How would you go about proving your hypothesis?

⚭ BACKGROUND ⚭

The gradual end of Reconstruction by the federal government left the South in the hands of political and economic leaders who chose to call themselves "Redeemers." Many of these men came from the same landowner and planter-lawyer groups that had led the South prior to the Civil War, thus giving the post–Reconstruction South a

high degree of continuity with earlier eras. Also important, however, was a comparatively new group of southerners, men who called for a "New South" that would be highlighted by increased industrialization, urbanization, and diversified agriculture.

In many ways, the New South movement was an undisguised attempt to imitate the industrialization that was sweeping through the North just prior to, during, and after the Civil War. Indeed, the North's industrial prowess had been one reason for its ultimate military victory. As Reconstruction gradually came to an end in the southern states, many southern bankers, business leaders, and editors became convinced that the South should not return to its previous, narrow economic base of plantations and one-crop agriculture but instead should follow the North's lead toward modernization through industry. Prior to the Civil War, many of these people had been calling for economic diversification, but they had been overwhelmed by the plantation aristocracy that controlled southern state politics and had used that control to further its own interests. By the end of Reconstruction, however, the planter elite had lost a good deal of its power, thus creating a power vacuum into which advocates of a New South could move.

Nearly every city, town, and hamlet of the former Confederacy had its New South boosters. Getting together in industrial societies or chambers of commerce, the boosters called for the erection of mills and factories. Why, they asked, should southerners export their valuable raw materials elsewhere, only to see them return from northern and European factories as costly finished products? Why couldn't southerners set up their own manufacturing establishments and become prosperous within a self-contained economy? And if the southerners were short of capital, why not encourage rich northern investors to put up

money in return for promises of great profits? In fact, the South had all the ingredients required of an industrial system: raw materials, a rebuilt transportation system, labor, potential consumers, and the possibility of obtaining capital. As they fed each other's dreams, the New South advocates pictured a resurgent South, a prosperous South, a triumphant South, a South of steam and power rather than plantations and magnolias.

Undoubtedly, the leading spokesman of the New South movement was Henry Grady, editor of the *Atlanta Constitution* and one of the most influential figures in the southern states. Born in Athens, Georgia, in 1850, Grady was orphaned in his early teens when his father was killed in the Civil War. Graduating from his hometown college, the University of Georgia, Grady began a long and not particularly profitable career as a journalist. In 1879, aided by northern industrialist Cyrus Field, he purchased a quarter interest in the *Atlanta Constitution* and became that newspaper's editor. From that position, he became the chief advocate of the New South movement.

Whether speaking to southern or northern audiences, Grady had no peer. Addressing a group of potential investors in New South industries in New York in 1886, he delighted his audience by saying that he was glad the Confederacy had lost the Civil War, for that defeat had broken the power of the plantation aristocracy and provided the opportunity for the South to move into the modern industrial age. Northerners, Grady continued, were welcome: "We have sown

CHAPTER 2

THE ROAD TO
TRUE FREEDOM:
AFRICAN
AMERICAN
ALTERNATIVES
IN THE NEW
SOUTH

towns and cities in the place of theories, and put business above politics . . . and have . . . wiped out the place where Mason and Dixon's line used to be."[3]

To those southerners who envisioned a New South, the central goal was a harmonious, interdependent society in which each person and thing had a clearly defined place. Most New South boosters stressed industry and the growth of cities because the South had few factories and mills and almost no cities of substantial size. But agriculture also would have its place, although it would not be the same as the cash-crop agriculture of the pre–Civil War years. Instead, New South spokesmen advocated a diversified agriculture that would still produce cash crops for export but would also make the South more self-sufficient by producing food crops and raw materials for the anticipated factories. Small towns would be used for collection and distribution, a rebuilt railroad network would transport goods, and northern capital would finance the entire process. Hence each part of the economy and, indeed, each person would have a clearly defined place and role in the New South, a place and role that would ensure everyone a piece of the New South's prosperity.

But even as Grady and his counterparts were fashioning their dreams of a New South and selling those dreams to both northerners and southerners, a less beneficial, less prosperous side of the New South was taking shape. In spite of the New South advocates' successes in establishing factories and mills (for example, Knoxville, Tennessee, witnessed the founding of more than ninety such enterprises in the 1880s alone), the post–Reconstruction South remained primarily agricultural. Furthermore, most of the farms were worked by sharecroppers or tenant farmers who eked out a bare subsistence while the profits went to the landowners or to the banks. This situation was especially prevalent in the lower South, where by 1890 a great proportion of farms were worked by tenants: South Carolina (61.1 percent), Georgia (59.9 percent), Alabama (57.7 percent), Mississippi (62.4 percent), and Louisiana (58.0 percent). Even as factory smokestacks were rising on portions of the southern horizon, a high percentage of southerners remained in agriculture and in poverty.

Undeniably, African Americans suffered the most. More than four million African American men, women, and children had been freed by the Civil War. During Reconstruction, some advances were made, especially in the areas of public education and voter registration. Yet even these gains were either impermanent or incomplete. By 1880 in Georgia, only 33.7 percent of the black school-age population was enrolled in school, and by 1890 (twenty-five years after emancipation) almost half of all black people ages ten to fourteen in the Deep South were still illiterate.[4] As for voting rights,

3. Grady's speech is in Richard N. Current and John A. Garraty, eds., *Words That Made American History* (Boston: Little, Brown, 1962), Vol. II, pp. 23–31.

4. Roger L. Ransom and Richard Sutch, *One Kind of Freedom: The Economic Consequences of Emancipation* (Cambridge: Cambridge University Press, 1977), pp. 28, 30.

the vast majority of African Americans chose not to exercise them, fearing intimidation and violence.

Many blacks and whites at the time recognized that African Americans would never be able to improve their situation economically, socially, or politically without owning land. Yet even many Radical Republicans were reluctant to give land to the former slaves. Such a move would mean seizing land from the white planters, a proposal that clashed with the notion of the sanctity of private property. As a result, most African Americans were forced to take menial, low-paying jobs in southern cities or work as farmers on land they did not own. By 1880, only 1.6 percent of the landowners in Georgia were black, and most of them owned the most marginal and least productive land.

As poor urban laborers or tenant farmers, African Americans were dependent on their employers, landowners, or bankers and prey to rigid vagrancy laws, the convict lease system, peonage, and outright racial discrimination. Moreover, the end of Reconstruction in the southern states was followed by a reimposition of rigid racial segregation, at first through a return to traditional practices and later (in the 1890s) by state laws governing nearly every aspect of southern life. For example, voting by African Americans was discouraged, initially by intimidation and then by more formal means such as poll taxes and literacy tests. African Americans who protested or strayed from their "place" were dealt with harshly. Between 1880 and 1918, more than twenty-four hundred African Americans were lynched by southern white mobs, each action being a grim reminder to African Americans of what could happen to those who challenged the status quo. For their part, the few southern whites who spoke against such outrages were themselves subjects of intimidation and even violence. Indeed, although most African American men and women undoubtedly would have disagreed, African Americans' relative position in some ways had deteriorated since the end of the Civil War.

Many New South advocates openly worried about how potential northern investors and politicians would react to this state of affairs. Although the dream of the New South rested on the concept of a harmonious, interdependent society in which each component (industry, agriculture, and so forth) and each person (white and black) had a clearly defined place, it appeared that African Americans were being kept in their "place" largely by intimidation and force. Who would want to invest in a region in which the status quo of mutual deference and "place" often was maintained by force? To calm northern fears, Grady and his cohorts assured northerners that African Americans' position was improving and that southern society was one of mutual respect between the races. "We have found," Grady stated, "that in the summing up the free Negro counts more than he did as a slave." Most northerners believed Grady because they wanted to, because they had no taste for another bitter Reconstruction, and in many cases because they shared white southerners' prejudice against African Americans. Grady was able to reassure them because they wanted to be reassured.

CHAPTER 2

THE ROAD TO
TRUE FREEDOM:
AFRICAN
AMERICAN
ALTERNATIVES
IN THE NEW
SOUTH

Thus for southern African Americans, the New South movement had done little to better their collective lot. Indeed, in some ways their position had deteriorated. Tied economically either to land they did not own or to the lowest-paying jobs in towns and cities, subjects of an increasingly rigid code of racial segregation and loss of political rights, and victims of an upswing in racially directed violence, African Americans in the New South had every reason to question the oratory of Henry Grady and other New South boosters. Jobs in the New South's mills and factories generally were reserved for whites, so the opportunities that European immigrants in the North had to work their way gradually up the economic ladder were closed to southern blacks.

How did African Americans respond to this deteriorating situation? In the 1890s, numerous African American farmers joined the Colored Alliance, part of the Farmers' Alliance Movement that swept the South and Midwest in the 1880s and 1890s. This movement attempted to reverse the farmers' eroding position through the establishment of farmers' cooperatives (to sell their crops together for higher prices and to purchase manufactured goods wholesale) and by entering politics to elect candidates sympathetic to farmers (who would draft legislation favorable to farmers). Many feared, however, that this increased militancy of farmers—white and black—would produce a political backlash that would leave them even worse off. Such a backlash occurred in the South in the 1890s with the defeat of the Populist revolt.

Wells, Washington, Turner, and Du Bois offered southern African Americans four other alternatives to meet the economic, social, and political problems they faced. And, as African American men and women soon discovered, there were other options as well.

Your task in this chapter is to analyze the evidence to answer the following central questions:

1. What were the different alternatives offered by Wells, Washington, Turner, and Du Bois?
2. Were there options those four spokespersons did not mention?
3. Which alternative do you think was the best one for African Americans in the South at the turn of the twentieth century?
4. How would you support your conclusion?

⚭ THE METHOD ⚭

In this chapter, the evidence is arranged chronologically. The piece by Ida B. Wells (Source 1) is from a pamphlet published simultaneously in the United States and England in 1892. It is likely that parts of the pamphlet were delivered as a speech by Wells earlier that year. The selections by Washington (Source 2) and Turner (Source 3) and the two selections by

Du Bois (Sources 4 and 5) are transcriptions, or printed versions, of speeches delivered in September 1895, December 1895, and 1903 and 1906, respectively. Finally, there is one set of statistics (Source 6) that suggests an additional alternative open to African Americans.

Ida Bell Wells was born a slave in Holly Springs, Mississippi, in 1862. After emancipation, her father and mother, as a carpenter and a cook, respectively, earned enough money to send her to a freedmen's school. In 1876, her parents died in a yellow fever epidemic. Only fourteen years old, Wells lied about her age and got a job teaching in a rural school for blacks, eventually moving to Memphis, Tennessee, to teach in the city's schools for African Americans. In 1884, she was forcibly removed from a railroad passenger car for refusing to move to the car reserved for "colored" passengers; she sued the railroad company.[5] About this time, Wells began writing articles for many black-owned newspapers, mostly on the subject of unequal educational opportunities for whites and blacks in Memphis. As a result, the Memphis school board discharged her, and she became a full-time journalist and lecturer. By 1892, she had become co-owner of the *Memphis Free Speech* newspaper. In 1895, she married black lawyer-editor Ferdinand Lee Barnett and from that time went by the name Ida Wells-Barnett, a somewhat radical practice in 1895.

Like Wells, Booker T. Washington was born a slave, in Franklin County,

5. The Tennessee Supreme Court ruled in favor of the Chesapeake and Ohio Railroad and against Wells in 1887.

Virginia. Largely self-taught before entering Hampton Institute, a school for African Americans, at age seventeen, he worked his way through school, mostly as a janitor. At age twenty-five, he was chosen to organize a normal school for blacks at Tuskegee, Alabama. Washington spent thirty-four years as the guiding force at Tuskegee Institute, shaping the school into his vision of what African Americans must do to better their lot. In great demand as a speaker to white and black audiences alike, Washington received an honorary degree from Harvard College in 1891. Four years later, he was chosen as the principal speaker at the opening of the Negro section of the Cotton States and International Exposition in Atlanta.

Henry McNeal Turner was born a free black near Abbeville, South Carolina. Mostly self-taught, he joined the Methodist Episcopal church, South, in 1848 and was licensed to preach in 1853. In 1858, he abandoned that denomination to become a minister in the African Methodist Episcopal (AME) church, and by 1862 he was the pastor of the large Israel church in Washington, D.C. In 1863, he became a chaplain in the Union army, assigned to the 1st U.S. Colored Regiment. After the war, he became an official of the Freedmen's Bureau in Georgia and afterward held a succession of political appointments. One of the founders of the Republican party in Georgia, Turner was made bishop of the AME church in Georgia in 1880. In that position, he met and became a friend of Ida B. Wells, who also was a member of the AME church.

CHAPTER 2

THE ROAD TO
TRUE FREEDOM:
AFRICAN
AMERICAN
ALTERNATIVES
IN THE NEW
SOUTH

William Edward Burghardt Du Bois was born in Great Barrington, Massachusetts, one of approximately fifty blacks in a town of five thousand people. He was educated with the white children in the town's public school and in 1885 was enrolled at Fisk University, a college for African Americans in Nashville, Tennessee. It was there, according to his autobiography, that he first encountered overt racial prejudice. Graduated from Fisk in 1888, he entered Harvard as a junior. He received his bachelor's degree in 1890 and his Ph.D. in 1895. His book *The Philadelphia Negro* was published in 1899. In this book, Du Bois asserted that the problems African Americans faced were the results of their history (slavery and racism) and environment, not of some imagined genetic inferiority.

This is not the first time that you have had to analyze speeches. Our society is almost literally bombarded by speeches delivered by politicians, business figures, educators, and others, most of whom are trying to convince us to adopt a set of ideas or actions. As we listen to such speeches, we invariably weigh the options presented to

us, often using other available evidence (in this case, the Background section of this chapter) to help us make our decisions. One purpose of this exercise is to help you think more critically and use evidence more thoroughly when assessing different options.

It is logical to begin by analyzing each of the speeches in turn. As you read each selection, make a rough chart like the one below to help you remember the main points. Then examine Source 6 for another option open to southern African Americans. Remember that when we analyze statistics, we need to ask three principal questions:

1. What is being measured?
2. How did that variable change over time?
3. How can that change be explained?

Once you have carefully defined the alternatives presented by Wells, Washington, Turner, Du Bois, and Source 6, return to the Background section of this chapter. As you reread that section, use your historical imagination to determine which was the best alternative.

African American Alternatives			
Speaker	Suggested Alternatives	How Does Speaker Develop Her/His Arguments?	Your Reaction (Fill in later)
Wells			
Washington			
Turner			
Du Bois			

∽ THE EVIDENCE ∼

Source 1 from Ida B. Wells, *United States Atrocities* (London: Lux Newspaper and Publishing Co., 1892), pp. 13–18. In the United States, the pamphlet was titled *Southern Horrors*. See Jacqueline Jones Royster, ed., *Southern Horrors and Other Writings: The Anti-Lynching Campaign of Ida B. Wells, 1892–1900* (Boston: Bedford Books, 1997), pp. 49–72.

1. Wells's *United States Atrocities*, 1892.

Mr. Henry W. Grady, in his well-remembered speeches in New England and New York, pictured the Afro-American as incapable of self-government. Through him and other leading men the cry of the South to the country has been "Hands off! Leave us to solve our problem." To the Afro-American the South says, "The white man must and will rule." There is little difference between the Ante-bellum South and the New South. Her white citizens are wedded to any method however revolting, any measure however extreme, for the subjugation of the young manhood of the dark race. They have cheated him out of his ballot, deprived him of civil rights or redress in the Civil Courts thereof, robbed him of the fruits of his labour, and are still murdering, burning and lynching him.

The result is a growing disregard of human life. Lynch Law has spread its insidious influence till men in New York State, Pennsylvania and on the free Western plains feel they can take the law in their own hands with impunity, especially where an Afro-American is concerned. The South is brutalised to a degree not realised by its own inhabitants, and the very foundation of government, law, and order are imperilled.

Public sentiment has had a slight "reaction," though not sufficient to stop the crusade of lawlessness and lynching. The spirit of Christianity of the great M. E. Church was sufficiently aroused by the frequent and revolting crimes against a powerless people, to pass strong condemnatory resolutions at its General Conference in Omaha last May. The spirit of justice of the grand old party[6] asserted itself sufficiently to secure a denunciation of the wrongs, and a feeble declaration of the belief in human rights in the Republican platform at Minneapolis, June 7th. A few of the great "dailies" and "weeklies" have swung into line declaring that Lynch Law must go. The President of the United States issued a proclamation that it be not tolerated in the territories over which he has jurisdiction. . . .

---

6. The Republican party.

CHAPTER 2

THE ROAD TO
TRUE FREEDOM:
AFRICAN
AMERICAN
ALTERNATIVES
IN THE NEW
SOUTH

These efforts brought forth apologies and a short halt, but the lynching mania has raged again through the past twelve months with unabated fury. The strong arm of the law must be brought to bear upon lynchers in severe punishment, but this cannot and will not be done unless a healthy public sentiment demands and sustains such action. The men and women in the South who disapprove of lynching and remain silent on the perpetration of such outrages are *particeps criminis*—accomplices, accessories before and after the fact, equally guilty with the actual law-breakers, who would not persist if they did not know that neither the law nor militia would be deployed against them.

In the creation of this healthier public sentiment, the Afro-American can do for himself what no one else can do for him. The world looks on with wonder that we have conceded so much, and remain law-abiding under such great outrage and provocation.

To Northern capital and Afro-American labour the South owes its rehabilitation. If labour is withdrawn capital will not remain. The Afro-American is thus the backbone of the South. A thorough knowledge and judicious exercise of this power in lynching localities could many times effect a bloodless revolution. The white man's dollar is his god, and to stop this will be to stop outrages in many localities.

The Afro-Americans of Memphis denounced the lynching of three of their best citizens, and urged and waited for the authorities to act in the matter, and bring the lynchers to justice. No attempt was made to do so, and the black men left the city by thousands, bringing about great stagnation in every branch of business. Those who remained so injured the business of the street car company by staying off the cars, that the superintendent, manager, and treasurer called personally on the editors of the *Free Speech,* and asked them to urge our people to give them their patronage again. Other business men became alarmed over the situation, and the *Free Speech* was suppressed that the coloured people might be more easily controlled. A meeting of white citizens in June, three months after the lynching, passed resolutions for the first time condemning it. *But they did not punish the lynchers.* Every one of them was known by name because they had been selected to do the dirty work by some of the very citizens who passed these resolutions! Memphis is fast losing her black population, who proclaim as they go that there is no protection for the life and property of any Afro-American citizen in Memphis who will not be a slave.

The Afro-American citizens of Kentucky, whose intellectual and financial improvement has been phenomenal, have never had a separate car law until now. Delegations and petitions poured into the Legislature against it, yet the Bill passed, and the Jim Crow Car of Kentucky is a legalised institution.

Will the great mass of Negroes continue to patronise the railroad? A special from Covington, Kentucky, says:—

"Covington, June 13th.—The railroads of the State are beginning to feel very markedly the effects of the separate coach Bill recently passed by the Legislature. No class of people in the State have so many and so largely attended excursions as the blacks. All these have been abandoned, and regular travel is reduced to a minimum." A competent authority says the loss to the various roads will reach 1,000,000 dols. this year.

A call to a State Conference in Lexington, Kentucky, last June, had delegates from every county in the State. Those delegates, the ministers, teachers, heads of secret and other orders, and the heads of families should pass the word around for every member of the race in Kentucky to stay off railroads unless obliged to ride. If they did so, and their advice was followed persistently, the Convention would not need to petition the Legislature to repeal the law or raise money to file a suit. The railroad corporations would be so affected they would, in self defence, "lobby" to have the separate car law repealed. On the other hand, as long as the railroads can get Afro-American excursions they will always have plenty of money to fight all the suits brought against them. They will be aided in so doing by the same partisan public sentiment which passed the law. White men passed the law, and white judges and juries would pass upon the suits against the law, and render judgment in line with their prejudices, and in deference to the greater financial power.

The appeal to the white man's pocket has ever been more effectual than all the appeals ever made to his conscience. Nothing, absolutely nothing, is to be gained by a further sacrifice of manhood and self-respect. By the right exercise of his power as the industrial factor of the South, the Afro-American can demand and secure his rights, the punishment of lynchers, and a fair trial for members of his race accused of outrage.

Of the many inhuman outrages of this present year, the only case where the proposed lynching did *not* occur, was where the men armed themselves in Jacksonville, Florida, and Paducah, Kentucky, and prevented it. The only times an Afro-American who was assaulted got away has been when he had a gun, and used it in self-defence. The lesson this teaches, and which every Afro-American should ponder well, is that a Winchester rifle should have a place of honour in every black home, and it should be used for that protection which the law refuses to give. When the white man, who is always the aggressor, knows he runs a great risk of biting the dust every time his Afro-American victim does, he will have greater respect for Afro-American life. The more the Afro-American yields and cringes and begs, the more he has to do so, the more he is insulted, outraged, and lynched. . . .

CHAPTER 2

THE ROAD TO
TRUE FREEDOM:
AFRICAN
AMERICAN
ALTERNATIVES
IN THE NEW
SOUTH

The assertion has been substantiated that the Press[7] contains unreliable and doctored reports of lynchings, and one of the most necessary things for the race to do is to get these facts before the public. The people must know before they can act, and there is no educator to compare with the Press.

The Afro-American papers are the only ones which will print the truth, and they lack means to employ agents and detectives to get at the facts. The race must rally a mighty host to the support of their journals, and thus enable them to do much in the way of investigation. . . .

Nothing is more definitely settled than that he must act for himself. I have shown how he may employ the "boycott," emigration, and the Press; and I feel that by a combination of all these agencies Lynch Law—the last relic of barbarism and slavery—can be effectually stamped out. "The gods help those who help themselves."

Source 2 from Louis R. Harlan, ed., *The Booker T. Washington Papers* (Urbana: University of Illinois Press, 1974), Vol. III, pp. 583–587.

2. The Standard Printed Version of Booker T. Washington's Atlanta Exposition Address.

[Atlanta, Ga., Sept. 18, 1895]

Mr. President and Gentlemen of the Board of Directors and Citizens:

One-third of the population of the South is of the Negro race. No enterprise seeking the material, civil, or moral welfare of this section can disregard this element of our population and reach the highest success. I but convey to you, Mr. President and Directors, the sentiment of the masses of my race when I say that in no way have the value and manhood of the American Negro been more fittingly and generously recognized than by the managers of this magnificent Exposition at every stage of its progress. It is a recognition that will do more to cement the friendship of the two races than any occurrence since the dawn of our freedom.

Not only this, but the opportunity here afforded will awaken among us a new era of industrial progress. Ignorant and inexperienced, it is not strange that in the first years of our new life we began at the top instead of at the bottom; that a seat in Congress or the state legislature was more sought than real estate or industrial skill; that the political convention or stump speaking had more attractions than starting a dairy farm or truck garden.

7. Wells was referring here to newspapers owned by whites.

A ship lost at sea for many days suddenly sighted a friendly vessel. From the mast of the unfortunate vessel was seen a signal, "Water, water; we die of thirst!" The answer from the friendly vessel at once came back, "Cast down your bucket where you are." A second time the signal, "Water, water; send us water!" ran up from the distressed vessel, and was answered, "Cast down your bucket where you are." And a third and fourth signal for water was answered, "Cast down your bucket where you are." The captain of the distressed vessel, at last heeding the injunction, cast down his bucket, and it came up full of fresh, sparkling water from the mouth of the Amazon River. To those of my race who depend on bettering their condition in a foreign land or who underestimate the importance of cultivating friendly relations with the Southern white man, who is their next-door neighbour, I would say: "Cast down your bucket where you are"—cast it down in making friends in every manly way of the people of all races by whom we are surrounded.

Cast it down in agriculture, mechanics, in commerce, in domestic service, and in the professions. And in this connection it is well to bear in mind that whatever other sins the South may be called to bear, when it comes to business, pure and simple, it is in the South that the Negro is given a man's chance in the commercial world, and in nothing is this Exposition more eloquent than in emphasizing this chance. Our greatest danger is that in the great leap from slavery to freedom we may overlook the fact that the masses of us are to live by the productions of our hands, and fail to keep in mind that we shall prosper in proportion as we learn to dignify and glorify common labour, and put brains and skill into the common occupations of life; shall prosper in proportion as we learn to draw the line between the superficial and the substantial, the ornamental gewgaws of life and the useful. No race can prosper till it learns that there is as much dignity in tilling a field as in writing a poem. It is at the bottom of life we must begin, and not at the top. Nor should we permit our grievances to overshadow our opportunities.

To those of the white race who look to the incoming of those of foreign birth and strange tongue and habits for the prosperity of the South, were I permitted I would repeat what I say to my own race, "Cast down your bucket where you are." Cast it down among the eight millions of Negroes whose habits you know, whose fidelity and love you have tested in days when to have proved treacherous meant the ruin of your firesides. Cast down your bucket among these people who have, without strikes and labour wars, tilled your fields, cleared your forests, builded your railroads and cities, and brought forth treasures from the bowels of the earth, and helped make possible this magnificent representation of the progress of the South. Casting down your bucket among my people, helping and encouraging them

CHAPTER 2

THE ROAD TO
TRUE FREEDOM:
AFRICAN
AMERICAN
ALTERNATIVES
IN THE NEW
SOUTH

as you are doing on these grounds, and to education of head, hand, and heart, you will find that they will buy your surplus land, make blossom the waste places in your fields, and run your factories. While doing this, you can be sure in the future, as in the past, that you and your families will be surrounded by the most patient, faithful, law-abiding, and unresentful people that the world has seen. As we have proved our loyalty to you in the past, in nursing your children, watching by the sick-bed of your mothers and fathers, and often following them with tear-dimmed eyes to their graves, so in the future, in our humble way, we shall stand by you with a devotion that no foreigner can approach, ready to lay down our lives, if need be, in defense of yours, interlacing our industrial, commercial, civil, and religious life with yours in a way that shall make the interests of both races one. In all things that are purely social we can be as separate as the fingers, yet one as the hand in all things essential to mutual progress.

There is no defense or security for any of us except in the highest intelligence and development of all. If anywhere there are efforts tending to curtail the fullest growth of the Negro, let these efforts be turned into stimulating, encouraging, and making him the most useful and intelligent citizen. Effort or means so invested will pay a thousand per cent interest. These efforts will be twice blessed—"blessing him that gives and him that takes."

There is no escape through law of man or God from the inevitable:—

"The laws of changeless justice bind
    Oppressor with oppressed;
And close as sin and suffering joined
    We march to fate abreast."

Nearly sixteen millions of hands will aid you in pulling the load upward, or they will pull against you the load downward. We shall constitute one-third and more of the ignorance and crime of the South, or one-third [of] its intelligence and progress; we shall contribute one-third to the business and industrial prosperity of the South, or we shall prove a veritable body of death, stagnating, depressing, retarding every effort to advance the body politic.

Gentlemen of the Exposition, as we present to you our humble effort at an exhibition of our progress, you must not expect overmuch. Starting thirty years ago with ownership here and there in a few quilts and pumpkins and chickens (gathered from miscellaneous sources), remember the path that has led from these to the inventions and production of agricultural implements, buggies, steam-engines, newspapers, books, statuary, carving, paintings, the management of drug stores and banks, has not been trodden without contact with thorns and thistles. While we take pride in what we exhibit as a result of our independent efforts, we do not for a moment forget that our part in this exhibition would fall far short of your expectations but for the constant help that has come to our educational life, not only from the Southern states, but especially from Northern philanthropists, who have made their gifts a constant stream of blessing and encouragement.

The wisest among my race understand that the agitation of questions of social equality is the extremest folly, and that progress in the enjoyment of all the privileges that will come to us must be the result of severe and constant struggle rather than of artificial forcing. No race that has anything to contribute to the markets of the world is long in any degree ostracized. It is important and right that all privileges of the law be ours, but it is vastly more important that we be prepared for the exercise of these privileges. The opportunity to earn a dollar in a factory just now is worth infinitely more than the opportunity to spend a dollar in an opera-house.

In conclusion, may I repeat that nothing in thirty years has given us more hope and encouragement, and drawn us so near to you of the white race, as this opportunity offered by the Exposition; and here bending, as it were, over the altar that represents the results of the struggles of your race and mine, both starting practically empty-handed three decades ago, I pledge that in your effort to work out the great and intricate problem which God has laid at the doors of the South, you shall have at all times the patient, sympathetic help of my race; only let this be constantly in mind, that, while from representations in these buildings of the product of field, of forest, of mine, of factory, letters, and art, much good will come, yet far above and beyond material benefits will be that higher good, that, let us pray God, will come, in a blotting out of sectional differences and racial animosities and suspicions in a determination to administer absolute justice, in a willing obedience among all classes to the mandates of law. This, coupled with our material prosperity, will bring into our beloved South a new heaven and a new earth.

Source 3 from Edwin S. Redkey, ed., *Respect Black: The Writings and Speeches of Henry McNeal Turner* (New York: Arno Press, 1971), pp. 167–171.

3. Turner's "The American Negro and His Fatherland," 1895.

It would be a waste of time to expend much labor, the few moments I have to devote to this subject, upon the present status of the Negroid race in the United States. It is too well-known already. However, I believe that the Negro

CHAPTER 2

THE ROAD TO
TRUE FREEDOM:
AFRICAN
AMERICAN
ALTERNATIVES
IN THE NEW
SOUTH

was brought to this country in the providence of God to a heaven-permitted if not a divine-sanctioned manual laboring school, that he might have direct contact with the mightiest race that ever trod the face of the globe.

The heathen Africans, to my certain knowledge, I care not what others may say, eagerly yearn for that civilization which they believe will elevate them and make them potential for good. The African was not sent and brought to this country by chance, or by the avarice of the white man, single and alone. The white slave-purchaser went to the shores of that continent and bought our ancestors from their African masters. The bulk who were brought to this country were the children of parents who had been in slavery a thousand years. Yet hereditary slavery is not universal among the African slaveholders. So that the argument often advanced, that the white man went to Africa and stole us, is not true. They bought us out of a slavery that still exists over a large portion of that continent. For there are millions and millions of slaves in Africa today. Thus the superior African sent us, and the white man brought us, and we remained in slavery as long as it was necessary to learn that a God, who is a spirit, made the world and controls it, and that that Supreme Being could be sought and found by the exercise of faith in His only begotten Son. Slavery then went down, and the colored man was thrown upon his own responsibility, and here he is today, in the providence of God, cultivating self-reliance and imbibing a knowledge of civil law in contradistinction to the dictum of one man, which was the law of the black man until slavery was overthrown. I believe that the Negroid race has been free long enough now to begin to think for himself and plan for better conditions [than] he can lay claim to in this country or ever will. *There is no manhood future in the United States for the Negro.* He may eke out an existence for generations to come, but he can never be a *man*—full, symmetrical and undwarfed. Upon this point I know thousands who make pretensions to scholarship, white and colored, will differ and may charge me with folly, while I in turn pity their ignorance of history and political and civil sociology. We beg here to itemize and give a cursory glance at a few facts calculated to convince any man who is not biased or lamentably ignorant. Let us note a few of them.

1. There is a great chasm between the white and black, not only in this country, but in the West India Islands, South America, and as much as has been said to the contrary, I have seen inklings of it in Ireland, in England, in France, in Germany, and even away down in southern Spain in sight of Morocco in Africa. We will not, however, deal with foreign nations, but let us note a few facts connected with the United States.

I repeat that a great chasm exists between the two race varieties in this country. The white people, neither North or South, will have social contact as a mass between themselves and any portion of the Negroid race. Although they may be as white in appearance as themselves, yet a drop of African blood imparts a taint, and the talk about two races remaining in the same country with mutual interest and responsibility in its institutions and progress, with no social contact, is the jargon of folly, and no man who has read the history of nations and the development of countries, and the agencies which have culminated in the homogeneity of racial variations, will proclaim such a doctrine. Senator Morgan,[8] of Alabama, tells the truth when he says that the Negro has nothing to expect without social equality with the whites, and that the whites will never grant it.

This question must be examined and opinions reached in the light of history and sociological philosophy, and not by a mere think-so on the part of men devoid of learning. When I use the term learning, I do not refer to men who have graduated from some college and have a smattering knowledge of Greek, Latin, mathematics and a few school books, and have done nothing since but read the trashy articles of newspapers. That is not scholarship. Scholarship consists in wading through dusty volumes for forty and fifty years. That class of men would not dare to predict symmetrical manhood for the Negroid race in this or any other country, without social equality. The colored man who will stand up and in one breath say that the Negroid race does not want social equality and in the next predict a great future in the face of all the proscription of which the colored man is the victim, is either an ignoramus, or is an advocate of the perpetual servility and degradation of his race variety.[9] I know, as Senator Morgan says, and as every white man in the land will say, that the whites will not grant social equality to the Negroid race, nor am I certain that God wants them to do it. And as such, I believe that two or three millions of us should return to the land of our ancestors, and establish our own nation, civilization, laws, customs, style of manufacture, and not only give the world, like other race varieties, the benefit of our individuality, but build up social conditions peculiarly our own, and cease to be grumblers, chronic complainers and a menace to the white man's country, or the country he claims and is bound to dominate.

The civil status of the Negro is simply what the white man grants of his own free will and accord. The black man can demand nothing. He is deposed from the jury and tried, convicted and sentenced by men who do not claim to be his peers. On the railroads, where the colored race is found in the

8. John Tyler Morgan (1824–1907), U.S. senator from 1877 to 1907. Morgan was an ardent expansionist and white supremacist. See Joseph A. Fry, *John Tyler Morgan and the Search for Southern Autonomy* (Knoxville: University of Tennessee Press, 1992).
9. The reference is to Booker T. Washington.

CHAPTER 2

THE ROAD TO
TRUE FREEDOM:
AFRICAN
AMERICAN
ALTERNATIVES
IN THE NEW
SOUTH

largest numbers, he is the victim of proscription, and he must ride in the Jim Crow car or walk. The Supreme Court of the United States decided, October 15th, 1883, that the colored man had no civil rights under the general government,[10] and the several States, from then until now, have been enacting laws which limit, curtail and deprive him of his civil rights, immunities and privileges, until he is now being disfranchised, and where it will end no one can divine.

They told me in the Geographical Institute in Paris, France, that according to their calculation there are not less than 400,000,000 of Africans and their descendants on the globe, so that we are not lacking in numbers to form a nationality of our own.

2. The environments of the Negroid race variety in this country tend to the inferiority of them, even if the argument can be established that we are equals with the white man in the aggregate, notwithstanding the same opportunities may be enjoyed in the schools. Let us not[e] a few facts.

The discriminating laws, all will concede, are degrading to those against which they operate, and the degrader will be degraded also. "For all acts are reactionary, and will return in curses upon those who curse," said Stephen A. Douglass [sic], the great competitor of President Lincoln. Neither does it require a philosopher to inform you that degradation begets degradation. Any people oppressed, proscribed, belied, slandered, burned, flayed and lynched will not only become cowardly and servile, but will transmit that same servility to their posterity, and continue to do so *ad infinitum,* and as such will never make a bold and courageous people. The condition of the Negro in the United States is so repugnant to the instincts of respected manhood that thousands, yea hundreds of thousands, of miscegenated will pass for white, and snub the people with whom they are identified at every opportunity, thus destroying themselves, or at least *unracing* themselves. They do not want to be black because of its ignoble condition, and they cannot be white, thus they become monstrosities. Thousands of young men who are even educated by white teachers never have any respect for people of their own color and spend their days as devotees of white gods. Hundreds, if not thousands, of the terms employed by the white race in the English language are also degrading to the black man. Everything that is satanic, corrupt, base and infamous is denominated *black,* and all that constitutes virtue, purity, innocence, religion, and that

10. On October 15, 1883, the Supreme Court handed down one decision that applied to five separate cases that had been argued before the Court, all of them having to do with racial segregation by private businesses (inns, hotels, theaters, and a railroad). Writing for the majority, Justice Joseph P. Bradley ruled that the Thirteenth, Fourteenth, and Fifteenth amendments did not give the federal government the power to outlaw discriminatory practices by private organizations, but only by states. See 109 U.S. 3, 3 S. Ct., 18, 27, L. Ed. 835 (1883).

which is divine and heavenly, is represented as *white*. Our Sabbath-school children, by the time they reach proper consciousness, are taught to sing to the laudation of white and to the contempt of black. Can any one with an ounce of common sense expect that these children, when they reach maturity, will ever have any respect for their black or colored faces, or the faces of their associates? But, without multiplying words, the terms used in our religious experience, and the hymns we sing in many instances, are degrading, and will be as long as the black man is surrounded by the idea that *white* represents God and black represents the devil. The Negro should, therefore, build up a nation of his own, and create a language in keeping with his color, as the whites have done. Nor will he ever respect himself until he does it.

3. In this country the colored man, with a few honorable exceptions, folds his arms and waits for the white man to propose, project, erect, invent, discover, combine, plan and execute everything connected with civilization, including machinery, finance, and indeed everything. This, in the nature of things, dwarfs the colored man and allows his great faculties to slumber from the cradle to the grave. Yet he possesses mechanical and inventive genius, I believe, equal to any race on earth. Much has been said about the natural inability of the colored race to engage in the professions of skilled labor. Yet before the war, right here in this Southland he erected and completed all of the fine edifices in which the lords of the land luxuriated. It is idle talk to speak of a colored man not being a success in skilled labor or the fine arts. What the black man needs is a country and surroundings in harmony with his color and with respect for his manhood. Upon this point I would delight to dwell longer if I had time. Thousands of white people in this country are ever and anon advising the colored people to keep out of politics, but they do not advise themselves. If the Negro is a man in keeping with other men, why should he be less concerned about politics than any one else? Strange, too, that a number of would-be colored leaders are ignorant and debased enough to proclaim the same foolish jargon. For the Negro to stay out of politics is to level himself with a horse or a cow, which is no politician, and the Negro who does it proclaims his inability to take part in political affairs. If the Negro is to be a man, full and complete, he must take part in everything that belongs to manhood. If he omits a single duty, responsibility or privilege, to that extent he is limited and incomplete.

Time, however, forbids my continuing the discussion of this subject, roughly and hastily as these thoughts have been thrown together. Not being able to present a dozen or two more phases, which I would cheerfully and gladly do if opportunity permitted, I conclude by saying the argument that

CHAPTER 2

THE ROAD TO
TRUE FREEDOM:
AFRICAN
AMERICAN
ALTERNATIVES
IN THE NEW
SOUTH

it would be impossible to transport the colored people of the United States back to Africa is an advertisement of folly. Two hundred millions of dollars would rid this country of the last member of the Negroid race, if such a thing was desirable, and two hundred and fifty millions would give every man, woman and child excellent fare, and the general government could furnish that amount and never miss it, and that would only be the pitiful sum of a million dollars a year for the time we labored for nothing, and for which somebody or some power is responsible. The emigrant agents at New York, Boston, Philadelphia, St. John, N.B., and Halifax, N.S., with whom I have talked, establish beyond contradiction, that over a million, and from that to twelve hundred thousand persons, come to this country every year, and yet there is no public stir about it. But in the case of African emigration, two or three millions only of self-reliant men and women would be necessary to establish the conditions we are advocating in Africa. . . .

Source 4 from Nathan Huggins, comp., *W. E. B. Du Bois Writings* (New York: Library of America, 1986), pp. 842, 846–848, 860–861.

4. Du Bois's "The Talented Tenth" (1903).

The Negro race, like all races, is going to be saved by its exceptional men. The problem of education, then, among Negroes must first of all deal with the Talented Tenth; it is the problem of developing the Best of this race that they may guide the Mass away from the contamination and death of the Worst, in their own and other races. Now the training of men is a difficult and intricate task. Its technique is a matter for educational experts, but its object is for the vision of seers. If we make money the object of man-training, we shall develop money-makers but not necessarily men; if we make technical skill the object of education, we may possess artisans but not, in nature, men. Men we shall have only as we make manhood the object of the work of the schools—intelligence, broad sympathy, knowledge of the world that was and is, and of the relation to men to it—this is the curriculum of that Higher Education which must underlie true life. On this foundation we may build bread-winning skill of hand and quickness of brain, with never a fear lest the child and man mistake the means of living for the object of life.

If this be true—and who can deny it—three tasks lie before me; first to show from the past that the Talented Tenth as they have risen among American Negroes have been worthy of leadership; secondly, to show how these men may be educated and developed; and thirdly, to show their relation to the Negro problem.

You misjudge us because you do not know us. From the very first it has been the educated and intelligent of the Negro people that have led and elevated the mass, and the sole obstacles that nullified and retarded their efforts were slavery and race prejudice; for what is slavery but the legalized survival of the unfit and the nullification of the work of natural internal leadership? . . .

It is the fashion of today to sneer at them and to say that with freedom Negro leadership should have begun at the plow and not in the Senate—a foolish and mischievous lie; two hundred and fifty years that black serf toiled at the plow and yet that toiling was in vain till the Senate passed the war amendments; and two hundred and fifty years more the half-free serf of today may toil at his plow, but unless he have political rights and righteously guarded civic status, he will still remain the poverty-stricken and ignorant plaything of rascals, that he now is. This all sane men know even if they dare not say it.

And so we come to the present—a day of cowardice and vacillation, of strident wide-voiced wrong and faint-hearted compromise; of double-faced dallying with the Truth and Right. Who are today guiding the work of the Negro people? The "exceptions" of course. And yet so sure as this Talented Tenth is pointed out, the blind worshippers of the Average cry out in alarm: "These are exceptions, look here at death, disease and crime—these are the happy rule." Of course they are the rule, because a silly nation made them the rule: Because for three long centuries this people lynched Negroes who dared to be brave, raped black women who dared to be virtuous, crushed dark-hued youth who dared to be ambitious, and encouraged and made to flourish servility and lewdness and apathy. But not even this was able to crush all manhood and chastity and aspiration from black folk. A saving remnant continually survives and persists, continually aspires, continually shows itself in thrift and ability and character. Exceptional it is to be sure, but this is its chiefest promise; it shows the capability of Negro blood, the promise of black men. Do Americans ever stop to reflect that there are in this land a million men of Negro blood, well-educated, owners of homes, against the honor of whose womanhood no breath was ever raised, whose men occupy positions of trust and usefulness, and who, judged by any standard, have reached the full measure of the best type of modern European culture? Is it fair, is it decent, is it Christian to ignore these facts of the Negro problem, to belittle such aspiration, to nullify such leadership and seek to crush these people back into the mass out of which by toil and travail, they and their fathers have raised themselves?

CHAPTER 2

THE ROAD TO
TRUE FREEDOM:
AFRICAN
AMERICAN
ALTERNATIVES
IN THE NEW
SOUTH

Can the masses of the Negro people be in any possible way more quickly raised than by the effort and example of this aristocracy of talent and character? Was there ever a nation on God's fair earth civilized from the bottom upward? Never; it is, ever was and ever will be from the top downward that culture filters. The Talented Tenth rises and pulls all that are worth the saving up to their vantage ground. This is the history of human progress; and the two historic mistakes which have hindered that progress were the thinking first that no more could ever rise save the few already risen; or second, that it would better the unrisen to pull the risen down.

How then shall the leaders of a struggling people be trained and the hands of the risen few strengthened? There can be but one answer: The best and most capable of their youth must be schooled in the colleges and universities of the land. We will not quarrel as to just what the university of the Negro should teach or how it should teach it—I willingly admit that each soul and each race-soul needs its own peculiar curriculum. But this is true: A university is a human invention for the transmission of knowledge and culture from generation to generation, through the training of quick minds and pure hearts, and for this work no other human invention will suffice, not even trade and industrial schools.

All men cannot go to college but some men must; every isolated group or nation must have its yeast, must have for the talented few centers of training where men are not so mystified and befuddled by the hard and necessary toil of earning a living, as to have no aims higher than their bellies, and no God greater than Gold. This is true training, and thus in the beginning were the favored sons of the freedmen trained.

Thus, again, in the manning of trade schools and manual training schools we are thrown back upon the higher training as its source and chief support. There was a time when any aged and wornout carpenter could teach in a trade school. But not so to-day. Indeed the demand for college-bred men by a school like Tuskegee, ought to make Mr. Booker T. Washington the firmest friend of higher training. Here he has as helpers the son of a Negro senator, trained in Greek and the humanities, and graduated at Harvard; the son of a Negro congressman and lawyer, trained in Latin and mathematics, and graduated at Oberlin; he has as his wife, a woman who read Virgil and Homer in the same class room with me; he has as college chaplain, a classical graduate of Atlanta University; as teacher of science, a graduate of Fisk; as teacher of history, a graduate of Smith,—indeed some thirty of his chief teachers are college graduates, and instead of studying French grammars in the midst of weeds, or buying pianos for dirty cabins, they are at Mr. Washington's right hand helping him in a noble work. And yet one of the effects of Mr. Washington's propaganda has been to throw doubt upon the expediency of such training for Negroes, as these persons have had.

Men of America, the problem is plain before you. Here is a race transplanted through the criminal foolishness of your fathers. Whether you like it or not the millions are here, and here they will remain. If you do not lift them up, they will pull you down. Education and work are the levers to uplift a people. Work alone will not do it unless inspired by the right ideals and guided by intelligence. Education must not simply teach work—it must teach Life. The Talented Tenth of the Negro race must be made leaders of thought and missionaries of culture among their people. No others can do this work and Negro colleges must train men for it. The Negro race, like all other races, is going to be saved by its exceptional men. . . .

Source 5 from Herbert Atheker, ed., *Pamphlets and Leaflets by W. E. B. Du Bois* (White Plains, N.Y.: Kraus-Thomson Organization Ltd., 1986), pp. 63–65.

5. Du Bois's Niagara Address (1906).[11]

. . . In detail our demands are clear and unequivocal. First, we would vote; with the right to vote goes everything: Freedom, manhood, the honor of your wives, the chastity of your daughters, the right to work, and the chance to rise, and let no man listen to those who deny this.

We want full manhood suffrage, and we want it now, henceforth and forever.

Second. We want discrimination in public accommodation to cease. Separation in railway and street cars, based simply on race and color, is un-American, undemocratic, and silly. We protest against all such discrimination.

Third. We claim the right of freemen to walk, talk, and be with them that wish to be with us. No man has a right to choose another man's friends, and to attempt to do so is an impudent interference with the most fundamental human privilege.

Fourth. We want the laws enforced against rich as well as poor; against Capitalist as well as Laborer; against white as well as black. We are not more lawless than the white race, we are more often arrested, convicted and mobbed. We want justice even for criminals and outlaws. We want the Constitution of the country enforced. We want Congress to take charge of Congressional elections. We want the Fourteenth Amendment carried out to the letter and every State disfranchised in Congress which attempts to

11. The Niagara Movement was organized by Du Bois in 1905. It called for agitation against all forms of segregation. This is a selection from Du Bois's address to the group in 1906.

CHAPTER 2

THE ROAD TO
TRUE FREEDOM:
AFRICAN
AMERICAN
ALTERNATIVES
IN THE NEW
SOUTH

disfranchise its rightful voters. We want the Fifteenth Amendment enforced and no State allowed to base its franchise simply on color.

The failure of the Republican Party in Congress at the session just closed to redeem its pledge of 1904 with reference to suffrage conditions [in] the South seems a plain, deliberate, and premeditated breach of promise, and stamps that party as guilty of obtaining votes under false pretense.

Fifth. We want our children educated. The school system in the country districts of the South is a disgrace and in few towns and cities are the Negro schools what they ought to be. We want the national government to step in and wipe out illiteracy in the South. Either the United States will destroy ignorance or ignorance will destroy the United States.

And when we call for education we mean real education. We believe in work. We ourselves are workers, but work is not necessarily education. Education is the development of power and ideal. We want our children trained as intelligent human beings should be, and we will fight for all time against any proposal to educate black boys and girls simply as servants and underlings, or simply for the use of other people. They have a right to know, to think, to aspire.

These are some of the chief things which we want. How shall we get them? By voting where we may vote, by persistent, unceasing agitation, by hammering at the truth, by sacrifice and work.

We do not believe in violence, neither in the despised violence of the raid nor the lauded violence of the soldier, nor the barbarous violence of the mob, but we do believe in John Brown, in that incarnate spirit of justice, that hatred of a lie, that willingness to sacrifice money, reputation, and life itself on the altar of right. And here on the scene of John Brown's martyrdom we reconsecrate ourselves, our honor, our property to the final emancipation of the race which John Brown died to make free.

Our enemies, triumphant for the present, are fighting the stars in their courses. Justice and humanity must prevail. We live to tell these dark brothers of ours—scattered in counsel, wavering and weak—that no bribe of money or notoriety, no promise of wealth or fame, is worth the surrender of a people's manhood or the loss of a man's self-respect. We refuse to surrender the leadership of this race to cowards and trucklers. We are men; we will be treated as men. On this rock we have planted our banners. We will never give up, though the trump of doom find us still fighting.

And we shall win. The past promised it, the present foretells it. Thank God for John Brown! Thank God for Garrison and Douglass! Sumner and Phillips, Nat Turner and Robert Gould Shaw,[12] and all the hallowed dead

12. Robert Gould Shaw was a Massachusetts white man who during the Civil War commanded African American troops. While leading those soldiers into battle, Shaw was killed on July 18, 1863. He was portrayed in the film *Glory*.

who died for freedom! Thank God for all those today, few though their voices be, who have not forgotten the divine brotherhood of all men, white and black, rich and poor, fortunate and unfortunate.

We appeal to the young men and women of this nation, to those whose nostrils are not yet befouled by greed and snobbery and racial narrowness: Stand up for the right, prove yourselves worthy of your heritage and whether born north or south dare to treat men as men. Cannot the nation that has absorbed ten million foreigners into its political life without catastrophe absorb ten million Negro Americans into that same political life at less cost than their unjust and illegal exclusion will involve?

Courage, brothers! The battle for humanity is not lost or losing. All across the skies sit signs of promise. The Slav is rising in his might, the yellow millions are tasting liberty, the black Africans are writhing toward the light, and everywhere the laborer, with ballot in his hand, is voting open the gates of Opportunity and Peace. The morning breaks over blood-stained hills. We must not falter, we may not shrink. Above are the everlasting stars.

Source 6 from Bureau of the Census, *Historical Statistics of the United States, Colonial Times to 1970* (Washington, D.C.: Government Printing Office, 1975), Vol. I, p. 95.

6. Estimated Net Intercensal Migration* of Negro Population by Region, 1870–1920 (in Thousands).

	1870–1880	1880–1890	1890–1900	1900–1910	1910–1920
New England[1]	4.5	6.6	14.2	8.0	12.0
Middle Atlantic[2]	19.2	39.1	90.7	87.2	170.1
East North Central[3]	20.8	16.4	39.4	45.6	200.4
West North Central[4]	15.7	7.9	23.5	10.2	43.7
South Atlantic[5]	−47.9	−72.5	−181.6	−111.9	−158.0
East South Central[6]	−56.2	−60.1	−43.3	−109.6	−246.3
West South Central[7]	45.1	62.9	56.9	51.0	−46.2

*A net intercensal migration represents the amount of migration that took place between United States censuses, which are taken every ten years. The net figure is computed by comparing in-migration with out-migration to a particular state. A minus figure means that out-migration from a state was greater than in-migration.
1. Maine, New Hampshire, Vermont, Massachusetts, Rhode Island, and Connecticut.
2. New York, New Jersey, and Pennsylvania.
3. Ohio, Indiana, Illinois, Michigan, and Wisconsin.
4. Minnesota, Iowa, Missouri, North Dakota, South Dakota, Nebraska, and Kansas.
5. Delaware, Maryland, District of Columbia, Virginia, West Virginia, North Carolina, South Carolina, Georgia, and Florida.
6. Kentucky, Tennessee, Alabama, and Mississippi.
7. Arkansas, Louisiana, Oklahoma, and Texas.

CHAPTER 2

THE ROAD TO
TRUE FREEDOM:
AFRICAN
AMERICAN
ALTERNATIVES
IN THE NEW
SOUTH

QUESTIONS TO CONSIDER

The Background section of this chapter strongly suggests that the prospects for African Americans in the post–Reconstruction South were bleak. Although blacks certainly preferred sharecropping or tenancy to working in gangs as in the days of slavery, neither sharecropping nor tenancy offered African Americans much chance to own their own land. Furthermore, the industrial opportunities available to European immigrants, which allowed many of them gradually to climb the economic ladder, for the most part were closed to southern blacks, in part because the South was never able to match the North in the creation of industrial jobs and in part because what jobs the New South industrialization did create often were closed to blacks. As we have seen, educational opportunities for African Americans in the South were severely limited—so much so that by 1890, more than 75 percent of the adult black population in the Deep South still was illiterate (as opposed to 17.1 percent of the adult white population). In addition, rigid segregation laws and racial violence had increased dramatically. Indeed, the prospects for southern blacks were far from promising.

Begin by analyzing Ida B. Wells's response (Source 1) to the deteriorating condition of African Americans in the South. In her view, how did blacks in Memphis and Kentucky provide a model for others? What was that model? In addition to that model, Wells tells us how blacks in Jacksonville, Florida, and Paducah, Kentucky, were able to prevent lynchings in those towns. What alternative did those blacks present? Was Wells advocating it? Finally, what role did Wells see the African American press playing in preventing lynchings?

The alternative offered by Booker T. Washington (Source 2) differs markedly from those offered by Wells. In his view, what *process* should African Americans follow to enjoy their full rights? How did he support his argument? What did Washington conceive the role of southern whites in African Americans' progress to be? Before you dismiss Washington's alternative, remember that his *goals* were roughly similar to those of Wells. Also use some inference to imagine how Washington's audiences would have reacted to his speech. How would southern whites have greeted his speech? Southern blacks? What about northern whites? Northern blacks? To whom was Washington speaking?

Now move on to Henry McNeal Turner's alternative (Source 3). At first Bishop Turner seems to be insulting blacks. What was he really trying to say? Why did he think that God ordained blacks to be brought to America in chains? In Turner's view, once blacks were freed, what was their best alternative? Why? Turner's view of whites is at serious odds with that of Washington. How do the two views differ on this point? How did Turner use his view of whites to support his alternative for blacks?

Taken together, the two speeches by Du Bois (Sources 4 and 5) present a consistent view, even though their subject matter and emphasis are different. What was the "talented tenth"? In Du Bois's view, what crucial role must that group play? How is that view at odds with Washington's view? In his Niagara Address of 1906, Du Bois states what the goals of the "talented tenth" should be. What are those objectives? How does his *process* differ from that of Washington? Furthermore, how does Du Bois's view differ from Washington's with respect to timing? Tactics? Tone? Remember, however, that the long-term goals of both men were similar.

Perhaps you have been struck by the fact that both Turner and Du Bois pinned their hopes for progress on African American *men*. Turner refers frequently to "manhood" and Du Bois to "exceptional men." Why do you think this was so? Why do you think the concept of African American manhood was important to these two thinkers?

Finally, examine Source 6. What additional alternative was open to African Americans? How did that alternative change over time? Can you use the other material in this chapter to suggest why such a change was taking place? What does this tell you about southern African Americans' reactions to the alternatives articulated by Wells, Washington, Turner, and Du Bois?

It is now time to assess the various options open to southern African Americans in the late nineteenth and twentieth centuries. To determine which option was best, you will have to answer the following questions:

1. How do I define "best"? More realistic? More morally defensible? Best in the long range? Best in the short range?

2. What would have happened if southern African Americans had come to adopt Wells's alternatives? Where might the process outlined by Wells have led? Were there any risks for African Americans? If so, what were they?

3. What would have happened if southern African Americans had adopted Washington's alternative? How long would it have taken them to realize Washington's goals? Were there any risks involved? If so, what were they?

4. What would have happened if southern African Americans had adopted Turner's alternative? Were there any risks involved? How realistic was Turner's option?

5. What would have happened if southern African Americans had adopted Du Bois's alternative? How long would Du Bois's process have taken? Were there any risks involved?

6. Was white assistance necessary according to Wells? To Washington? To Turner? To Du Bois? How did each spokesperson perceive the roles of the federal government and the federal courts? How did the government and courts stand on this issue at the time? [*Clue:* What was the Supreme Court decision in *Plessy v. Ferguson* (1896)?]

No one living in the latter part of the twentieth century can assess with absolute objectivity which of the options available to African Americans in the South almost a century before was the best one. Nor is it possible to put ourselves completely in the shoes of these men and women. Yet a thorough examination of the positive points and liabilities of each option

CHAPTER 2

THE ROAD TO
TRUE FREEDOM:
AFRICAN
AMERICAN
ALTERNATIVES
IN THE NEW
SOUTH

can give us a closer approximation of which alternative was the most attractive. As you do this, do not neglect the statistical evidence or the material provided in the Background section of this chapter or in other material you read.

EPILOGUE

For the advocates of a New South, the realization of their dream seemed to be just over the horizon, always just beyond their grasp. Many of the factories did make a good deal of money. But profits often flowed out of the South to northern investors. And factory owners often maintained profits by paying workers pitifully low wages, which led to the rise of a poor white urban class that lived in slums and faced enormous problems of malnutrition, poor health, family instability, and crime. To most of those who had left their meager farms to find opportunities in the burgeoning southern cities, life there appeared even worse than it had been in the rural areas. Many whites returned to their rural homesteads disappointed and dispirited by urban life.

For an increasing number of southern African Americans, the solution seemed to be to abandon the South entirely. Beginning around the time of World War I (1917–1918), a growing number of African Americans migrated to the industrial cities of the Northeast, Midwest, and West Coast. But there, too, they met racial hostility and racially inspired riots.

At least in the North, African Americans could vote and thereby influence public policy. By the late 1940s, it had become clear that northern urban African American voters, by their very number, could force American politicians to deal with racial discrimination. By the 1950s, it was evident that the South would have to change its racial policies, if not willingly then by force. It took federal courts, federal marshals, and occasionally federal troops, but the crust of discrimination in the South began to be broken in the 1960s. Attitudes changed slowly, but the white southern politician draped in the Confederate flag and calling for resistance to change became a figure of the past. Although much work still needed to be done, changes in the South had been profound, laying the groundwork for more changes ahead. Indeed, by the 1960s the industrialization and prosperity (largely through in-migration) of the Sunbelt seemed to show that Grady's dream of a New South might become a reality.

And yet, for all the hopeful indications (black voting and officeholding in the South, for instance), in many ways the picture was a somber one. By the 1970s, several concerned observers, both black and white, feared that the poorest 30 percent of all black families, instead of climbing slowly up the economic ladder, were in the process of forming a permanent underclass, complete with a social pathology that included broken families, crime, drugs, violence, and grinding poverty. Equally disturbing in the 1980s was a new wave of racial intolerance among whites, a phenomenon that even invaded many American colleges and universities. In short, although much progress had been made since the turn of the century, in many ways, as in the New South, the dream of equality and tolerance remained just over the horizon.

By this time, of course, Wells, Washington, Turner, and Du Bois were dead. Wells continued to write militant articles for the African American press, became deeply involved in the women's suffrage movement, and carried on a successful crusade to prevent the racial segregation of the Chicago city schools. She died in Chicago in 1931. For his part, Washington clung stubbornly to his notion of self-help, even though he realized privately that whites could use him as an apologist for the status quo and a supporter of racial segregation. He died in Tuskegee, Alabama, in 1915.

Turner's dream of thousands of blacks moving to Africa never materialized. In response, he grew more strident and was especially critical of African Americans who opposed his ideas. In 1898, Turner raised a storm of protest when his essay "God Is a Negro" was published. The essay began, "We have as much right . . . to believe that God is a Negro, as you buckra, or white, people have to believe that God is a fine looking, symmetrical and ornamented white man." He died while on a speaking trip to Canada in 1915. As for Du Bois, he also grew more embittered over the years, turning toward Marxism and pan-Africanism when he believed "the system" had failed him and his people. He died in Africa in 1963.

In their time, Wells, Washington, Turner, and Du Bois were important and respected figures. Although often publicly at odds, privately they shared the same dream of African Americans living with pride and dignity in a world that recognized them as complete men and women. In an era in which few people championed the causes of African American people, these four spokespersons stood as courageous figures.

CHAPTER 3

HOW THEY LIVED: MIDDLE-CLASS LIFE, 1870–1917

 THE PROBLEM

In the 1870s, Heinrich Schliemann, a middle-aged German archaeologist, astonished the world with his claim that he had discovered the site of ancient Troy. As all educated people of the time knew, Troy was the golden city of heroes that the blind poet Homer (seventh century B.C.) made famous in his *Iliad* and *Odyssey*. Although archaeologists continued to argue bitterly about whether it was really Troy or some other ancient city that Schliemann was excavating, the general public was fascinated with the vases, gold and silver cups, necklaces, and earrings that were unearthed.

Not only the relics and "treasure" interested Americans, however. As the magazine *Nation* pointed out in 1875, these discoveries offered an opportunity to know about Troy as it had actually existed and to understand something about the daily lives of the inhabitants. Nineteenth-century Americans were intensely curious about the art, religion, burial customs, dress, and even the foods of the ancient Greeks. "Real Trojans," noted a magazine editor in 1881, "were very fond of oysters." (He based his conclusion on the large amounts of oyster shells uncovered at the archaeological digs.)

Material culture study is the use of artifacts to understand people's lives. In this chapter, you will be looking at some artifacts of the late nineteenth and early twentieth centuries—advertisements and house plans—to try to reconstruct the lives of middle-class white Americans during a period when the country was changing rapidly. What were Americans' hopes and fears during this era? What were their values?

∽ BACKGROUND ∾

The age from approximately 1870 to 1900 was characterized by enormous and profound changes in American life. Unquestionably, the most important changes were the nation's rapid industrialization and urbanization. Aided and accelerated by the rapid growth of railroads, emerging industries could extend their tentacles throughout the nation, collecting raw materials and fuel for the factories and distributing finished products to the growing American population. By 1900, that industrial process had come to be dominated by a few energetic and shrewd men, captains of industry to their friends and robber barons to their enemies. Almost every conceivable industry, from steel and oil to sugar refining and meat packing, was controlled by one or two gigantic corporations that essentially had the power to set prices on the raw materials bought and the finished products sold. In turn, the successes of those corporations created a new class of fabulously rich industrialists, and names like Swift, Armour, Westinghouse, Pillsbury, Pullman, Rockefeller, Carnegie, and Duke literally became almost household words, as much for the notoriety of the industrialists as for the industries and products they created.

As America became more industrialized, it also became more urban. In the past, the sizes of cities had been limited by the availability of nearby food, fuel, and employment opportunities. But the network of railroads and the rise of large factories had removed those limitations, and American cities grew phenomenally. Between 1860 and 1910, urban population increased sevenfold, and by 1920 more than half of all Americans lived in cities.[1] These urban complexes not only dominated the regions in which they were located but eventually set much of the tone for the entire nation as well.

Both processes—industrialization and urbanization—profoundly altered nearly every facet of American life. Family size began to decrease; the woman who might have had five or six children in 1860 was replaced by the "new" woman of 1900 who had only three or four children. The fruits of industrialization, distributed by new marketing techniques, could be enjoyed by a large portion of the American population. Electric lights, telephones, and eventually appliances virtually revolutionized the lives of the middle and upper classes, as did Ford's later mass production of the Model T automobile.

The nature of the work also was changed because factories required a higher degree of regimentation than did farm work or the "putting-out" system. Many industries found it more profitable to employ women and children than adult males, thus altering the home lives of many of the nation's working-class citizens. Moreover, the lure of employment brought millions of immigrants to the United States, most of whom huddled together in

1. The census defined *city* as a place with a population over twenty-five hundred people. Thus, many of the cities referred to in this exercise are what we would call towns, or even small towns.

cities, found low-paying jobs, and dreamed of the future. And as the cities grew grimy with factory soot and became increasingly populated by laborers, immigrants, and what one observer referred to as the "dangerous classes," upper- and middle-class Americans began to abandon the urban cores and retreat to fashionable suburbs on the peripheries, to return to the cities either in their automobiles or on streetcars only for work or recreation. In fact, the comforts of middle-class life were made possible, in part, by the exploitation of industrial workers.

Industrialization and urbanization not only changed how most Americans lived but how they *thought* as well. Faith in progress and technology was almost boundless, and there was widespread acceptance of the uneven distribution of wealth among Americans. Prior to the turn of the century, many upper- and middle-class Americans believed that life was a struggle in which the fittest survived. This concept, which applied Charles Darwin's discoveries about biological evolution to society, was called social Darwinism. The poor, especially the immigrant poor, were seen as biologically and morally inferior. It followed, then, that efforts to help the less fortunate through charity or government intervention were somehow tampering with both God's will and Darwinian evolution. In such a climate of opinion, the wealthy leaders of gigantic corporations became national heroes, superior in prestige to both preachers and presidents.

The response of the working classes varied; although many workers rejected the concepts of social Darwinism and Victorian morality, others aspired to middle-class status. In spite of long hours, low pay, and hazardous conditions, the men and women of the working classes engaged in a series of important labor protests and strikes during this period. A rich working-class culture developed in the saloons, vaudeville theaters, dance halls, and streets of medium-size and larger cities. Many workers sought alternatives in some form of socialism; many others, however, strove to achieve the standard of living of the rapidly expanding middle class. Across the country, young boys read the rags-to-riches tales of Horatio Alger, and girls learned to be "proper ladies" so that they would not embarrass their future husbands as they rose in society together.

Social critics and reformers of the time were appalled by the excesses of the "fabulously rich" and the misery of the "wretchedly poor." And yet a persistent belief in the opportunity to better oneself (or one's children's position) led many people to embrace an optimistic attitude and to focus on the acquisition of material possessions. New consumer goods were pouring from factories, and the housing industry was booming. Middle-class families emulated the housing and furnishing styles of the wealthy, and skilled blue-collar workers and their families aspired to own modest suburban homes on the streetcar line.

After 1900, widespread concern about the relationship of wages to the cost of maintaining a comfortable standard of living led to numerous studies of working-class families in various parts of the country. Could workers realistically hope to own homes and achieve decent standards of living as a result of their labor? In 1909, economist Robert Coit Chapin estimated that a family of five needed an annual income of about $900 to live in a decent home or apartment in New York City. A follow-up study of Philadelphia in 1917 estimated that same standard of living at approximately $1,600. Yet the average annual pay of adult male wage workers during these years ranged from only $600 to $1,700. Several other factors affected family income, however. Average wages are misleading, since skilled workers earned significantly more than unskilled or semiskilled workers. Even within the same industry and occupation, midwestern workers earned more than northeastern workers, and southern workers earned the lowest wages of all. Adult women workers, 80 percent of whom lived with families as wives or unmarried daughters, added their wages (approximately $300 to $600 a year) to the family income, as did working children. Many families, especially those of recent immigrants, also took in boarders and lodgers, who paid rent.

Finally, the cost of land and building materials was much more expensive in large cities than in smaller cities and towns. In his investigation of New York, Chapin found that 28 percent of working-class families in nine upstate cities owned their own homes, compared with only 1 percent in New York City. Another study in 1915 also sharply illustrated regional differences in home ownership. Twenty percent of Paterson, New Jersey, silk workers were homeowners, but only 10 percent of Birmingham, Alabama, steelworkers owned homes. Nineteen percent of Milwaukee's working-class families owned their own homes, compared to 4.4 percent of Boston's working-class families. Nor were all these homes in the central city. Working-class suburbs expanded along streetcar lines or were developed near industries on the fringes of a city, such as the suburb of Oakwood just outside Knoxville, Tennessee.[2] In this community near textile mills and a major railroad repair shop, house lots measuring 50 by 140 feet sold for less than one hundred dollars; most homes were built for under one thousand dollars. Nearly half of the one thousand families who moved to Oakwood between 1902 and 1917 came from the older industrial sections of Knoxville.

Completely reliable income and cost statistics for early twentieth-century America do not exist, but it seems reasonable to estimate that at least one-fourth of working-class families owned or were paying for homes and that many more aspired to homeownership. But fully half of all working-class families, usually concentrated in large cities, lived in or near poverty and could not hope to own their own homes. Those with middle-class white-collar occupations were more fortunate. Lawyers, doctors, businessmen, ministers, bank tellers, newspaper editors, and even schoolteachers could—through careful budgeting and saving—realistically expect to buy or build a house.

2. Knoxville's population in 1900 was 32,637; the city had experienced a 237 percent growth in population from 1880 to 1900.

Although technological advances and new distribution methods put many modern conveniences and new products within the reach of all but the poorest Americans, the economic growth of the period was neither constant nor steady. The repercussions from two major depressions—one in 1873 and one in 1894—made "getting ahead" difficult, if not impossible, for many lower-middle-class and blue-collar families. Furthermore, at times everything seemed to be changing so rapidly that many people felt insecure. Yet within middle-class families, this sense of insecurity and even fear often coexisted with optimism and a faith in progress.

One way to understand the lives of middle-class Americans during the post–Civil War era is to look at the *things* with which they surrounded themselves: their clothes, the goods and services they bought, and even their houses. Why did such fashions and designs appeal to Americans of the late nineteenth and early twentieth centuries? What kind of an impression were these people trying to make on other people? How did they really feel about themselves? Sometimes historians, like archaeologists, use artifacts such as clothes, furniture, houses, and so forth to reconstruct the lives of Americans in earlier times. Indeed, each year many thousands of tourists visit historic homes such as Jefferson's Monticello, retrace the fighting at Gettysburg, or stroll through entire restored communities such as Colonial Williamsburg. But historians of the post–Civil War period also may use advertisements (instead of the products or services themselves) and house plans (instead of the actual houses) to understand how middle-class Americans lived and what their values and concerns were.

Every day, Americans are surrounded, even bombarded, by advertising that tries to convince them to buy some product, use some service, or compare brand X with brand Y. Television, radio, billboards, magazines, and newspapers spread the message to potential consumers of a variety of necessary—and unnecessary—products. Underlying this barrage of advertisements is an appeal to a wide range of emotions: ambition, elitism, guilt, and anxiety. A whole new "science" has arisen, called market research, that analyzes consumers' reactions and predicts future buying patterns.

Yet advertising is a relatively new phenomenon, one that began to develop after the Civil War and did not assume its modern form until the 1920s. P. T. Barnum, the promoter and impresario of mid-nineteenth-century entertainment, pointed the way with publicity gimmicks for his museum and circuses and, later, for the relatively unknown Swedish singer Jenny Lind. (Barnum created such a demand for Lind's concert tickets that they sold for as much as two hundred dollars each.) But at the time of the Civil War, most merchants still announced special sales of their goods in simple newspaper notices, and brand names were virtually unknown.

Businesses, both large and small, expanded enormously after the Civil War. Taking advantage of the country's greatly improved transportation and communication systems, daring business leaders established innovative ways to distribute products, such as the mail-order firm and the department store. Sears Roebuck & Co. was founded in 1893, and its "wish book," or catalogue, rapidly became popular reading for millions of people, especially those who lived in rural areas. Almost one thousand pages long, these catalogues offered a dazzling variety of consumer goods and were filled with testimonial letters from satisfied customers. Lewis Thomas from Jefferson County, Alabama, wrote in 1897,

> I received my saddle and I must say that I am so pleased and satisfied with my saddle, words cannot express my thanks for the benefit that I received from the pleasure and satisfaction given me. I know that I have a saddle that will by ordinary care last a lifetime, and all my neighbors are pleased as well, and I am satisfied so well that you shall have more of my orders in the near future.

And from Granite, Colorado, Mrs. Laura Garrison wrote, "Received my suit all right, was much pleased with it, will recommend your house to my friends."

For those who lived in cities, the department store was yet another way to distribute consumer goods. The massive, impressively decorated buildings erected by department store owners were often described as consumer "cathedrals" or "palaces." In fact, no less a personage than President William Howard Taft dedicated the new Wanamaker's department store in Philadelphia in 1911. "We are here," Taft told the crowd, "to celebrate the completion of one of the most important instrumentalities in modern life for the promotion of comfort among the people."

Many of the products being manufactured in factories in the late nineteenth and early twentieth centuries represented items previously made at home. Tinned meats and biscuits, "store-bought" bread, ready-made clothing, and soap all represent the impact of technology on the functions of the homemaker. Other products were new versions of things already being used. For example, the bathtub was designed solely for washing one's body, as opposed to the large bucket or tub in which one collected rainwater, washed clothes, and, every so often, bathed. Still other products and gadgets (such as the phonograph and the automobile) were completely new, the result of a fertile period of inventiveness (1860 to 1890) that saw more than ten times more patents issued than were issued during the entire period up to 1860 (only 36,000 patents were issued prior to the Civil War, but 440,000 were granted during the next thirty years).

There was no question that American industry could produce new products and distribute them nationwide. But there *was* a problem: how could American industry overcome the traditional American ethic of thrift and create a demand for products that might not have even existed a few years earlier? It was this problem that the new field of advertising set out to solve.

America in 1865 was a country of widespread, if uneven, literacy and a vast variety of newspapers and magazines, all competing for readership.

Businesses quickly learned that mass production demanded a national, even an international, market, and money spent on national advertising in newspapers and magazines rose from $27 million in 1860 to more than $95 million in 1900. By 1929, the amount spent on advertising had climbed to more than $1 billion. Brand names and catchy slogans vied with one another to capture the consumer's interest. Consumers could choose from among many biscuit manufacturers, as the president of National Biscuit Company reported to his stockholders in 1901: "We do not pretend to sell our standard goods cheaper than other manufacturers of biscuits sell their goods. They always undersell us. Why do they not take away our business?" His answer was fourfold: efficiency, quality goods, innovative packaging, and advertising. "The trademarks we adopted," he concluded, "their value we created."

Advertising not only helped differentiate one brand of a product from another, but it also helped break down regional differences as well as differences between rural and urban lifestyles. Women living on farms in Kansas could order the latest "New York–style frocks" from a mail-order catalogue, and people in small towns in the Midwest or rural areas in the South could find the newest furniture styles, appliances, and automobiles enticingly displayed in mass-circulation magazines. In this era, more and more people abandoned the old ways of doing things and embraced the new ways of life that resulted from the application of modern technology, mass production, and efficient distribution of products. Thus, some historians have argued that advertising accelerated the transition of American society from one that emphasized production to one that stressed consumption.

The collective mentality, ideas, mood, and values of the rapidly changing society were reflected in nearly everything the society created, including its architecture. During the period from approximately 1865 to 1900, American architects designed public buildings, factories, banks, apartment houses, offices, and residential structures, aided by technological advances that allowed them to do things that had been impossible in the past. For instance, as American cities grew in size and population density, the value of real estate soared. Therefore, it made sense to design higher and higher buildings, taking advantage of every square foot of available land. The perfection of central heating systems; the inventions of the radiator, the elevator, and the flush toilet; and the use of steel framing allowed architects such as William Le Baron Jenney, Louis Sullivan, and others of the Chicago school of architecture to erect the modern skyscraper, a combined triumph of architecture, engineering, ingenuity, and construction.

At the same time, the new industrial elite were hiring these same architects to build their new homes—homes that often resembled huge Italian villas, French chateaux, and even Renaissance palaces. Only the wealthy, however, could afford homes individually designed by professional architects. Most people relied on contractors, builders, and carpenters who adapted drawings from books or magazines to suit their clients' needs and tastes. Such "pattern books," published by men like Henry Holly, the Palliser brothers, Robert Shoppell, and the Radford Architectural Company, were extremely popular. It is estimated that in the mid-1870s, at least one hundred homes a year were being built from plans published in one women's magazine, *Godey's Lady's Book,* and thousands of others were built from pamphlets provided by lumber and plumbing fixture companies and architectural pattern books. Eventually, a person could order a complete home through the mail; all parts of the prefabricated house were shipped by railroad for assembly by local workers on the owner's site. George Barber of Knoxville, Tennessee, the Aladdin Company of Bay City, Michigan, and even Sears Roebuck & Co. were all prospering in mail-order homes around the turn of the century.

From the historian's viewpoint, both advertising and architecture created a wealth of evidence that can be used to reconstruct our collective past.

By looking at and reading advertisements, we can trace Americans' changing habits, interests, and tastes. And by analyzing the kinds of emotional appeals used in the advertisements, we can begin to understand the aspirations and goals as well as the fears and anxieties of the people who lived in the rapidly changing society of the late nineteenth and early twentieth centuries.

Unfortunately, most people, including professional historians, are not used to looking for values and ideas in architecture. Yet every day we pass by houses and other buildings that could tell us a good deal about how people lived in a particular time period, as well as something about the values of the time. In this chapter, you will be examining closely both advertisements and house plans to reconstruct partially how middle-class Americans of the late nineteenth and early twentieth centuries lived.

❧ THE METHOD ❧

No historian would suggest that the advertisements of preceding decades (or today's advertisements, for that matter) speak for themselves—that they tell you how people actually lived. Like almost all other historical evidence, advertisements must be carefully analyzed for their messages. Advertisements are intended to make people want to buy various products and services. They can be positive or negative. Positive advertisements show the benefits—direct or indirect, explicit or implicit—that would come

from owning a product. Such advertisements depict an ideal. Negative or "scare" advertisements demonstrate the disastrous consequences of not owning the product. Some of the most effective advertisements combine both negative and positive approaches ("I was a lonely 360-pound woman before I discovered Dr. Quack's Appetite Suppressors—now I weigh 120 pounds and am engaged to be married!"). Advertisements also attempt to evoke an emotional response from potential consumers that will encourage the purchase of a particular product or service.

Very early advertisements tended to be primarily descriptive, simply picturing the product. Later advertisements often told a story with pictures and words. In looking at the advertisements in this chapter, first determine whether the approach used is positive, negative, or a combination of both factors. What were the expected consequences of using (or not using) the product? How did the advertisement try to sell the product or service? What emotional response(s) were expected?

The preceding evaluation is not too difficult, but in this exercise you must go even further with your analysis. You are trying to determine what each advertisement can tell you about earlier generations of Americans and the times in which they lived. Look at (and read) each advertisement carefully. Does it reveal anything about the values of the time period in which the advertisements appeared? About the roles of men and women? About attitudes concerning necessities and luxuries? About people's aspirations or fears?

House plans also must be analyzed if they are to tell us something about how people used to live. At one time or another, you have probably looked at a certain building and thought, "That is truly an ugly, awful-looking building! Whatever possessed the lunatic who built it?" Yet when that building was designed and built, most likely it was seen as a truly beautiful structure and may have been widely praised by its occupants as well as by those who merely passed by. Why is this so? Why did an earlier generation believe the building was beautiful?

All of us are aware that standards for what is good art, good music, good literature, and good architecture change over time. What may be pleasing to the people of one era might be considered repugnant or even obscene by those of another time. But is this solely the result of changing fads, such as the sudden rises and declines in the popularity of movie and television stars, rock 'n' roll groups, or fashionable places to vacation?

The answer is partly yes, but only partly. Tastes do change, and fads such as the Hula-Hoop and the yo-yo come and inevitably go. However, we must still ask why a particular person or thing becomes popular or in vogue at a certain time. Do these changing tastes in art, music, literature, and architecture *mean* something? Can they tell us something about the people who embraced these various styles? More to the point, can they tell us something about the *values* of those who embraced them? Obviously, they can.

In examining these middle-class homes, you should first look for common exterior and interior features. Then look at the interior rooms and their functions, comparing them with rooms in American homes today. You also must try to imagine what impression these houses conveyed to people in the late nineteenth and early twentieth centuries. Finally, you will be thinking about all the evidence—the advertisements and the house plans— as a whole. What is the relationship between the material culture (in this case, the advertisements and the house plans) and the values and concerns of Americans in the late nineteenth and early twentieth centuries?

Sources 1 through 3 from Sears Roebuck & Co. catalogues, 1897 and 1902.

1. Children's Reefer Jackets (1897) and Children's Toys (1902).

SEARS ROEBUCK & CO. INC

85¢ $1.50

24171   24172

REEFER JACKETS FOR CHILDREN FROM 1 TO 5 YEARS OLD.

Do not forget to mention age and color desired when ordering.

Reefer Jackets for little toddlers, from one to four years, nobby, stylish little coats at little bits of prices. As usual S. R. & Co. will save you money on these goods.

DRESSED SAILOR DOLLS.
Sailor Girl Dolls.
No. 29R735 Sailor Girl Doll, bisque head, flowing hair, solid eyes, dressed to represent a girl in sailor costume. A very pretty doll. Length, 13 inches.
Price, each..................50c

Sailor Boy Dolls.
No. 29R739 Sailor Boy Doll, dressed to represent a boy in sailor costume, companion doll to sailor girl. Length, 13 inches.
Price, each.......................50c

The Penny Saver.
No. 29R147 A perfect registering bank; no key, no combination. Each time a cent is dropped into the bank the bell rings and the register indicates. Opens automatically at each 50 cents. The total always in sight. They are attractive and interesting to children. The mechanism is made of steel, and will not break or get out of order. It is highly interesting to children, and for this reason will encourage them to save. Shipping weight, 5 pounds. Price, each.........85c

PENNY SAVER

2. Boys' Wash Suits and Girls' Wash Dresses[3] (1902).

BOYS' WASH SUITS.

The extraordinary value we offer in Boys' Wash Suits can only be fully appreciated by those who order from this department. A trial order will surely convince you that we are able to furnish new, fresh, up to date, stylish and well made wash suits at much lower prices than similar value can be had from any other house.

NOTE.—Boys' wash suits can be had only in the sizes as mentioned after each description. Always state age of boy and if large or small of age.

Boy's
Wash
Crash
Suit,
35 Cents.

Navy Blue and White Percale Wash Suit, 40 Cents.

38R2128
98c

38R2130
$1.39

38R2131
$1.48

GIRLS' WASH DRESSES.

AGES FROM 4 TO 14 YEARS.

WHEN ORDERING please state Age, Height, Weight and Number of Inches around Bust.

SCALE OF SIZES, SHOWING PROPORTION OF BUST AND LENGTH TO THE AGE OF CHILD

Age	4	6	8	10	12	14
Bust	24	27	28	29	30	31
Skirt length	18	20	22	24	26	28

No. 38R2126 GIRLS' DRESS. Some made of Madras and some made of gingham in fancy stripes and plaids, round yokes, "V" shape yokes, some trimmed with braid, ruffles and embroidery. We show no illustration of this number on account of the differ

3. Washable, casual clothing.

3. Hip Pad and Bustle, 1902.

Parisienne Hip Pad and Bustle.

No. 18R4880 The
Parisienne Hip
Pad and Bustle,
made of best tem-
pered, black enam-
eled, woven wire
with hip pads of
padded cloth. Per-
fect in shape, and
light in weight.
Very durable.
Price, each...40c
If by mail, postage extra, each, 10 cents.

Source 4 from 1893 advertisement.

4. Corset (1893).

DOCTORS RECOMMEND REAST'S PATENT

INVIGORATOR CORSETS.

FOR LADIES, MAIDS, BOYS, GIRLS, AND CHILDREN.

Dr. M. O. B. NEVILLE, L.R.C.P., Edin. Medical Officer of Health, says, Nov. 1st, 1890:—

"From a scientific point of view, I am of opinion that your Corset is the only one that gives support without unduly compressing important organs. Its elasticity, in a great measure, prevents this. I am satisfied, by its support of back and shoulders, that it is a material help to expanding the chest."

"Mrs. WELDON'S FASHION JOURNAL," says July '90:—

"Undoubtedly supplies a long-felt want for ensuring an upright form and graceful carriage, COMBINES ELEGANCE of FORM WITH COMFORT. It renders a corset what it should be, comfort, and support to the wearer, strengthening the spine, expanding the chest, and giving necessary support without tight lacing or undue pressure."

PRICES.
Child's under 5 years, 3/4; Boys' and Girls' over 5 years, 4/6; Maids, 5/6; Ladies', 6/6, 8/6, 12/9, 18/6, 22/6, 63/-.

SOLD BY ALL DRAPERS, OR SEND P.O. TO
REAST, 15, CLAREMONT, HASTINGS, ENGLAND.
FOR LICENSE FOR MANUFACTURING, OR SALE OF AMERICAN PATENT APPLY AS ABOVE.

Source 5 from an 1884 advertisement.

5. Beauty Advice Book.

A SCRAP-BOOK
FOR
"HOMELY WOMEN" ONLY.

We dedicate this collection of toilet secrets, not to the pretty women (they have advantages enough, without being told how to double their beauty), but to the plainer sisterhood, to those who look in the glass and are not satisfied with what they see. To such we bring abundant help.

CONTENTS. Part 1--Part 2.

Practical devices for ugly ears, mouths, fingertips, crooked teeth. To reduce flesh, etc. How to bleach and refine a poor skin. Freckles, Pimples, Moles, etc. Mask of Diana of Poictiers. Out of 100 Cosmetics, which to choose. How to make and apply them for daylight, evening, and the stage (one saves two thirds, and has a better article by making instead of buying Cosmetics). What goes to constitute a belle. Madame Vestris's methods for private Theatricals. How to sit for a photograph successfully, and other toilet hints.

Send $1.00, 2 two-cent stamps, and an envelope addressed to yourself.

BROWN, SHERBROOK, & CO.,
27 Hollis Street, Boston, Mass.

Source 6 from a 1912 advertisement.

6. Massage Cream for the Skin.

"Mother, here she is"

OF all moments the most trying—when the son brings *her* to his mother, of all critics the most exacting. Mother-love causes her to look with penetrating glance, almost *trying* to find flaws. No quality of beauty so serves to win an older woman as a skin smooth, fresh and healthy *in a natural way*, as easily provided by

POMPEIAN MASSAGE CREAM

Where artificial beautifiers—cosmetics and rouges—would only antagonize; and an uncared-for, pallid, wrinkled skin prove a negative influence—the Pompeian complexion immediately wins the mother, as it does in every other instance in social or business life.

You can have a beautiful complexion—that greatest aid to woman's power and influence. A short use of Pompeian will surprise you and your friends. It will improve even the best complexion, and retain beauty and youthful appearance against Time's ravages.

"Don't *envy* a good complexion; use Pompeian and *have* one."

Pompeian is not a "cold" or "grease" cream, nor a rouge or cosmetic, and positively can not grow hair on the face. Pompeian simply affords a natural means toward a complete cleanliness of the facial pores. And in pores that are "Pompeian clean" lies skin health.

TRIAL JAR

sent for 6c (stamps or coin). Find out for yourself, now, why Pompeian is used and prized in a million homes where the value of a clear, fresh, youthful skin is appreciated. Clip coupon now.

All dealers 50c, 75c, $1

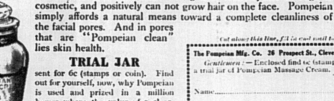

Cut along this line, fill in and mail today!

The Pompeian Mfg. Co. 36 Prospect St., Cleveland, Ohio

Gentlemen :—Enclosed find 6c (stamps or coin) for a trial jar of Pompeian Massage Cream.

Name..

Address.......................................

City.................................. State...............

Source 7 from 1895, 1888, and 1912 advertisements.

7. Croup Remedy (1895), Garment Pins (1888), and Boys' Magazine (1912).

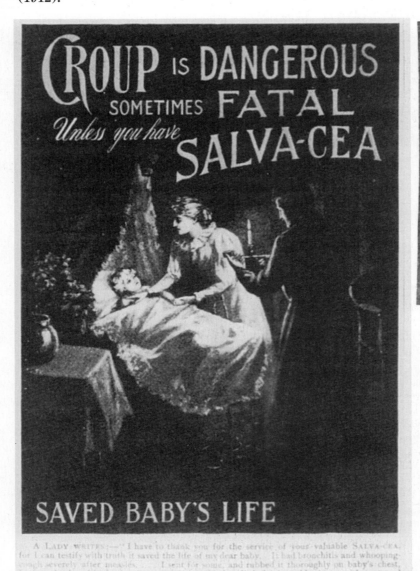

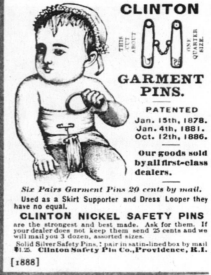

8. Ladies' and Men's Hats (1897).

LATEST DESIGNS IN STYLISH TRIMMED HATS.

AT 99 CENTS, $2.35, $3.25 AND UPWARDS.

WE SUBMIT ON THESE FOUR PAGES, the very newest effects in fashionable trimmed hats made especially for us from original designs, the same styles as will be shown by fashionable city milliners in large cities; styles that it will be impossible for you to secure in the stores in smaller towns, such goods as can be had only from the big millinery emporiums in metropolitan cities and there at two to three times our prices. These illustrations are made by artists direct from the hats, but it is impossible in a plain black and white drawing to give you a fair idea of the full beauty of these new hat creations. We ask you to read the descriptions carefully, note the illustrations and send us your order with the understanding that if the hat, when received, is not all and more than we claim for it, perfectly satisfactory, you are at liberty to return it to us at our expense and we will immediately return your money.

Wonderful Value.

99c

No. 39R101 Is a black dress shape fancy straw, slightly raised on the left. Very tastefully trimmed in the front with six large muslin roses and shaded foliage. Trimmed high to the right is a large rosette consisting of silk finished pink mull in half wheel effect, same extending all around the crown and falling over the back and caught on bandeau with loops of the same material. A very stylish young or middle aged ladies' hat. Shape can be ordered only in black or white, trimmings in any color desired, but looks very handsome as described. Price, each........ ....99c

$1.95

No. 39R107 This is a hand made fancy straw braid dress hat, drooping slightly to front and back. The wire frame is covered with an imported hand made straw braid, trimmed fully to the left with artistically designed rosettes draped in plume effect. The entire crown is covered with an imported tinted foliage and buds. The facing is neat drawn work of narrow folds of pink silk finished mull, and the bandeau is covered with nicely made loops of the same material. An exceedingly becoming and effectively designed hat. Can be ordered in all colors, Price, each................. ....$1.95

...HAT DEPARTMENT...

DO NOT BE SATISFIED WITH ANY STYLE HAT when you can have at no additional expense a hat that will be becoming and at the same time stylish and in good form. Different sections of the country have their styles, due mainly to their difference in occupation and environment. If you live on a ranch and want the proper hat for such a life, we have it. If you wish the fashionable derby or stiff hat, we can supply this.

OUR LINE OF SOFT AND FEDORA SHAPES CANNOT BE EXCELLED.

VALUE. We can sell you a hat at almost any price, but by our manufacturer to the wearer plan we are able to sell to you at almost the same price your home merchant pays for the same quality. We want your order, because we can save you 25 to 40 per cent, and at the same time fill your order with NEW, CLEAN, UP TO DATE GOODS.

MEN'S DERBY OR STIFF HATS, $1.50.

No. 33R2010 Young Men's Stiff Hat, in fashionable shape. Is a very neat block, not extreme, but stylish. Crown, 4¾inches; brim, 1¾ inches. Fine silk band and binding. Colors, black or brown. Sizes, 6¾ to 7½. Price, each.... $1.50 If by mail, postage extra, 34 cents. **A Fashionable Block in Men's Stiff Hats for $2.00.**

Men's Large or Full Shape Stiff Hats.

No. 33R2040 A style particularly suited to large men. A shapely, staple hat, as shown in illustration. Crown, 5½ inches; brim, 2¾ inches. Fine silk band and binding. Sizes, 6¾ to 7¾. Color, black only. Each.... $1.50 If by mail, postage extra, 34 cents.

Our Men's $2.25 Quality Full Shape Hat.
No. 33R2046 Men's Full Shape Hat, same style and dimensions as the above, in the high grade nonbreakable stock, with very fine silk band and binding; imported leather sweatband. Color, black only. Sizes, 6¾ to 7¾. Price, each.............$2.25 If by mail, postage extra, 34 cents.

9. Men's Underwear (1902).

MEN'S UNDERWEAR.

ASTONISHING TEMPTATIONS FOR ALL MANKIND.

QUALITIES THAT WILL SURPRISE YOU,

PRICES THAT WILL CONVINCE YOU.

MAKE A CHANGE. Off with the Old, on with the New. Prudence suggests it, your health demands it. Our prices protect you from over profit paying. We handle more Underwear and Hosiery than any one concern in the World. We save you nearly 50 per cent. on your purchases and give you better values than you could possible obtain anywhere else either wholesale or retail. Every garment we quote is guaranteed to be exactly as represented or money refunded. **EVERY PRICE WE QUOTE IS A REVELATION.**

OUR TERMS ARE LIBERAL. All goods sent C. O. D., subject to examination, on receipt of $1.00, balance and express charges payable at express office. **Three per cent.** Discount allowed if cash in full accompanies your order. **Nearly All Our Customers Send Cash in Full.**

Ventilated Health Underwear.

Summer Weight Balbriggan.

No. 2830 Men's Ventilated Natural Gray Mixed Summer Undershirts. The most comfortable as well as the most healthful balbriggan underwear ever made; fine gauge and soft finish; fancy collarette neck, pearl buttons and ribbed cuffs; ventilated all over with small drop stitch openings. Highly recommended by the best physicians as conducive to good health. Sizes 34 to 42 only. Price each..**$0.58**

MEN'S FANCY UNDERWEAR.

Men's Striped Balbriggan Underwear, 41 Cents.

No. 16R5078 Men's Fine Fancy Balbriggan Undershirts, knit from fine Egyptian cotton, made in a very narrow ½-inch alternating white and blue stripe. A very pretty garment that never fails to give satisfaction. Fast color. Trimmed with collarette neck and pearl buttons. Perfect fitting ribbed cuffs. Never retails for less than 50 to 65 cents. Stitched throughout with never-rip seams. Sizes, 34 to 44 breast measure.
Price, each......................**41c**

Source 10 from an 1893 advertisement.

10. Shaving Soaps.

WILLIAMS' SHAVING SOAPS have enjoyed an unblemished reputation for excellence—for over HALF A HUNDRED YEARS—and are to-day the *only* shaving soaps—of absolute purity, with well-established claims for healing and antiseptic properties.

"CHEAP" and impure Shaving Soaps—are composed largely of refuse animal fats—abound in scrofulous and other disease germs—and if used—are almost sure to impregnate the pores of the skin—resulting in torturing cutaneous eruptions and other forms of blood-poisoning.

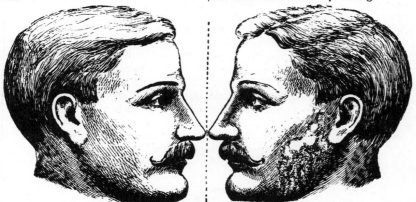

This view shows face—as shaved daily for years—with the famous WILLIAMS' Shaving Soap—always soft—fresh—bright and healthy. Not a sore or pimple in over 20 years of Shaving Experience.

This view shows the effect of being shaved ONCE with an impure—so-called "Cheap" Shaving Soap. Blood-poison—caused by applying impure animal fats to the tender cuticle of the face.

MR. CHAS. A. FOSTER,
34 SAVIN STREET,
BOSTON, MASS., writes:

"Never again will I allow a Barber to shave me unless I am *sure* he is using the only safe and reliable shaving soap made—namely **WILLIAMS'.** The other day—being in a hurry—I went into a shop near the Boston and Maine depot—to get a shave.

"I noticed a rank odor when the lather was put on my face, and asked the Barber if he used WILLIAMS' Shaving Soap. He said, 'No—I do not—because it costs a little more than other kinds.'

"A few days after this experience—my face was all broken out—terribly sore and smarting like fire.

"I consulted my Physician who told me it was a bad case of 'BARBER'S ITCH'—caused by the use of the Cheap Shaving Soap—containing diseased animal fats.

"I have suffered the worst kind of torture for two weeks—but I have learned a lesson."

QU–?

Ask your Barber if *he* uses WILLIAMS'. Take no chances. Blood-poisoning—in some form or other is the almost sure result of using a cheaply made and impure Shaving Soap. While shaving—the pores of the Skin are open—and quickly drink in—any of the disease germs which may be contained in the diseased animal fats—so largely used in all "cheap"—inferior Toilet and Shaving Soaps. Ask for WILLIAMS'—and *insist* that you have it—and enjoy a feeling of SECURITY—as well as of comfort—while shaving or being shaved.

In providing for the safety and comfort of visitors—it has been officially ordered that

WILLIAMS' SHAVING SOAPS

shall be used EXCLUSIVELY—in all of the Barber Shops located on the Grounds of the World's Columbian Exposition. Thus AT THE VERY START—it receives the highest possible Honor.

WILLIAMS' "JERSEY CREAM" TOILET SOAP.

Something new with us. The result of 50 years of costly and laborious experiment. Send for circular.
A most exquisite—healing and beautifying toilet soap. Containing the rich yellow cream of *our own herd* of imported Jersey Cattle. A full size cake mailed to any address for 25c. in stamps.
Do not fail to try it. Ask your Druggist—or send to us.—Address,

The J. B. Williams Co., Glastonbury, Conn., U. S. A.

"WILLIAMS' SOAPS have for a foundation—over half a hundred years of unblemished reputation."

Source 11 from a 1908 advertisement.

11. Safety Razor.

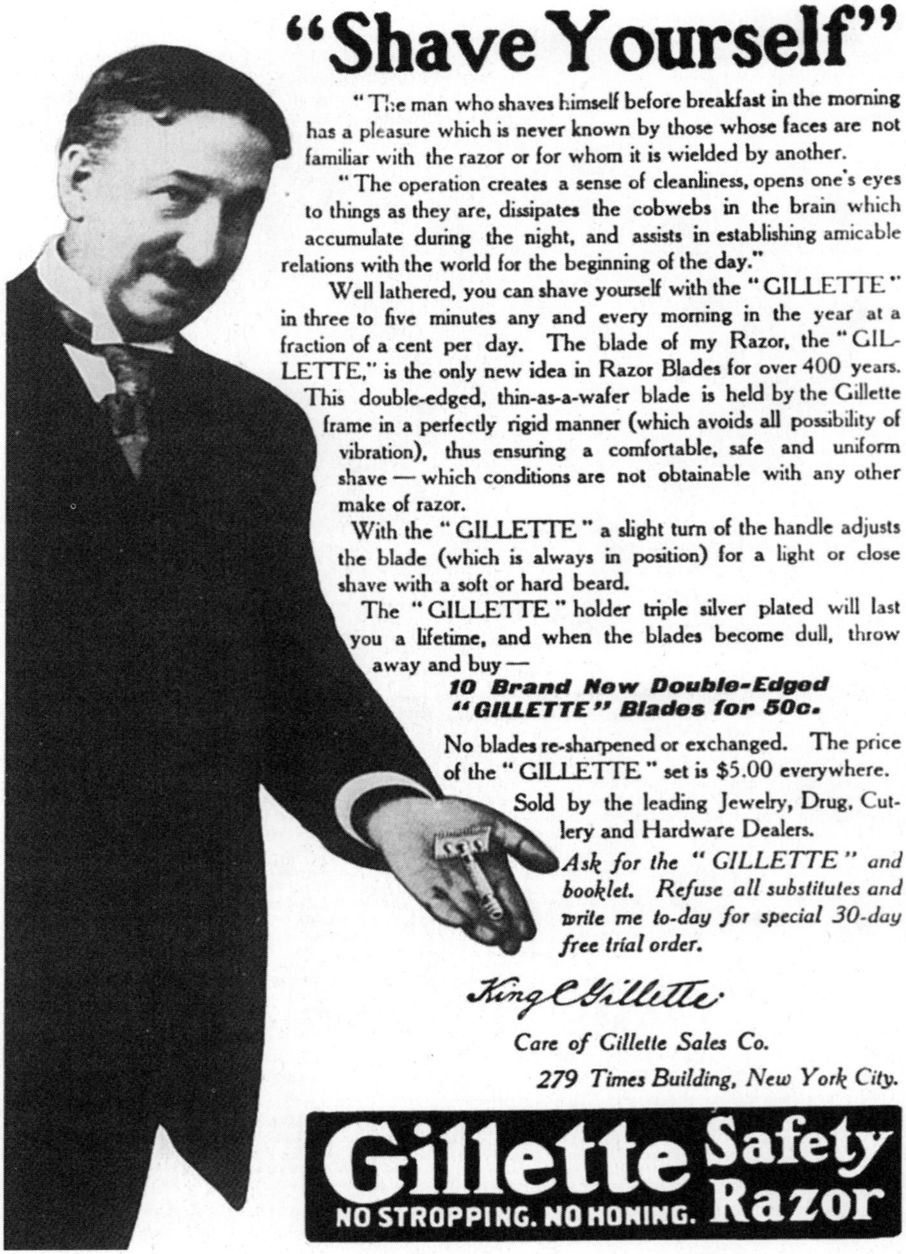

Source 12 from a 1912 advertisement.

12. Watch Chains.

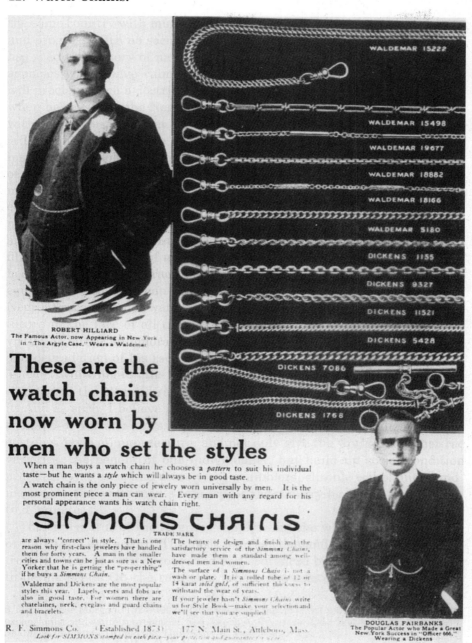

Source 13 from 1916 advertisement.

13. Colt Revolver (1916).

Source 14 from an 1891 advertisement.

14. One-Volume Book.

NONE ARE TOO BUSY TO READ

IN ONE VOLUME.

"The Best Fifty Books of the Greatest Authors."

CONDENSED FOR BUSY PEOPLE.

BENJAMIN R. DAVENPORT, EDITOR.

NO EXCUSE FOR IGNORANCE.

Born 1564.   William Shakespeare.   Died 1616.

THIS WORK of 771 pages covers the whole range of Literature from Homer's Iliad, B. C. 1200 to Gen. Lew. Wallace's Ben Hur, A. D. 1880, including a Brief Biographical Sketch and FINE FULL-PAGE PORTRAIT OF EACH AUTHOR. Every one of the Fifty Books being so thoroughly reviewed and epitomized, as to enable the READERS OF THIS VOLUME TO DISCUSS THEM FULLY, making use of Familiar Quotations properly, and knowing the connection in which they were originally used by their Great Authors.

THIS BOOK is made from material furnished by Homer, Shakespeare, Milton, Bunyan, Dickens, Stowe, Gen. Lew. Wallace. and the other great authors of thirty centuries.

BY IT A LITERARY EDUCATION MAY BE ACQUIRED WITHIN ONE WEEK, ALL FROM ONE VOLUME.

A BOOK FOR BUSY AMERICANS.
TIME SAVED. MONEY SAVED.
KNOWLEDGE IN A NUTSHELL.

NEW YORK WORLD, March 15th.—"The book is one destined to have a great sale, because it supplies, IN THE FULLEST SENSE, A LONG FELT LITERARY WANT."

Born 1783.   Washington Irving.   Died 1859.

Opinions expressed by practical, busy and successful self-made men, as to the great value and merit of Mr. Davenport's condensations:

Mr. PHILIP D. ARMOUR writes: "I am pleased to own 'Fifty Best Books.' It certainly should enable the busy American, at small expenditure of time, to gain a fairly comprehensive knowledge of the style and scope of the authors you have selected."

GEN. RUSSELL A. ALGER writes: "I have received the beautiful volume. It is surely a very desirable work."

GOV. JOSEPH E. BROWN, of Georgia, writes: "You have shown great power of condensation. This is eminently a practical age; men engaged in the struggle for bread have no time to enter much into details in literature. What the age wants is to get hold of the substance of a book. This work entitles you to be understood as a benefactor."

Born 1812.   Charles Dickens.   Died 1870.

BOSTON DAILY GLOBE, April 2, 1891. — "Men of the present generation have not time to wade through from 2,000 to 3,000 pages of any of literature's standard volumes, and as a result they do not undertake it at all, and are often placed in an embarrassing position."

BUFFALO EXPRESS, March 1st.—"The Best Fifty Books of the Greatest Authors. Condensed for Busy People," edited by Benjamin R. Davenport, deserves high praise. It not only gives busy people an introduction to literature, but takes them to its very sanctum sanctorum and bids them be at home. The editor has selected his best fifty books with the advice of the most eminent literary men in England and America. These masterpieces, from Homer's 'Iliad' to Lew. Wallace's 'Ben Hur,' he has condensed into one volume of 771 pages, working in all of the famous passages and supplying a narrative in good, straightforward, unpretentious English. The story of each book is accompanied with a brief biographical sketch and a portrait of each author. No matter how familiar one is with any of these fifty books, be it for instance, 'Don Quixote,' 'Rasselas,' 'Les Miserables,' 'Paradise Lost,' or any other, he will be forced to admit, after reading the dozen pages devoted to each one in this condensation, that there is little, if anything, to add, either with regard to plot, characters, scenes, situations, quotations, or anything else that is ever discussed by people. The result of days or weeks of reading will be the possession of hardly one single bit of information or one tangible idea concerning the book in hand that is not to be acquired by reading the dozen pages in this condensation within a half hour."

SOLD BY SUBSCRIPTION ONLY.   AGENTS WANTED EVERYWHERE.
CANVASSERS who desire to represent a book which sells rapidly and without argument should send for CIRCULARS. Books forwarded, postage paid, to any address upon receipt of price.

Fine English Muslin, Sprinkled Edges, $3 75.   Full Sheep, Library Style, Marbled Edges, $4.75.
Seal Russia, Gilt Edges, $6.75.

19th CENTURY BOOK CONCERN, 40 Exchange St., Buffalo, N. Y.
1891]

Source 15 from a 1906 advertisement.

15. Correspondence School.

What are You Worth

From The NECK UP?

It is estimated that the average man is worth $2.00 a day from the neck *down*—what is he worth from the neck *up?*

That depends entirely upon training. If you are trained so that you can plan and direct work you are worth ten times as much as the man who can work only under orders.

The **International Correspondence Schools** go to the man who is struggling along on small pay and say to him, "We will train you for promotion right where you are, or we will qualify you to take up a more congenial line of work at a much higher salary."

What the I. C. S. says it can do, it *will* do. It has already done it for others and will do it for *you,* if you only show the inclination.

Thousands of ambitious men, realizing this fact, have marked the I. C. S. coupon, and multiplied their wages many times. During March, 403 students voluntarily reported an increase in salary and position as the direct result of **I. C. S.** training.

In this day of demand for leaders, a young man ought to be ashamed to be satisfied with small wages when he has the I. C. S. ready to qualify him for a higher salary.

Mark the coupon at once and mail it. You need not leave your present work, or your own home, while the I. C. S. prepares you to advance.

Back your *trained hand* with a *trained head!* It pays big. This coupon is for you. *Will you use it?*

International Correspondence Schools,
Box 815, SCRANTON, PA.
Please explain without further obligation on my part, how I can qualify for a larger salary in the position before which I have marked X

Bookkeeper	Mechanical Draftsman
Stenographer	Telephone Engineer
Advertisement Writer	Elec. Lighting Supt.
Show Card Writer	Mecha. Engineer
Window Trimmer	Surveyor
Commercial Law	Stationary Engineer
Illustrator	Civil Engineer
Civil Service	Building Contractor
Chemist	Architec'l Draftsman
Textile Mill Supt.	Architect
Electrician	Structural Engineer
Elec. Engineer	Bridge Engineer
	Mining Engineer

Name

Street and No.

City_____ State

Source 16 from a 1906 advertisement.

16. Typewriter.

A Course in Practical Salesmanship
Tuition FREE~All Expenses Paid

IN these times of keen business rivalry, the services of the Trained Salesman command a high premium.

The Oliver Sales Organization is the finest body of Trained Salesmen in the world. It is composed of picked men, and is under the guidance of Sales Experts.

In less than ten years it has placed the Oliver Typewriter where it belongs—in a position of absolute leadership.

Its aggregate earnings are enormous and the individual average is high.

The scope of its activities is as wide as civilization and the greatest prizes of the commercial world are open to its membership.

The organization is drilled like an army. It affords a liberal education in actual salesmanship, and increases individual earning power many per cent, by systematic development of natural talents.

Its ranks are recruited from every walk of life. Men who had missed their calling and made dismal failures in the over-crowded professions have been developed in the Oliver School of Practical Salesmanship into phenomenal successes.

Because every Business Executive is interested in the very things the Oliver stands for—economy of time and money—increase in efficiency of Correspondence and Accounting Departments.

The OLIVER Typewriter

The Standard Visible Writer

is simple in principle, compactly built, durable in construction, and its touch is beautifully elastic and most responsive.

In versatility, legibility, perfect alignment, visibility, etc., it is all that could be desired in a writing machine.

It's a constant source of inspiration to the salesman, as every day develops new evidence of its wide range of usefulness.

Just as the winning personality of a human being attracts and holds friends, so does the Oliver, by its responsiveness to all demands, gain and hold an ever-widening circle of enthusiastic admirers.

If you wish to learn actual salesmanship and become a member of the Oliver Organization, send in your application **immediately,** as the ranks are rapidly being filled.

You can take up this work in spare time, or give us your entire time, just as you prefer.

Whether you earn $300 a year, or **twelve times** $300 a year, depends entirely upon **yourself.**

We offer to properly qualified applicants the opportunity to earn handsome salaries and to gain a knowledge of salesmanship that will prove of inestimable value.

Can you afford to vegetate in a poorly-paid position, when the way is open to a successful business career?

Address at once.

The Oliver Typewriter puts the salesman in touch with the men worth knowing—the human dynamos who furnish the brain power of the commercial world.

THE OLIVER TYPEWRITER CO., 161 Wabash Ave., Chicago

WE WANT LOCAL AGENTS IN THE UNITED STATES AND CANADA.
PRINCIPAL FOREIGN OFFICE—75 QUEEN VICTORIA ST., LONDON.

Source 17 from a 1908 advertisement.

17. Life Insurance.

Don't Depend on Your Relatives When You Get Old

If you let things go kind o' slip-shod *now*, you may later have to get out of the 'bus and set your carpet-bag on the stoop of some house where your arrival will hardly be attended by an ovation.

If you secure a membership in the Century Club this sad possibility will be nipped in the bud. It is very, very comfortable to be able to sit under a vine and fig-tree of your own.

The Club has metropolitan headquarters and a national member-ship of self-respecting women and men who are building little fortunes on the monthly plan. Those who have joined thus far are a happy lot—it would do your heart good to read their letters.

We would just as soon send our particulars to you as to anybody else, and there is no reason in the world why you shouldn't know all about everything. You'll be glad if you do and sorry if you don't.

Be kind to those relatives—*and to yourself.*

Address, stating without fail your occupation and the exact date of your birth,

Century Life-Insurance Club
Section O

5, 7 and 9 East 42d Street, New York

RICHARD WIGHTMAN, Secretary

Source 18 from 1881 and 1885 advertisements.

18. Bicycles (1881) and Tricycles (1885).

Source 19 from 1896 and 1914 advertisements.

19. Gramophone (1896) and Victrola (1914).

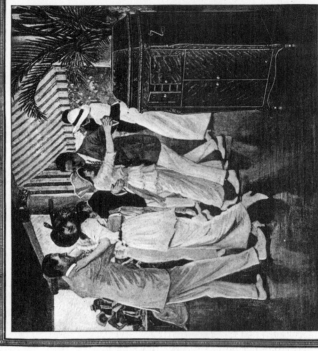

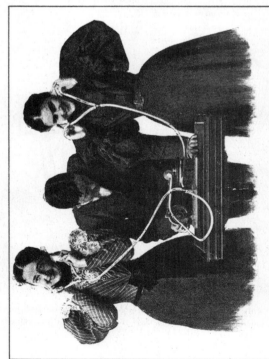

20. Ford Automobile (1907) and Electric Car for Women (1912).

FORD RUNABOUT
"Built for Two"

Two's company and a crowd frequently spoils a motoring trip.

When you have a large car you feel like filling up the seats—seems stingy for two to usurp so much luxury; so your tonneau is always full. Everybody's happy but—

Did you ever feel as if you'd just like to go alone—you and she—and have a day all your own? Go where you please, return when you please, drive as fancy dictates, without having to consult the wishes or the whims of others?

Ford Runabouts are ideal for such trips. Just hold two comfortably; ride like a light buggy, control easily and you can jog along mile after mile and enjoy the scenery.

Of course you can scorch if you want to—40 miles an hour easily—but you won't want to. You'll get used to the soft purr of the motor and the gentle motion of the car over the rolling country roads and—well, it's the most luxurious sensation one can imagine.

"We've enjoyed motoring more since we've had the Ford Runabout than we ever did before," says one lady whose purse can afford anything she desires. "Got the big car yet, but 'two's company,' and most times that's the way we go."

$600,
F.O.B. Detroit

Model N. 4 Cyl. 15 H.P.

FORD MOTOR COMPANY,
25 Piquette Ave., - Detroit, Mich.

BRANCH RETAIL STORES—New York, Philadelphia, Boston, Chicago, Buffalo, Cleveland, Detroit and Kansas City. Standard Motor Co., San Francisco, Oakland and Los Angeles, distributors for California. Canadian trade supplied by Ford Motor Company of Canada, Walkerville, Ont.

The Automobile for Women

Electrically Started and Lighted — *Inter-State* — **Controls Itself Pumps Its Own Tires**

THE advent of the Inter-State, with its marvelously simple mechanism, its electrical self-starter and its self-controller has brought a revolution in motoring. Now the powerful and magnificent Inter-State starts and obeys the will of the woman driver as readily, as easily and as simply as an electric coupe. Without moving from the driver's seat or shifting gears she starts the engine by a turn of the switch — regulates the mixture by a simple movement of the lever on the steering column, and the magnificent Inter-State is under way

No labor to start the Inter-State

and under perfect and absolute control, with no more trouble than turning on an electric light. The Inter-State electric self-starter is **part of the system** and **built into it,** and the motor dynamo turns the engine itself until it picks up under its own power.

Electric Lights as in Your Own Home

ONE of the greatest features of the Inter-State is its electric light system—not a single light or two—but an entire and reliable system, front —side—rear, all correlated and so arranged that by a turn of the switch, without leaving the driver's seat, any or all of the lights may be turned on in all their brilliancy. No more gas tanks, no more oil filling, no more lamp trimming or adjusting. The system is simply perfect. The front head-lights are provided with a dimming feature so that driving in city streets may be done with a medium diffused light.

Any or all lights on by turning switch

Write Today for Art Catalog

This describes fully the six 40 and 50 H. P. completely equipped Models which cost from $2,400 to $3,400. Gives complete details of all the equipment and features, and also shows the Inter-State Models 30-A and 32-B, 40 H. P., costing $1,750 and $1,700 respectively.

THAT greatest nuisance of motoring—tire pumping—is *totally eliminated* with the Inter-State equipment. Any woman can attach the valve to the tire, turn on the pump and in a few minutes have tires just as solid and as perfectly filled as if done by the greatest tire expert in the world.

The Inter-State *does* the work. You *direct* it. There is nothing to it at all and you are fore-armed for any emergency with the complete and thorough equipment of the Inter-State.

Inter-State Tire Pumping—No Work

Motoring Now All Pleasure

THIS great car performs all the labor itself—electrically self-started—electric lights and ignition, tire pumping and the automatic regulation of fuel consumption.

For the first time in the history of the automobile, electricity plays its *real part* in the entire mechanism. The Inter-State Electric System is really the *nerve system* commanding the energy and motion of the powerful steel muscles that make the Inter-State such a masterpiece of construction. Every conceivable accessory and feature is built into or included in the Inter-State. The Inter-State is truly the *only complete car* in this country or abroad —and this statement is made advisedly.

The Only Complete Car—Equipment and Features Unequalled

INTER-STATE AUTOMOBILE COMPANY, Dept. X, Muncie, Indiana
Boston Branch: 153 Massachusetts Avenue   *Omaha Branch:* 310 South 18th Street

Source 21 from a 1913 advertisement.

21. Auto Horn.

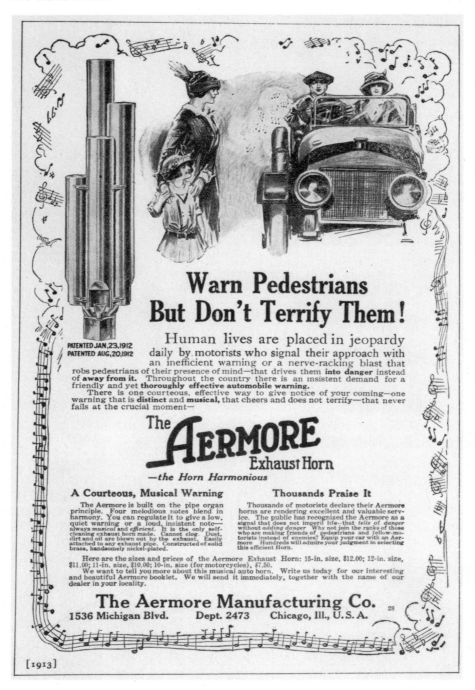

22. Stove (1884) and Washer and Wringer (1908).

ASK YOUR DEALER FOR THE
"GLENWOOD"

WITH PATENT MAGIC GRATE.

There is nothing more essential to the healthy happy home than well cooked food—which you may always be sure of by using the **Glenwood Range. 100 styles!** Illustrated Circular and Price List sent free.
WEIR STOVE CO., Taunton, Mass.

The Electric Washer and Wringer

YOU can now have your washings done by electricity.
The 1900 Electric Washer Outfit (Washer, Wringer and Motor complete) does all the heavy work of washing and wrings out the clothes.
Any electric light current furnishes the power needed. You connect up the washer the same way you put an electric light globe into its socket. Then all there is to do to start the washer is—turn on the electricity. The motion of the tub (driven by the electricity) and the water and soap in the tub wash the clothes clean. Washing is done quicker and easier, and more thoroughly and economically this way than ever before.

Washing

30 Days' FREE Trial—Freight Prepaid

Wringing

Servants will stay contented—laundry bills will be saved—clothes will last twice as long—where there is a 1900 Electric Washer to do the washing.
These washers save so much work and worry and trouble, that they *sell themselves.* This is the way of it—
We ship you an Electric Washer and *prepay the freight.*
Use the washer a month. Wash your linens and laces—wash your blankets and quilts—wash your rugs.
Then—when the month is up, if you are not convinced the washer is all we say—don't keep it. Tell us you don't want the washer and that will settle the matter. We won't charge anything for the use you have had of it.
This is the *only* washer outfit that does *all* the drudgery of the washing—*washes* and *wrings* clothes—saves them from wear and tear—and keeps your servants contented.
Our Washer Book tells how our washers are made and how they work. Send for this book today.
Don't mortgage your pleasure in life to dread of wash-day and wash-day troubles with servants. Let the 1900 Electric Washer and Wringer shoulder your wash-day burden—save your clothes and money, and keep your servants contented.
Write for our Washer Book at once. Address—
The 1900 Washer Co. 3133 Henry Street, Binghamton, N. Y. (If you live in Canada, write to the Canadian 1900 Washer Co., 355 Yonge Street, Toronto, Ont.)

23. Vacuum Cleaner (1909) and Bathroom Closet (1913).

Why stir up the Dust Demon to Frenzy like this?

THE IDEAL VACUUM CLEANER

The Man

always wonders why some way of cleaning can't be found without tormenting him with choking clouds of dust.

You can Escape all this for $25

EVERY MAN AND WOMAN

The Woman

thinks she is performing praiseworthy and necessary work in an unavoidable manner.

should now realize that such laborious and tormenting "cleaning" methods, not only are absolutely unnecessary, but are **a relic** of barbarism, **a mockery and a farce.** "Cleaning" with broom and carpet-sweeper merely scatters more of the dirt over a wider area. Old dirt has to be *rehandled again and again.* The house is never thoroughly clean. Disease germs are left to multiply, then are sent flying to infect all those whose powers of resistance may be lowered.

Operated by Hand puts no tax on the strength.

Price $25

(Fully Protected by Patents)

"IT EATS UP THE DIRT"

literally sucks out all the dust, grit, germs, moths and eggs of vermin that are *on* the object as well as *in* it—gobbles them down into its capacious maw, never to trouble you again.

This machine places in your hands a method of cleaning carpets, rugs, curtains, upholstery, wall decorations, etc., that hitherto has been limited to the very rich. It does exactly the same work as the Vacuum Cleaning systems that cost from $500 up—*and does it better and with more convenience.*

The Ideal Vacuum Cleaner is the perfection of the Vacuum Cleaning principle.

Or by Electric Motor, at a cost of 2 cents per hour.

Price $55 or $60

OPERATED BY HAND

Weighs only 20 pounds. Anybody can use it. Everybody can afford it. Compared with sweeping

It is ease itself.

It is absolutely dustless.

Every machine guaranteed.

Our free Illustrated Booklet tells an interesting story of a remarkable saving in money, time, labor, health, and strength. Send for it to-day.

The American Vacuum Cleaner Company

225 Fifth Avenue, New York City

PRICE $55 or $60

SIWELCLO Noiseless Siphon Jet CLOSET

The Noiselessness of the Siwelclo Is an Advantage Found in No Other Similar Fixture.

This appeals particularly to those whose sense of refinement is shocked by the noisy flushing of the old style closet. The Siwelclo was designed to prevent such embarrassment and has been welcomed whenever its noiseless feature has become known. When properly installed it cannot be heard outside of its immediate environment.

Every sanitary feature has been perfected in the Siwelclo—deep water seal preventing the passage of sewer gas, thorough flushing, etc.

The Siwelclo is made of Trenton Potteries Co. Vitreous China, with a surface that actually repels dirt like a china plate. It is glazed at a temperature 1000 degrees higher than is possible with any other material.

The most sanitary and satisfactory materials for all bathroom, kitchen and laundry fixtures are Trenton Potteries Co. Vitreous China and Solid Porcelain. Your architect and plumber will recommend them. If you are planning a new house or remodeling, you ought to see the great variety and beauty of design such as are shown in our new free booklet S13 "Bathrooms of Character." Send for a copy now.

The Trenton Potteries Co.

Trenton, N. J., U. S. A.

The largest manufacturers of sanitary pottery in the U.S.A.

24. Musical Organ.

"LIBRARY ORGAN."

Containing the Celebrated Carpenter Organ Action.

Something Entirely New! The Æsthetic Taste Gratified!

THIS IS ONLY ONE OF ONE HUNDRED DIFFERENT STYLES.

THIS effective and beautiful design in the modern Queen Anne Style is intended to meet the demands of those desiring an instrument of special elegance, and in harmony with the fittings and furnishings of the Study or Library Room, combining as it does, in a substantial and tasteful manner, the Organ, the Library cases, and the cabinet for bric-a-brac and articles of virtu.

It is well adapted to find favor in homes of culture and refinement, and will be championed by the music lover and connoisseur.

The composition is one of well balanced proportions, chaste subordination of ornamentation, and of artistic arrangement in constructive details, imparting to the design a rich simplicity and substantial worth

This beautiful organ contains the Celebrated Carpenter Organ Action. The action is to an Organ what the works are to a watch. The merits of the Carpenter Organ were fully proved on page 158 of the YOUTH'S COMPANION of April 20th, to which special attention is directed.

A beautiful 80-page Catalogue, the finest of its kind ever published, is now ready and will be sent free to all applying for it.

Nearly all reliable dealers sell the Carpenter Organs, but if any do not have them to show you, write to us for a Catalogue and information where you can see them. DO NOT BUY ANY ORGAN UNTIL YOU HAVE EXAMINED "THE CARPENTER." In writing for a Catalogue always state that you saw this advertisement, in the *Youth's Companion.*

Address or call on E. P. CARPENTER, Worcester, Mass., U. S. A.

Source 25 from a 1909 advertisement.

25. Reed and Rattan Furniture.

ESTABLISHED 1826

Heywood-Wakefield

TRADE MARK

FACSIMILE OF OUR TAG

THE name *Heywood-Wakefield* appearing on Reed and Rattan Furniture signifies quality, style, and workmanship, that individualizes our brands of goods and has made them world-renowned. The best in Rattan Furniture is *not* the best unless it bears the tag *Heywood-Wakefield*

Our furniture enhances the beauty of any home. Its presence lends an influence of dignity, comfort, and artisticness that harmonizes with any color treatment or architectural effect. So numerous are the styles made by us in Reed and Rattan Furniture, covering every known desire for the household, club, or hotel, and to which our design creators are constantly adding new effects in shapes and patterns, that you are practically sure of possessing, when selecting our goods, ideas that are exclusive and original.

We are also producers of the well-known line of

Heywood *Wakefield*

go-carts and baby carriages. Made in every conceivable style, including our celebrated collapsible, room-saving go-carts.

We have prepared attractive illustrated catalogs showing and describing our Reed and Rattan Furniture. Before purchasing, *write for catalog G.*

We also furnish, free, interesting catalog of our go-carts and baby carriages. If interested, *write for catalog 7.*

Write to our nearest store.

HEYWOOD BROTHERS AND WAKEFIELD COMPANY

BOSTON, BUFFALO, NEW YORK, PHILADELPHIA, BALTIMORE, CHICAGO. SAN FRANCISCO, LOS ANGELES, PORTLAND, ORE.

J. C. PLIMPTON & CO., Agts.
LONDON AND LIVERPOOL, ENG.

Style 6830 B

26. Houses in New York (1887) and Tennessee (1892). Exterior View and Floor Plan.

* * * This marvelous house has been built more than 300 times from our plans; *it is so well planned* that it affords ample room even for a large family. 1st floor shown above; on 2d floor are 4 bedrooms and in attic 2 more. Plenty of Closets. The whole warmed by one chimney.

Large illustrations and full description of the above as well as of 39 other houses, ranging in cost from $400 up to $6,500, may be found in "SHOPPELL'S MODERN LOW-COST HOUSES," a large quarto pamphlet, showing also how to select sites, get loans, &c. Sent postpaid on receipt of 50c. Stamps taken, or send $1 bill and we will return the change. Address, BUILDING PLAN ASSOCIATION. (Mention this paper.) 24 Beekman St. (Box 2702,) N. Y.

Source 27 from a *Ladies' Home Journal* advertisement, 1909.

27. Advice for Couples Buying a Home.

This is the house the young couple saved and paid for in five years.

A Young Couple
Were Married 5 Years Ago

He had a moderate salary. They started simply and saved. But they didn't skimp. They gave little dinners and heard the best lectures. In five years they had saved enough to pay for the house at the head of this page.

Another Young Couple Were Married, Too

They put by $7 a week, and the house at the bottom of this page is now theirs, —entirely paid for. A third young couple's income was $16 per week. They saved $8 of it, and bought and paid for the house at the bottom of this page.

How these and 97 others did it, step by step, dollar by dollar, is all told in the great series, "*How We Saved For a Home,*"— 100 articles by 100 people who saved for and now own their own homes on an

Average Salary of $15 a Week: None Higher Than $30

This great series will run for an entire year in

The Ladies' Home Journal

For ONE DOLLAR, for a year's subscription, you get the whole series.

THE CURTIS PUBLISHING COMPANY, PHILADELPHIA, PA.

This is the house saved for on $7 a week and now all paid for.

This is the house paid for out of a salary of $16 per week, saving $8.

Sources 28 through 31 from *Palliser's Model Homes,* 1878.

28. Cottage for a Mill Hand at Chelsea, Mass. (Cost $1,200).

This is a very attractive design, and intended to give ample accommodation at a low cost for an ordinary family.

The cellar is placed under the Kitchen and Hall, which was thought in this instance to be sufficient to meet all requirements, though it is generally considered, in the Eastern States at least, to be poor economy not to have a cellar under the whole house, as it only requires about one foot in depth of additional stone work to secure a cellar, it being necessary to put down the stone work in any case, so that it will be beyond the reach of frost. The Kitchen is without a fire-place, the cooking to be done by a stove, which, if properly contrived, is a very effective ventilator, and preferred by many housekeepers for all Kitchen purposes.

The Parlor and Dining-room or general Living-room are provided with the healthy luxury of an open fire-place, and we know of no more elegant, cleanly and effective contrivance for this purpose than the one adopted in this instance; they are built of buff brick, with molded jambs and segment arch, and in which a basket grate or fire dogs can be placed for the desired fire, and in this way large rooms are kept perfectly comfortable in cold weather without heat from any other source. These fire-places are also provided with neat mantels constructed of ash, and which are elegant compared with the marbelized slate mantel, which is a sham, and repulsive to an educated taste.

On entering nearly every house in the land we find the same turned walnut post at the bottom of the stairs with tapering walnut sticks all the way up, surmounted with a flattened walnut rail having a shepherd's crook at the top; however, in this instance it is not so, but the staircase is surmounted with an ash rail, balusters and newel of simple, though unique design; and now that people are giving more attention to this important piece of furniture, we may look for a change in this respect.

This house is supplied with a cistern constructed with great care, the Kitchen sink being supplied with water by a pump, and there is no more easy method of procuring good water for all purposes of the household.

For a compact, convenient Cottage with every facility for doing the work with the least number of steps, for a low-priced elegant Cottage, we do not know of anything that surpasses this. Cost, $1,200.

Mr. E. A. Jones of Newport, Ohio, is also erecting this Cottage with the necessary changes to suit points of compass. Such a house as this if taste-fully furnished, and embellished with suitable surroundings, as neat and well-kept grounds, flowers, etc., will always attract more attention than the uninviting, ill-designed buildings, no matter how much money may have been expended on them.

It is not necessary that artistic feeling should have always a large field for its display; and in the lesser works and smaller commissions as much art may find expression as in the costly façades and more pretentious structures.

29. Floor Plan of Cottage for a Mill Hand.

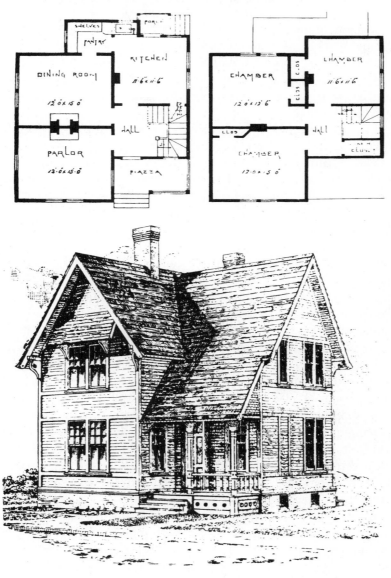

30. Residence of Rev. Dr. Marble, Newtown, Conn. (Cost $2,925).

This house commands a particularly fine view from both sides and the front, and is situated in one of the pleasantest country towns in New England, the hotels of this town being crowded during the summer months with people from the cities.

The exterior design is plain, yet picturesque, and at once gives one an idea of ease and comfort. The roofing over the Hall and Sitting-room is a particularly fine feature, and the elevation of the rear is very striking, the roof over the porch being a part of the main roof.

The interior arrangements are very nice, the Hall being very spacious, and in it we have a very easy and handsome stair-case of plain design, constructed of Georgia pine; the newel extends up to ceiling of first floor, while the other two posts extend up to ceiling of second floor. In all country houses one of the first things to be aimed at is to secure ample stair-cases, and until a man can afford space for an easy ascent to a second floor he should stay below; and to-day we find in houses, where there is no necessity for it, stairs that are little better than step-ladders, making a pretence of breadth at the bottom with swelled steps, and winding the steps on approaching the floor above, thus making a trap for the old and for the children.

The corner fire-place between Parlor and Dining-room is a feature we indulge in to a great extent in these days of economy, sliding doors and fire-places, although we sometimes have clients who object to this, thinking it would not look as well as when placed in center of side wall; but when they are asked how this and that can be provided for with the best and most economical results, they readily give in.

There is no water-closet [toilet] in the house, but an Earth-Closet is provided in the rear Hall, which is thoroughly ventilated.

The Dining-room is a very cheerful room and the Kitchen is reached through a passage also connecting with side veranda. The pantry is lighted with a window placed above press; each fire-place is furnished with a neat hard-wood mantel, and the Hall is finished in Georgia pine, the floor being laid with this material, and finished in natural color.

The exterior is painted as follows: Ground, light slate; trimmings, buff, and chamfers, black. Cost, $2,925.

The sight of this house in the locality in which it is built is very refreshing, and is greatly in advance of the old styles of rural box architecture to be found there. When people see beautiful things, they very naturally covet them, and they grow discontented in the possession of ugliness. Handsome houses, other things equal, are always the most valuable. They sell quickest and for the most money. Builders who feign a blindness to beauty must come to grief.

31. Floor Plan of a Clergyman's Residence.

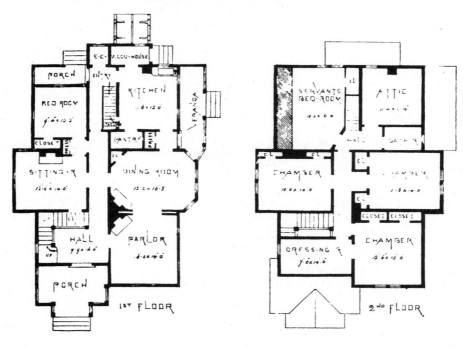

32. Perspective View and Floor Plans for a Suburban Middle-Class Home (Cost $3,600).

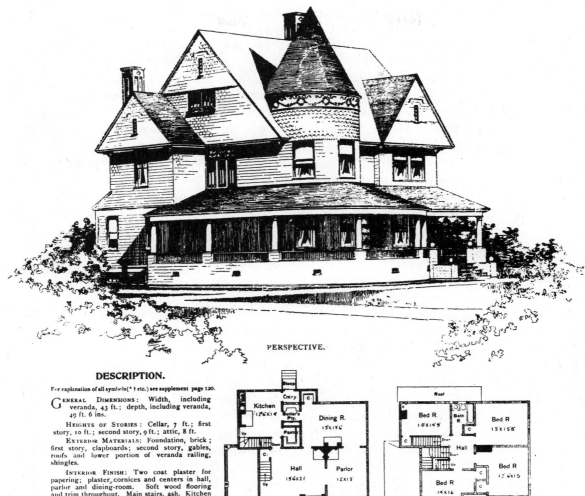

PERSPECTIVE.

DESCRIPTION.

For explanation of all symbols(* † etc.) see supplement page 120.

GENERAL DIMENSIONS: Width, including veranda, 43 ft.; depth, including veranda, 49 ft. 6 ins.

HEIGHTS OF STORIES: Cellar, 7 ft.; first story, 10 ft.; second story, 9 ft.; attic, 8 ft.

EXTERIOR MATERIALS: Foundation, brick; first story, clapboards; second story, gables, roofs and lower portion of veranda railing, shingles.

INTERIOR FINISH: Two coat plaster for papering; plaster, cornices and centers in hall, parlor and dining-room. Soft wood flooring and trim throughout. Main stairs, ash. Kitchen and bath-room, wainscoted. Chair-rail in dining-room. Picture molding in hall, parlor and dining-room. All interior woodwork grain filled and finished with hard oil.

COLORS: All clapboards, first story, Colonial yellow. Trim, including water-table, corner boards, casings, cornices, bands, veranda posts and rails, outside doors, conductors, etc., ivory white. Veranda floor and ceiling, oiled. Shingles on side walls and gables stained dark yellow. Roof shingles, dark red.

ACCOMMODATIONS: The principal rooms, and their sizes, closets, etc., are shown by the floor plans. Cellar under whole house with inside and outside entrances and concrete floor. One room finished in attic, remainder of attic floored for storage. Double folding doors between parlor and hall and parlor and dining-room. Direct communication from hall with dining-room, parlor and kitchen. Bathroom, with complete plumbing, in second story. Open fire-places in dining-room, parlor and hall. Wide veranda. Bay-window in hall and bed-room over. Two stationary wash-tubs in cellar under kitchen.

COST: $3,600, including mantels, range and heater. The estimate is based on † New York prices for labor and materials.

Price of working plans, specifications, detail drawings, etc., $35.

Price of †† bill of materials, ... 10.

FEASIBLE MODIFICATIONS: General dimensions, materials and colors may be changed. Cellar may be decreased in size or wholly omitted. Sliding doors may be used in place of folding doors. Portable range may be used instead of brick-set range. Servants' water-closet could be introduced in cellar. Fireplaces may be reduced in number.

The price of working plans, specifications, etc., for a modified design, varies according to the alterations required and will be made known upon application to the Architects.

Address, CO-OPERATIVE BUILDING PLAN ASSOCIATION, Architects, 203 Broadway and 164-6-8 Fulton Street, New York, N. Y.

FIRST FLOOR.

SECOND FLOOR.

33. The New Business of Advertising.

"Photographs in Advertising," *Printers' Ink,* August 17, 1898, p. 18.

It may have been noticed that the trend of modern magazine advertising is toward the use of photographs. . . . An advertisement that contains the photograph of a beautiful woman is certain to be attractive, and consequently its success is largely guaranteed. . . . But there are a host of articles on the market that can be advertised to great advantage by the introduction of a lady into the picture, and many advertisers have already seen this. . . .

But though the photographs of pretty women are only supposed to be attractive to the male sex, the picture of a baby or "cute" child will immediately captivate ninety-nine per cent of humanity. . . . Whatever he or she is supposed to advertise, we feel kindly toward, even if it is only for introducing us to the baby. . . .

Earnest Elmo Calkins, *The Business of Advertising* (New York: D. Appleton and Co., 1915 [1920 reprint]), pp. 1, 9.

It is hard to find a satisfactory definition of advertising. A picturesque way of putting it is to call it business imagination, an imagination that sees in a product possibilities which can be realized only by appealing to the public in new ways to create a desire where none existed before. . . .

Advertising modifies the course of the people's daily thoughts, gives them new words, new phrases, new ideas, new fashions, new prejudices and new customs. In the same way it obliterates old sets of words and phrases, fashions and customs. It may be doubted if any other one force, the school, the church and the press excepted, has so great an influence as advertising. To it we largely owe the prevalence of good roads, rubber tires, open plumbing, sanitary underwear, water filters, hygienic waters, vacuum cleaners, automobiles, kitchen cabinets, pure foods. These are only a few of the things which the public has been taught by advertising to use, to believe in, and to demand.

S. Roland Hall, *The Advertising Handbook: A Reference Work Covering the Principles and Practice of Advertising* (New York: McGraw-Hill, 1921), pp. 79–80, 101–103.

In other words, certain thoughts have become fixed in our minds in connection with certain other thoughts, and when we bring up one end of the connection the other is likely to follow. . . .

There is a motive, and a good one, in calling an automobile the "Lincoln," for that suggests sturdy, honest qualities.

No writer would undertake to make a real hero out of a character known as "Percy," for this name suggests "sissiness.". . .

Man is the stronger, as a rule. He is the bread-winner, to a large extent. His job is more in the outside world. He grows up to severer tasks, as a rule. He is more accustomed to rebuffs.

Though woman has progressed a long way in taking her place on an equal plane with that of man in business, politics and the professions, yet she is still to a large extent more sheltered than man. Her affairs are more within the home. Her sex makes her interest in clothes, home-furnishings, and the like keener than man's as a general thing. . . .

Because of her years of comparative non-acquaintance with mechanical matters, woman is generally less apt in understanding mechanical description and directions, and such advertisers must use greater care when appealing to women. . . .

On the other hand it is generally admitted that men are more democratic, more gregarious, than women—that women move more within their own circle or "clique."

A man is not likely to care if several other men in his circle have a hat exactly like his own. A woman would hardly care to buy a hat exactly like one worn by several other women in her town or community. A woman ordinarily will think nothing of shopping at several places to look at hats. A man is likely to visit only one shop. . . .

Claude C. Hopkins, *My Life in Advertising* (1927), reprinted as Claude C. Hopkins, *My Life in Advertising and Scientific Advertising* (Chicago: Advertising Publications, 1966), pp. 8–9, 119.

I am sure that I could not impress the rich, for I do not know them. I have never tried to sell what they buy. . . . But I do know the common people. I love to talk to laboring-men, to study housewives who must count their pennies, to gain the confidence and learn the ambitions of poor boys and girls. Give me something which they want and I will strike the responsive chord. My words will be simple, my sentences short. Scholars may ridicule my style. The rich and vain may laugh at the factors which I feature. But in millions of humble homes the common people will read and buy. They will feel that the writer knows them. And they, in advertising, form 95 per cent of our customers. . . .

People are like sheep. They cannot judge values, nor can you and I. We judge things largely by other's impressions, by popular favor. We go with the crowd. So the most effective thing I have ever found in advertising is the trend of the crowd.

QUESTIONS TO CONSIDER

For convenience, the evidence is divided into three sections. Sources 1 through 25 are advertisements from popular magazines and the 1897 and 1902 Sears Roebuck & Co. catalogues. The prices probably seem ridiculously low to you, but these items were reasonably priced and affordable—although not really cheap—for most middle-class Americans in cities and towns and on farms. Sources 26 through 32 all deal with houses and buying a house, including house plans readily available by mail and through pattern books. Again, the prices seem very low, but working-class homes could be built for less than one thousand dollars (excluding the cost of the land) and middle-class homes for as little as two thousand dollars during this period.

As you read each advertisement, you will find it helpful to jot down notes. First, try to determine the message of the ad. What is the advertiser trying to sell? What emotion(s) does the ad appeal to? What fears? What hopes? Then ask what the ad tells you about society during that time. Does it tell you anything about men's roles? About women's roles? About the relationships between men and women? Does it tell you anything about children or young people? About adults' concerns about young people? About old people? Finally, do you see any changes occurring during the time period—for example, in the two ads for the Gramophone and the Victrola (Source 19) or in the ads for automobiles (Source 20)? If so, what do these changes tell you about the roles of men, women, and young people between the 1880s and 1917?

Source 26 contains two advertisements for houses. Source 27 is an advertisement for a magazine series giving advice on how to buy a home. What do they tell you about people's needs and wants with regard to housing? What advice is offered to young married people? What values are emphasized by these advertisements for housing? Sources 28 through 32 consist of house plans and descriptions from architectural pattern books, arranged chronologically from 1878 to 1900. Look carefully at the exterior features of these houses. How would you describe them to a student who had not seen the pictures? Next, look at the interior rooms and their comparative sizes. What use or uses would each room probably have had? What rooms did these houses have that our own modern houses do not have? Do modern houses have rooms that these houses lacked? What similarities do you find in all the houses, from the mill hand's cottage ($1,200) in Source 28 to the suburban middle-class home ($3,600) in Source 32? What differences are there? Finally, what kinds of things seemed to be important to the owners of these houses? What kind of impression did they wish to make on other people?

The excerpts in Source 33 are drawn from an advertising journal, two textbooks, and the autobiography of a famous advertising pioneer. *Printers' Ink* was a weekly journal of advertising founded in the second half of the nineteenth century. What kinds of photographs does the author recommend using? Why? What is the relationship between the photographs and the item being sold? Earnest Calkins first published a book on "modern" advertising in 1895, which he later rewrote as a textbook, *The Business of Advertising*. How does he define advertising? In what ways does he believe that advertising affects people?

S. Roland Hall had worked in advertising and later taught both salesmanship and advertising. Why does he believe that the names of products are important? What does he think are the major differences between men and women? How might these differences affect people who wrote advertisements? Finally, Claude Hopkins was a self-made man who became one of the highest-paid advertising copywriters of the late nineteenth and early twentieth centuries, at one time earning over $100,000 a year. In this excerpt from his autobiography, he explains the basic elements in his approach to advertising. To what factors does he attribute his success?

To conclude, consider what you have learned from the evidence as a whole. Can you describe how white middle-class Americans lived during this period? How the new business of advertising promoted material goods and houses? What these advertisements reveal about white middle-class values, hopes, and fears during this era of rapid changes?

∽ EPILOGUE ∾

Of course, not all Americans could live like the middle-class families you just studied. The poor and the immigrants who lived in the cities were crowded into windowless, airless tenement buildings that often covered an entire block. Poor rural black and white sharecroppers in the South lived in one- or two-room shacks, and many farmers in the western plains and prairies could afford to build only sod houses. During the Great Depression of the 1930s, many people, including middle-class families, lost their homes entirely through foreclosure, and the 1960s and 1970s saw the price of houses increase so rapidly that many families were priced out of the housing market. Even today, the problem of the homeless has not been solved.

The early twentieth century saw the captains of industry come under attack for what many came to believe were their excesses. Evidence of their disdain for and defiance of the public good, as well as of their treatment of workers, their political influence, and their ruthless business practices, came more and more to light due to the efforts of reformers and muckraking journalists. The society that once had venerated the industrial barons began to worry that they had too much power and came to believe that such power should be restricted.

Architecture also was undergoing a rapid transformation. Neoclassical, Georgian, colonial, and bungalow styles signaled a shift toward less ostentation and increased moderation in private dwellings. Perhaps the most striking work was done by Chicago architect Frank Lloyd Wright, who sought to give functional and social meaning to his designs and to make each structure blend into its unique landscape. According to Wright's concepts, there was no standard design for the "perfect house." Wright's ideas formed the basis for a series of movements that ultimately changed the perspective and direction of American architecture.

Progressive muckrakers also criticized advertising, particularly the claims of patent medicine advertisements. Such salesmanship, however, was described as "the brightest hope of America" by the 1920s. Bruce Barton, a talented salesman and founder of a huge advertising agency, even discovered "advertisements" in the Bi-

ble, which he described as the first "best seller." Although its image was slightly tarnished by the disillusionment accompanying the Great Depression, advertising helped "sell" World War II to the American public by encouraging conservation of scarce resources, and it emerged stronger and more persuasive than ever in the 1950s. Americans were starved for consumer goods after wartime rationing, and their rapid acceptance of a new entertainment medium—television—greatly expanded advertising opportunities.

But advertising still had (and has) its critics. Writing in 1954, historian David Potter, in *People of Plenty*, characterized advertising as the basic "institution of abundance." Advertising, he maintained, had become as powerful as religion or education had been in earlier eras. Advertising, he said, now actually *created* the standards and values of our society. Because advertising lacked social goals or social responsibility, however, he believed that its power was dangerous. We must not forget, Potter warned, "that it ultimately regards man as a consumer and defines its own mission as one of stimulating him to consume."

CHAPTER 4

JUSTIFYING AMERICAN IMPERIALISM: THE LOUISIANA PURCHASE EXPOSITION, 1904

∽ THE PROBLEM ∽

On April 30, 1904, in the White House in Washington, D.C., President Theodore Roosevelt pressed a telegraph key. Over 750 miles away, in St. Louis, Missouri, Roosevelt's signal officially opened the Louisiana Purchase International Exposition, in terms of acreage the largest world's fair that has ever been held. At the president's signal, a battery of artillery fired a salute in the direction of the nation's capital, ten thousand flags were unfurled, bands struck up their numbers, fountains sprayed into the air, and the opening day crowd of 200,000 people heard Missouri governor David R. Francis exclaim, "Enter here, ye sons of men." The 1904 St. Louis World's Fair was underway.[1]

1. The actual centennial of the Louisiana Purchase was 1903, but construction of the

From the formal end of Reconstruction in 1877 to the United States' entry into the First World War in 1917, Americans appeared to fall in love with world's fairs. Between 1876 and 1916, various United States cities hosted fourteen international expositions that were attended by nearly 100 million eager visitors.[2] Intended to

fair was so vast that the exposition opened one year late. The St. Louis Exposition commemorated the acquisition of the Louisiana Territory from France. The treaty between the United States and France was signed in Paris on April 30, 1803; the U.S. Senate ratified the treaty on October 20, 1803; and the United States took formal possession of the Louisiana Territory on December 20, 1803.

2. The first international exposition was held in London's Crystal Palace in 1851. Between 1876 and 1916, American expositions were held in Philadelphia, New Orleans, Chicago, Atlanta, Nashville, Buffalo, Charleston, St.

CHAPTER 4

JUSTIFYING
AMERICAN
IMPERIALISM:
THE LOUISIANA
PURCHASE
EXPOSITION,
1904

stimulate economic development in the host cities as well as provide opportunities for manufacturers to show their newest products to millions of potential consumers, these expositions or world's fairs also acquainted provincial Americans with machines and technology (the Corliss engine, electric lights, the air brake, refrigeration, the dynamo, x-rays, the telephone), new delights (the Ferris wheel, ice cream cones, the hoochie-koochie dance), and spectacular architecture, art, and historical artifacts (the Liberty Bell was brought from Philadelphia to both the New Orleans and Atlanta expositions). As President William McKinley commented at the 1901 Pan-American Exposition in Buffalo (where he was soon after assassinated), "Expositions are the time keepers of progress."

Visitors to the Louisiana Purchase Exposition in St. Louis in 1904 saw all this and more. More than 19 million people[3] attended the largest world's fair ever held (1,272 acres, 75 buildings, 70,000 exhibits). Visitors could examine a display of one hundred automobiles or watch demonstrations of totally electric cooking. But the highlight of the St. Louis Exposition was its Anthropology Department, headed by the preeminent Smith-

sonian Institution ethnologist W. J. McGee. The department brought to St. Louis representatives of "all the races of the world," who lived on the fairgrounds in villages designed to reproduce their "native habitats." For example, twelve hundred people were brought from the Philippine Islands, an area acquired from Spain in the Spanish-American War of 1898 and where American soldiers recently (1902) had subdued a Filipino rebellion. On a 47-acre site, six villages were constructed for these people, where American visitors could observe them and their customs.

In this chapter, you will be analyzing several photographs taken at the 1904 Louisiana Purchase Exposition in St. Louis. As noted earlier, in 1898 the United States had acquired a colonial empire from Spain as a result of the Spanish-American War. How did the exhibits at the 1904 St. Louis Exposition attempt to justify America's rise as an imperialist power? How do you think American visitors might have reacted to these exhibits?

This chapter also shows how imaginative historians can analyze public events such as world's fairs, parades, patriotic celebrations, and so forth to understand the thoughts and attitudes of the events' organizers, participants, and audience. Such analyses are especially valuable in uncovering the collective mentality of people at a particular point in time. As you examine evidence from the Louisiana Purchase International Exposition of 1904, think of how the methods you are using might be applied to other large public events.

Louis, Jamestown, Portland, Seattle, San Francisco, and San Diego. Numerous regional expositions and fairs also were held.
3. Nineteen million people (the official count; others were lower) represented 23.1 percent of the total U.S. population in 1904. Of course, not all visitors were Americans, and some people visited the exposition more than once and thus were counted more than once in the total figure.

∞ BACKGROUND ∞

Until the late nineteenth century, the United States' transoceanic foreign policy clearly had been of minor concern to the nation's citizens. Westward expansion and settlement, the slavery controversy and the Civil War, postwar reconstruction of the republic, and industrialization and urbanization had alternately captured the attention of Americans and pushed foreign affairs into the background. But beginning in the late nineteenth century, several factors prompted Americans to look beyond their own shores, and by the end of the century, the United States had become a world power complete with a modest empire.

Initially, the American business community opposed this drift toward expansion and colonialism, believing that American industry would do well just meeting the needs of the rapidly growing population and fearing that a colonial empire would mean large armies and navies, increased government expenses, and the possibility of the nation's involvement in war. However, by the mid-1890s, American business leaders were beginning to have second thoughts. The apparent cycle of economic depressions (1819, 1837, 1857, 1873, 1893) made some businessmen believe that American prosperity could be maintained only by selling surpluses of manufactured goods in foreign markets. Business leaders also were constantly looking for areas in which to invest their surplus capital. Investments beyond the borders of the United States, they be-

lieved, would be more secure if the American government would act to stabilize the areas in which they invested. In 1895, the newly organized National Association of Manufacturers sounded both those chords at its convention, where the keynote speaker was soon-to-be-president William McKinley, an Ohio governor with decided expansionist leanings.

Yet it would be wrong to see American expansion and colonialism strictly as a scheme to better the nation's industrial and commercial interests. A number of other intellectual currents dovetailed with American commercial interests to create a powerful and popular urge toward imperialism. For example, those who advocated military growth (especially of a large, steam-powered navy) saw in American expansion a perfect justification for their position. Their interests were represented by increasingly influential lobbies in Washington. Especially important was Captain Alfred Thayer Mahan, whose book *The Influence of Sea Power Upon History* (published in 1890) argued persuasively that national self-preservation depended on international trade protected by a large and powerful navy with worldwide bases and refueling stations. Two of Mahan's disciples, Theodore Roosevelt and Henry Cabot Lodge, eventually achieved positions whereby they could put Mahan's philosophy to work, Roosevelt as president and Lodge as a powerful U.S. senator from Massachusetts.

CHAPTER 4

JUSTIFYING
AMERICAN
IMPERIALISM:
THE LOUISIANA
PURCHASE
EXPOSITION,
1904

Another current influencing American expansion was the dramatic increase in religious missionary zeal in the late nineteenth century. Working through both individual denominations and powerful congressional lobbies, missionaries argued that it was their duty to "Christianize" the world.[4] In the United States, Methodists, Baptists, Presbyterians, and Congregationalists were especially active, giving money and attention to their denominational missionary boards as well as to those who went out to convert the "heathen." In large part, these missionaries were selfless, committed men and women. Some, however, attempted to Westernize as well as Christianize their flocks, often denigrating or destroying indigenous cultures and traditions even as they brought modern health and educational institutions with them. All argued for the U.S. government to protect the missionaries more actively and open up other areas around the world to missionary work.

Accompanying this religious zeal were two other intellectual strains that in some ways were contradictory but that both justified American expansion. The first was that of social Darwinism. An application of Charles Darwin's theories of biological evolution to human affairs, social Darwinism taught that peoples, like species, were engaged in a life-or-death struggle to determine the "survival of the fittest." Those classes or nations that

emerged triumphant in this struggle were considered the best suited to carry on the evolution of the human race. Therefore, the subjugation of weak peoples by strong ones was not only in accordance with the laws of nature but bound to result in a more highly civilized world as well. Most celebrated among the social Darwinists was the Englishman Herbert Spencer, a diminutive and eccentric man who became a worldwide celebrity through his writings. (A letter was once addressed to him, "Herbert Spencer. England. And if the postman doesn't know the address, he ought to." It was delivered.)

Although Spencer himself disapproved of imperialism, it is easy to see how his writings could be used as a justification for empire building, not only in the United States but in Western Europe as well (which at this time was furiously engaged in imperialistic adventures). One reflection of the intellectual strain of social Darwinism was reflected in the writings of the American author Josiah Strong. As he predicted in his book *Our Country: Its Possible Future and Its Present Crisis* (1885),

this race of unequaled energy . . . will spread itself over the earth. If I read not amiss, this powerful race will move down upon Mexico, down upon Central and South America, out upon the islands of the sea, over upon Africa and beyond. And can anyone doubt that the result of this competition of races will be the "survival of the fittest"?

Paralleling this notion of struggle for survival between the "fittest" and the "unfit" (a doctrine with strong

4. Because the majority of Filipinos were Roman Catholics (making the Philippines the only Christian "nation" in Asia), obviously American missionaries to the Philippines after 1899 meant *Protestantize* when they said "Christianize."

racist overtones) was the concept of the "White Man's Burden." This concept held that it was the duty of the "fittest" not so much to destroy the "unfit" as to "civilize" them. White people, according to this view, had a responsibility to educate the rest of the world to the norms of Western society. As racist as social Darwinism, the belief in the White Man's Burden downplayed the idea of a struggle for survival between peoples and emphasized the "humanitarian" notion of bringing the benefits of "civilization" to the "uncivilized." Using this argument, many in the West justified imperialism as an obligation, a sacrifice that God had charged the "fittest" to make. Although the doctrine differs in tone from that of social Darwinism, one can see that its practical results might well be the same.

All these ideological impulses (economic, military, religious, "scientific," paternalistic) rested on one common assumption: that the world was a great competitive battlefield and that those nations that did not grow and expand would wither and die. Indeed, this "growth mania," or fascination with growth and the measurement of growth, was perhaps the most powerful intellectual strain in all of American society. For those who accepted such an assumption, the world was a dangerous, competitive jungle in which individuals, races, religions, nations, corporations, and cities struggled for domination. Those that grew would continue to exist; those that did not grow would die.

The convergence of these intellectual strains in the late nineteenth century prompted Americans to view the outside world as an area into which the United States' influence should expand. This expansionist strain was not an entirely new phenomenon; it had been an almost regular feature of American life nearly since the nation's beginning. Yet except for the purchase of Alaska, this was the first time that large numbers of Americans seemed to favor the extension of U.S. influence into areas that would not be settled subsequently by Americans and would not eventually become states of the Union. In that sense, the American imperialism of the late nineteenth century was a new phenomenon, different from previous expansionist impulses. Instead, it more nearly resembled the "new" imperialism that engulfed European nations in the late nineteenth and early twentieth centuries, in which those nations rushed to carve out colonies or spheres of influence in Africa and Asia.

The Spanish-American War of 1898 was the event that helped the various impulses for U.S. expansion and colonization to converge. When Cubans began a revolt to secure their independence from Spain in 1895, most Americans were genuinely sympathetic toward the Cuban underdogs. Those genuine feelings were heightened by American newspaper reporters and editors, some of whom wrote lurid (and knowingly inaccurate) accounts of the Spanish "monsters" and the poor, downtrodden Cubans. President William McKinley tried to pressure Spain into making concessions and sent the American battleship *Maine* to Havana on a "courtesy call," an obvious move to underscore the United States' position toward Spain. But on February 15, 1898, the *Maine* blew up in Havana harbor. Although

CHAPTER 4

JUSTIFYING
AMERICAN
IMPERIALISM:
THE LOUISIANA
PURCHASE
EXPOSITION,
1904

we now know (as a result of a 1976 study) that the explosion on the *Maine* was an internal one, almost surely the result of an accident, at the time many Americans, fired up by the press, were convinced that the Spanish had been responsible. Yet war with Spain did not come immediately and, in the opinion of some, was not inevitable, even after the *Maine* incident. However, on April 11, 1898, after two months of demands, negotiations, and arguments in which it sometimes appeared that war might be avoided, McKinley asked Congress for authorization to intervene in Cuba "in the name of humanity and civilization." On April 20, Congress granted authorization, and the Spanish-American War began.

If the Spanish-American War had not begun as an imperialistic venture, the convergence of the economic, military, religious, and racist impulses mentioned previously and the weak condition of Spain gave American leaders the opportunity to use the war and victory for expansionist purposes. Once the United States had achieved a comparatively bloodless[5] victory against nearly impotent Spain, a general debate began over whether the United States should demand from Spain the surrender of its colonial empire, the jewels of which were Cuba and the Philippine Islands. Although President McKinley admitted that he had to consult a globe to find out where the Philippine Islands were, he was never in doubt that they should become a part of a new American empire. McKinley thus pressured the Spanish to include the surrender of their empire in the peace treaty (signed in Paris on December 10, 1898) and submitted that treaty to the U.S. Senate on January 4, 1899. After a brisk debate in which opponents of acquisition charged that acquiring colonies went against America's history and morality, that acquiring the Philippines would embroil the United States in future wars, and that Filipinos would be able to migrate to the United States, where they would compete with American labor, on February 6, 1899, the Senate ratified the treaty by a vote of 57–27, just one vote more than the two-thirds necessary for ratifying a treaty.[6] Learning of the vote, an exultant McKinley boasted that the Philippines would become

a land of plenty and increasing possibilities; a people redeemed from savage and indolent habits, devoted to the arts of peace, in touch with commerce and trade of all nations, enjoying the blessings of freedom, of civil and religious liberty, of education, and of homes, and whose children's children shall for ages hence bless the American republic because it emancipated their fatherland, and set them in the pathway of the world's best civilization.

The Senate vote, however, did not end the debate over whether the United States should become a colonial power. Two days before the Sen-

---

5. The Spanish-American War lasted less than three months. The United States suffered only 362 battle or battle-related deaths (an additional 5,100 died of either disease or food poisoning), and the war cost only $250 million.

6. Outside the Senate, opponents of imperialism included Carl Schurz, William James, Mark Twain, Andrew Carnegie, Charles Francis Adams, Jane Addams, and William Jennings Bryan.

ate voted, fighting broke out between U.S. troops and Filipinos under Emilio Aguinaldo, who had helped American soldiers overthrow the Spanish and who expected the United States to grant the Philippines immediate independence. Before the United States broke Aguinaldo's insurrection, approximately 125,000 American troops served in the Philippines, 4,200 were killed in action, and 2,800 were wounded, but an alleged 220,000 Filipinos died in battle, from disease and famine, and through torture. Government censors kept war-related atrocities from the American people. By 1902, the Philippine insurrection had been broken.

In 1900, Democratic presidential nominee William Jennings Bryan campaigned against McKinley on an anti-imperialist platform. The incumbent won easily (probably because of the fairly widespread prosperity that American voters enjoyed in 1900), but Bryan carried 45.5 percent of the vote, a better showing for a loser than in all but four presidential elections from 1900 to the present. By the time the St. Louis Exposition opened in 1904, anti-imperialist rhetoric had lost much of its appeal, but the issue was far from dead.

At the St. Louis Exposition, the "Philippine Reservation" was sponsored almost totally by the U.S. government. (It cost approximately

$1 million.) Undoubtedly, this delighted the exposition's organizers, for they knew that similar attractions (called ethnological villages) had been extremely popular at the Paris Exposition of 1889, the Columbian Exposition of 1893, and the Pan-American Exposition of 1901. Former civil governor of the Philippines William Howard Taft (who in 1904 became secretary of war) supported the Philippine Reservation completely, as did Pedro A. Paterno, president of the Philippine Senate, who hoped that such an exhibit would attract investment capital to the islands. Federal agents scoured the Philippines, collecting materials to exhibit and "inviting" various Filipinos to journey to St. Louis. Those who agreed to come were allowed to make money by diving for coins, selling handicrafts, demonstrating their prowess with bows and arrows, and having their photographs taken with visitors to the exposition.

As expected, the Philippine Reservation was one of the highlights of the St. Louis Exposition. How did the Philippine Reservation seek to justify American imperialism? How do you think visitors might have reacted to what they saw? According to a 1904 *Harper's* magazine article, the St. Louis Exposition "fills a visitor full of pictures . . . that keep coming up in his mind for years afterwards." What were those pictures?

THE METHOD

According to historian Robert W. Rydell, who wrote an excellent book about American international expo-

sitions in the late nineteenth and early twentieth centuries, expositions "propagated the ideas and values of

CHAPTER 4

JUSTIFYING
AMERICAN
IMPERIALISM:
THE LOUISIANA
PURCHASE
EXPOSITION,
1904

the country's political, financial, corporate, and intellectual leaders and offered these ideas as the proper interpretation of social and political reality."[7] In other words, the millions of Americans who visited exhibits that the Anthropology Department had created at the 1904 exposition saw what someone else wanted them to see. At the Philippine Reservation, visitors made their way through six Filipino villages erected by the U.S. government in which representatives of "all the races of the Philippine Islands" could be "studied" by scientists and where most Americans had their only opportunity to see Filipinos with their own eyes. This allowed the American government to use the reservation to justify its imperialistic ventures in the Philippines and elsewhere.

The evidence that you will be examining and analyzing in this chapter consists of fourteen photographs taken at the Louisiana Purchase International Exposition and an excerpt from an essay by W. J. McGee, head of the fair's Anthropology Department (Source 15). Through photographs taken by official exposition photographers, you will see some of what the fair's visitors saw. Similarly, McGee's essay is intended to help you understand some of the thinking behind the Anthropology Department's exhibits.

As you examine the photographs in Sources 1 through 14, keep in mind that you are seeing what someone else wants you to see. The Philippine Is-

lands in 1904 contained an enormous diversity of peoples, from the most "primitive" to the most technologically and culturally sophisticated. About seventy-five linguistic groups were represented, as well as a plethora of Western and non-Western religious (under Spanish rule, most Filipinos had become Roman Catholics) and social customs. Yet of the many peoples who inhabited the Philippine Islands, the U.S. government selected only six groups to inhabit the reservation's villages. Five of the six groups are photographically depicted in Sources 5 through 13.[8] Why do you think each group was selected to go to St. Louis? What impressions do you think each group left in the minds of American visitors?

A second problem you will confront is the photographer's bias. As do journalists, photojournalists have a particular point of view or bias toward or against their subjects. These biases often affect the *way* subjects are presented to the viewers of the photographs. As you examine each photograph, think about the photographer's bias, including whether the subjects are presented in a favorable or an unfavorable light.

Although you may not be used to thinking of photographs as historical evidence, photographs and other visual documents (drawings, paintings, movies) often can yield as much information as more traditional sources. As Charles F. Bryan, Jr., and Mark V. Wetherington note,

7. Robert W. Rydell, *All the World's a Fair: Visions of Empire at American International Expositions, 1876–1916* (Chicago: University of Chicago Press, 1984), p. 3.

8. Negro pygmies (or Negritos), Igorots, Tagalos, Bontocs, and Visayans. The sixth group was the Moros.

Through the eye of the camera, the researcher can examine people and places "frozen" in time. . . . Photographs can tell us much about the social preferences and pretensions of their subjects, and can catch people at work, at play, or at home. In fact, you can "read" a photograph in much the same manner as any other historical document.[9]

When a historian "reads" a photograph, it means that he or she puts the photograph into words, describing it in terms of its intent, specific details about it, and the overall impression it makes.

For you to read the photographs, you will have to subject each one to the following questions (take notes as you go):

1. What "message" is the photographer attempting to convey? How does the photographer convey that message (there may well be more than one way)?
2. Is the photographer biased in any way? How? What is the purpose of the photograph?
3. Are there buildings in the photograph? What impressions of these buildings does the photographer intend that viewers should get? How does the photograph seek to elicit those impressions?
4. Are there people in the photograph? Are they posed or "natural"? How has the photographer portrayed these people? What are the people doing (if anything)? What impressions of these people does the photographer intend that viewers of the photograph should retain?
5. Examine the people in more detail. What about their clothing? Their facial expressions? *Note:* Because photographers expected their subjects to strike artificial poses in order to be photographed, many of the pictures appear rigid and posed. Indeed, they were. If you have an old family album, see how similar some of the poses are to those in these photographs.

After you have examined each photograph, look at all the photographs together. What "message" is the photographer (or photographers) intending to convey? Most professional photographers judge whether a photograph is good or poor by the responses it evokes in the viewer's mind. What is the relationship between the responses you imagine these photographs might have elicited with America's justification for imperialism? The excerpt from McGee's essay also is extremely illuminating. Can you identify any cultural bias or prejudice in his thinking?

9. Charles F. Bryan, Jr., and Mark V. Wetherington, *Finding Our Past: A Guidebook for Group Projects in Community History* (Knoxville: East Tennessee Historical Society, 1983), p. 26.

Sources 1–3 from *The World's Fair, Comprising the Official Photographic Views of the Universal Exposition Held in St. Louis, 1904* (St. Louis: N. D. Thompson Publishing Co., 1903), pp. 6, 56, 67.

1. Opening Day Ceremonies, April 30, 1904, in the Plaza of St. Louis (Palace of Varied Industries in the Background).

2. Palace of Liberal Arts (the United States Government Building in the Background).

3. Palace of Machinery and Palace of Electricity (260-Foot-High Ferris Wheel in the Background).

Source 4 from J. W. Buel, ed., *Louisiana and the Fair: An Exposition of the World, Its People, and Their Achievements* (St. Louis: World's Progress Publishing Co., 1904), Vol. V, frontispiece. Photo: Missouri Historical Society.

4. Types and Development of Man.

CHAPTER 4

JUSTIFYING
AMERICAN
IMPERIALISM:
THE LOUISIANA
PURCHASE
EXPOSITION,
1904

Source 5 from Robert W. Rydell, *All the World's a Fair: Visions of Empire at American International Expositions, 1876–1916* (Chicago: University of Chicago Press, 1984), p. 175. Photo: Library of Congress.

5. Negrito Tribesman from the Philippines (Exposition Officials Named This Man "Missing Link").

Source 6 from *The World's Fair, Comprising the Official Photographic Views*, p. 149. Photo: Missouri Historical Society.

6. Igorots from the Philippines.

Sources 7 and 8 from Buel, ed., *Louisiana and the Fair,* Vol. V, p. 1721. Photos: Missouri Historical Society.

7. Tagalo Women Washing.

8. Igorots Performing a Festival Dance.

Source 9 from Rydell, *All the World's a Fair,* p. 174. Photo: Library of Congress.

9. Igorot Dance and Spectators.

Source 10 from Buel, ed., *Louisiana and the Fair,* Vol. V, p. 1737. Photo: Missouri Historical Society.

10. Igorots Preparing a Feast of Dog.

Source 11 from *The World's Fair, Comprising the Official Photographic Views,* p. 169. Photo: Missouri Historical Society.

11. Bontoc Head-Hunters from the Philippines.

Sources 12 and 13 from *The World's Fair, Comprising the Official Photographic Views,* pp. 161, 163, 152–153. Photos: Missouri Historical Society.

12. Visayan Mothers with Their Children (Two of Whom Were Born at the Exposition).

CHAPTER 4

JUSTIFYING
AMERICAN
IMPERIALISM:
THE LOUISIANA
PURCHASE
EXPOSITION,
1904

13. A Visayan Troupe of Singers, Dancers, and Orchestra.

Source 14 from Rydell, *All the World's a Fair*, p. 176. Photo: Missouri Historical Society.

14. Reproduction of an American School in the Philippines.

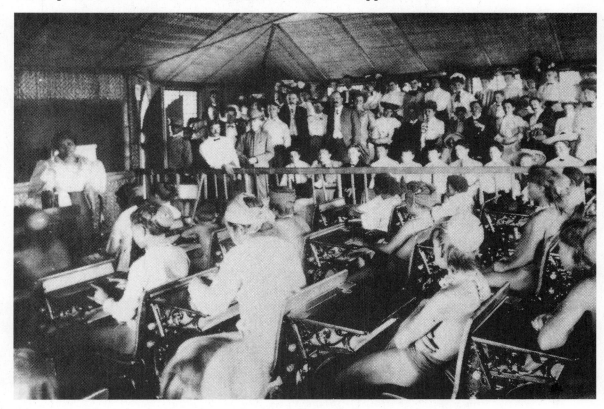

CHAPTER 4

JUSTIFYING
AMERICAN
IMPERIALISM:
THE LOUISIANA
PURCHASE
EXPOSITION,
1904

Source 15 from Buel, ed., *Louisiana and the Fair*, Vol. V, pp. 1567–1572.

15. W. J. McGee, "Anthropology—A Congress of Nations at the Fair."

It is possible for the naturalist to build from the smallest bone of an extinct animal the very form, size, appearance, in short a reconstruction and reproduction of the animal as it appeared in life. So it is possible for the ethnologist to estimate, from any object fashioned by the art of man, the degree of civilization that produced it, and in many cases to establish a reasonable hypothesis respecting the customs, the religion, and even the achievements of the people of which the object referred to is a relict.

The story of the birth of man cannot be told in geologic records, but his growth from primitive savagery to the attainments that distinguish and aggrandize our times may be closely followed by the evidences of his existence and his crafts scattered along the highway of the ages. To tell the story, however, is much less impressive and far less convincing than is production of the proofs of scientific deductions and conclusions in the form of specimens of handiwork, and with this thoroughly understood the anthropological department of the Louisiana Purchase Exposition was made a museum of objects rather than a school dependent upon pictographic art for the elucidation of theory.

In pursuing the study of mankind's development one very important fact must be kept well in view, viz., that it is not possible to measure the growth of the world's civilization with that precision which may be applied in estimating the periods of geology, during which the processes of nature reduced the earth to a habitable condition. For it is well to consider that in different localities two or more ages, so to speak, have always co-existed. The mind of man is so constituted that each individual presents special characteristics, so that there is perpetual conflict in concept and endless antagonisms in conclusions. A superior mind may point the way to higher and better conditions, but it does not follow that his counsel will be obeyed; and it is equally probable that the voice of one least qualified to give advice will be heeded as that of a leader. Thus it happens with families, clans, tribes and nations, for which reason development may be advanced or retarded as circumstances favor or hinder. In our own day, acquainted with and enjoying a high degree of civilization, we know that there are other countries in which barbarism still exists; even in almost primitive savagery; such for example as the Terre del Fuegans, the Seri Indians, on the Gulf of California, and the Ainu, of the Kurile Islands, north of Japan. If such low types, of which there are many more examples than the three noted, can exist in an age distinguished for great achievements in industry, commerce, art, science, we must, in justice to previous ages, believe that disparities equally great characterized all other periods; that the stone age, bronze age, the iron age, co-existed, though divided by lines geographic, tribal, and national; that man's growth has been indigenous and adventitious, dependent upon conditions of mind, environment, and climate. For these reasons, to know the human race in its multiplied aspects, past and present, we must specialize, since generalization leads inevitably into a labyrinth of uncertainties respecting origin, distribution, and development of peoples.

It is to make the study of mankind at once interesting and clearly understandable that the anthropological department was established at the World's Fair, in the elaboration of which reliance was placed in specialization and objective demonstration; thus, early man was a cave dweller, whose weapons were flint and stone, and whose appearance bore hairy resemblance to the wild beasts with which he contended. This description presents an image to the reader, who constructs according to preconceived opinions, and the vividness of his imagination. Similarly mere descriptions, or even drawings, of people, implements, and utensils, convey no more than a general idea, which being unsubstantial soon vanishes, like a vision, leaving no permanent impression.

The Anthropological exhibit at the St. Louis Fair represented the sum of human knowledge respecting races, presented in a concrete form by the exhibition of actual objects recovered from the graves of centuries; resurrections from the tombs of long ago civilizations; exhumations from the cemeteries wherein were laid the bones and relics of primitive man as he existed in all countries. To this interesting showing many nations contributed the most rare and precious specimens which scientists, archaeologists, and explorers have discovered, bearing in any wise upon the subject of primitive, prehistoric, savage and strange peoples that have inhabited the earth. This department of the Fair was accordingly a world's museum of human relics, and a congress of living examples of various human types, brought from the most remote parts of the globe.

A general survey of the anthropological department revealed to the visitor the appearance, habits, surroundings and every day life of early man, such as lived in caves, burrowed like wild animals, dwelt in trees, and existed in the primal state of savagery more than ten thousand, aye, perhaps fifty thousand years ago. And in the showing the ancient Egyptian reappeared, out of the spiced and pitched cerements that wrapped his body in preservatives long before the time of Noah—even from millenniums when human hands fashioned the first mud hut that stood upon the banks of the Nile.

The Assyrian, earliest of the tribe of Asshur, was there, mute of lip for a period so great that hoary antiquity cannot measure it, to remind beholders of the first monarchy of history; and the Babylonian was present, out of the

CHAPTER 4

JUSTIFYING
AMERICAN
IMPERIALISM:
THE LOUISIANA
PURCHASE
EXPOSITION,
1904

cradle of civilization, with specimens of his workmanship and evidences of his marked attainments in sculpture, architecture, literature, religion, 6500 years ago in the far away and now desert land where the Garden of Eden is supposed to have been planted. It was resurrection and revivification of the most antique races of the world, brought forth from sepulchers of the nameless past, to be reviewed by the living present that the secrets of existence in the unnumbered ages might be exposed.

In the procession of peoples, extinct and living, that represented all the periods of human life on our planet, there appeared examples from orient, occident, continent and island the wide world over; tree dwellers from New Guinea; lake dwellers from the Orinoco valley; head hunters from Borneo; cannibals from Africa; hairy men from the Kuriles; devil worshipers from Saghalien; giants from Patagonia; pygmies from Africa; Eskimos from Arctic regions; in short, the exhibition was a congress of typical peoples from every corner and part of the earth, and a museum of humanity so comprehensive that it was possible for the visitor to gain therefrom a perception and mental grasp of man as he appeared in all ages, conditions, and countries. The showing being thus complete it was made comparatively easy to trace man's progress from his earliest manifestation through all the pauses, periods, and epochs of his advance even to the heights of his accomplishments in the dawn of the twentieth century, in the culmination of effort, as illustrated in the greatest and latest of Expositions. . . .

∞ QUESTIONS TO CONSIDER ∞

As you examine the photographs, first look for the photographer's intent and biases in each one. What "message" was the photographer trying to communicate? How might that message be used as a justification for American imperialism in the Philippines? For example, examine Sources 1 through 3, which show some of the majestic buildings at the exposition. What reactions did the fair's organizers hope that visitors would have to the buildings in Sources 1 through 3? Awe? Pride? What impressions (amuse-ment, awe, disgust, etc.) might viewers have had of these edifices? Now compare the structures in Sources 1 through 3 with those in Sources 6 through 9. What message did photographers hope that viewers would receive?

The caption for Source 4 (from the official history of the Louisiana Purchase Exposition) reads in part, "The photogravure herewith is from an excellent specially prepared drawing which very accurately illustrates, as nearly as the science of ethnology is able to do, the characteristic types of mankind arranged in a progressive order of development from primitive or prehistoric man to the highest example of modern civilization." How does this photograph of a painting (which was on display at the exposition) help you assess the intent of all the photographers?

Sources 5 through 11 are of posed Philippine men and women from the Negrito, Igorot, Tagalo, and Bontoc tribes. These groups were among the most "primitive" of all Filipinos. Why did U.S. government officials select these people to appear at the St. Louis Exposition? How are these peoples portrayed by photographers? How are they dressed? What are they doing? What impressions might visitors or viewers of the photographs have had of these peoples? When there are American visitors in the photographs (as in Sources 9 and 14), what are they doing? Why did photographers place them in these pictures?

Sources 12 and 13 are photographs of Visayans, a people quite different from the Negritos, Igorots, Tagalos, and Bontocs. What was different about them? How might you account for these differences?[10] How might American visitors to the village and viewers of these photographs have reacted to the Visayans as compared with other Filipino peoples at the exposition? What impressions would the Visayans have made? How might the Visayans have been used to justify American imperialism in the Philippines?

Source 14 is a photograph depicting a replica of an American school for Filipinos in the Philippines. What was the purpose of the photographer who took this picture? What is the photograph's message? What impressions would viewers have had?

Once you have examined the photographs individually, analyze them collectively. What was their collective message? How does that message relate to American actions in the Philippines from 1898 to the exposition in 1904? Could these photographs or word descriptions of them have been used to justify American imperialism in the Philippines? How? Refer to specific photographs to prove your points.

In Source 15, the excerpt from his essay on the fair's Anthropology Department, W. J. McGee boasts that, in addition to relics, the department has created "a congress of living examples of various human types, brought from the most remote parts of the globe." By 1904, nearly all scientists had accepted Darwin's theory of evolution. To McGee, however, how could the world of 1904 simultaneously be home to "primitive savagery" and the Western "attainments that distinguish and aggrandize our times"? Was evolution a universal phenomenon that affected all subgroups of a species? If not, did the "fittest" (to use Spencer's word) owe anything to their "unfit" brethren? How could McGee's essay be used as a justification for imperialism?

---

10. The Visayans were Roman Catholics, whereas all the other Filipinos brought to St. Louis practiced non-Western religions or held on to native Filipino religious customs. What does this tell you about the Visayans?

CHAPTER 4

JUSTIFYING
AMERICAN
IMPERIALISM:
THE LOUISIANA
PURCHASE
EXPOSITION,
1904

≪∽ EPILOGUE ∽≫

At the Louisiana Purchase Exposition in 1904, American visitors saw countless exhibits that communicated very strong messages. Arranged and erected by the nation's corporate, intellectual, and political leaders, the exhibits nevertheless were what Americans wanted to see. These exhibits trumpeted America's own scientific, technological, and cultural prowess while at the same time offering living proof that it was the United States' economic, political, and moral duty to become a colonial power. In addition to Filipino villages, villages had been set up for Native Americans and Alaskan Eskimos, who, like the Filipinos, were wards of the United States. It was as powerful a visual justification for American imperialism as could possibly have been contrived.

Once the Philippine revolt was broken in 1902, the United States invested considerable time and energy in trying to Americanize the Filipinos, largely through education and giving Filipinos an increasing voice in their own affairs. In 1913, President Woodrow Wilson appointed Francis B. Harrison governor general of the Philippines, with the explicit instructions to prepare the Filipinos for their ultimate independence (a promise Congress gave its assent to in 1916, noting that independence would be granted "as soon as a stable government can be established"). Schools were set up throughout the islands, and by the 1930s, almost 50 percent of the population was literate. Gradually American officials increased the percentage

of Filipinos in the civil service, from 49 percent in 1903 to 94 percent in 1923. Elections were held for a Philippine legislature, although the real power remained in the hands of Americans.

In economic matters, the Americans' record in the Philippines was not so impressive. Economic power remained in the hands of a small, native Philippine landed elite, who, with the cooperation of Americans, continued to dominate the Philippine economy. Between 1900 and 1935, poverty became more widespread, real wages actually declined, and sharecropping (like that in the American South) doubled. This was the situation when the Japanese attacked the Philippine Islands on December 8, 1941. Emilio Aguinaldo, leader of the Philippine independence movement that the United States had crushed, sided with the Japanese.

With the defeat of Japan in 1945, the United States moved quickly to grant independence to the Philippines (which occurred on July 4, 1946), although America's economic and military presence in the new nation remained strong. Favorable leases on military and naval bases were negotiated, and the Central Intelligence Agency closely monitored Philippine elections and on occasion secretly backed candidates for office.

In 1965, campaigning against widespread government corruption and favoritism to the landed elite, Ferdinand Marcos was elected president of the Philippines. A much-lauded war hero,

Marcos had entered politics in 1949, when he had become the youngest person ever elected to the Philippine Congress. As president, Marcos increased the power of his office to virtual one-man rule, largely by hobbling or eradicating the other branches of government and by a brutal policy of political repression, with more than fifty thousand political prisoners and numerous reported incidents of assassinations and torture. Even so, Marcos's rule was insecure. In the nation's economic expansion, profits went to a very few, usually Marcos's associates (in 1972, the poorest 20 percent of Filipinos received only 4.4 percent of the nation's income), and a population boom (2.5 percent per year) increased poverty and unemployment.

Things began coming apart for Marcos on August 21, 1983, when his principal political rival, Benigno Aquino, was shot and killed at the Manila airport as he was returning to the Philippines to lead an anti-Marcos political movement. Public opinion in both the Philippines and the United States was that Marcos had been responsible for Aquino's death. By 1984, opinion polls in the Philippines showed a serious erosion of support for the Marcos government.

In 1986, Marcos was challenged for the presidency by Corazon Aquino, the widow of the killed opposition leader. The election results were clouded by charges of fraud, and both Marcos and Aquino claimed victory. By this time, the aging and ill Marcos had become increasingly isolated from the people, as he and his wife, Imelda, remained cloistered in the presidential palace. In February 1986, a general strike by Aquino supporters, the army's turning against the government, and the increasing displeasure of the Reagan administration finally toppled Marcos, who fled the Philippines for American protection in Hawaii. Corazon Aquino became president, only to face the nation's severe economic and political problems. Her term expired in 1992, and she did not seek reelection, having survived numerous coup attempts. She left a nation that was more democratic but still economically and politically unstable.

Filipinos were not the only people "displayed" at the St. Louis Exposition. Indeed, the same economic, political, and intellectual strains that supported America's overseas imperialism also were evident in the conquest and subjugation of Native Americans, the growing efforts to exclude certain immigrants (the Chinese Exclusion Act of 1882, for example), the rising tide of American nativism, and the successful legal and extralegal methods southern whites used to deprive African Americans of their economic and civil rights. Not surprisingly, both Geronimo and Chief Joseph were extremely popular "attractions" at the exposition, as were the Sioux men and women pictured in Source 16. What similarities can you see between Source 16 and the photographs of Filipinos? Undoubtedly, ethnologist W. J. McGee, head of the exposition's Anthropology Department, spoke for most white Americans when he remarked that *white* and *strong* are synonymous terms."

In one sense, the Louisiana Purchase Exposition of 1904 marked the

Source 16 from *The World's Fair, Comprising the Official Photographic Views,*
p. 137. Photo: Library of Congress.

16. Sioux Men and Women.

high point of Americans' interest in international expositions and world's fairs. As Americans became less provincial, especially after the introduction of modern communications media, attendance at such events declined. As a result, such expositions became smaller (as opposed to the St. Louis Exposition, which covered 1,272 acres, the Knoxville, Tennessee, world's fair of 1982 was held on less than 70 acres). Moreover, the purpose of American expositions changed. Rather than being celebrations of the nation's technological might or justifications for American imperialism, world's fairs were viewed by their backers as massive urban renewal projects, in which the city government would come into possession of valuable acreage to be used for economic development. Such was the goal of recent fairs in Portland, Knoxville, and New Orleans. Finally, increased costs and lower attendance figures meant that such expositions were not economical. The New Orleans World's Fair lost millions of dollars. As a result, Chicago, which had planned to host an international exposition in 1992, had second thoughts.

In 1904, however, millions of Americans came to St. Louis to visit the Louisiana Purchase Exposition, a massive reinforcement of their own ideas about American superiority and the rectitude of Euro-American world domination. At the same time, the ideas that spurred and justified imperialism similarly spurred and justified increasingly harsh treatment of Native Americans, African Americans, Hispanics, Asian Americans, and recent immigrants from southern and eastern Europe. In a nation and a world filled with opportunities, few Americans realized that their own ideology and attitudes not only did not carry them forward but in many ways actually held them back.

CHAPTER 5

HOMOGENIZING A PLURALISTIC CULTURE: PROPAGANDA DURING WORLD WAR I

❧ THE PROBLEM ❧

One week after Congress approved the war declaration that brought the United States into World War I, President Woodrow Wilson signed Executive Order 2594, which created the Committee on Public Information, designed to mobilize public opinion behind the war effort. Apparently there was considerable worry in the Wilson administration that the American public, which had supported neutrality and noninvolvement, would not rally to the war effort.

Wilson selected forty-one-year-old journalist and political ally George Creel to head the Committee on Public Information. Creel rapidly established voluntary press censorship, which made the committee essentially the overseer of all war and war-related news. The committee also produced films, engaged some seventy-five thousand lecturers (called "Four Minute Men") who delivered approximately 7.5 million talks, commissioned posters intended to stir up support for the war and sell war bonds (seven hundred poster designs were submitted, and more than 9 million posters were printed in 1918 alone), and engaged in numerous other activities to blend this ethnically and ideologically diverse nation into a homogeneous nation in support of the country's war effort and to discredit any potential opposition to America's entry into the war.

In this chapter, you will analyze the propaganda techniques of a modern nation at war. The evidence contains material sponsored or commissioned by the Committee on Public Information (posters, newspaper advertisements, selections of speeches by Four Minute Men) as well as privately produced works (musical lyrics and commercial films) that tended to parallel the committee's efforts. Essentially, the question you are to answer is this: How did the United States mobilize public opinion in support of the nation's participation in World War I? In addition, what were the consequences, positive and negative, of this mobilization of public opinion?

On a larger scale, you should be willing to ponder other questions as well, although they do not relate directly to the evidence you will examine. To begin with, is government-sponsored propaganda during wartime a good thing? When it comes into conflict with the First Amendment's guarantees of freedom of speech, which should prevail? Finally, is there a danger that government-sponsored propaganda can be carried too far? Do you think that was the case during World War I?

BACKGROUND

By the early twentieth century, the United States had worldwide economic interests and even had acquired a modest colonial empire, but many Americans wanted to believe that they were insulated from world affairs and impervious to world problems. Two great oceans seemed to protect the nation from overseas threats, and the enormity of the country and comparative weakness of its neighbors appeared to secure it against all dangers. Let other nations waste their people and resources in petty wars over status and territory, Americans reasoned. The United States should stand above such greed or insanity, and certainly should not wade into foreign mud puddles.

To many Americans, European nations were especially suspect. For centuries, European nations had engaged in an almost ceaseless round of armed conflicts—wars for national unity, territory, or even religion or empire.

Moreover, in the eyes of many Americans, these bloody wars appeared to have solved little or nothing, and the end of one war seemed to be but a prelude to the next. Ambitious kings and their plotting ministers seemed to make Europe the scene of almost constant uproar, an uproar that many Americans saw as devoid of reason and morality. Nor did it appear that the United States, as powerful as it was, could have any effect on the unstable European situation.

For this reason, most Americans greeted news of the outbreak of war in Europe in 1914 with equal measures of surprise and determination not to become involved. They applauded President Wilson's August 4 proclamation of neutrality, his statement (issued two weeks later) urging Americans to be impartial in thought as well as in deed, and his insistence that the United States continue neutral commerce with all the belligerents. Few

CHAPTER 5

HOMOGENIZING
A PLURALISTIC
CULTURE:
PROPAGANDA
DURING WORLD
WAR I

Americans protested German violation of Belgian neutrality. Indeed, most Americans (naively, as it turned out) believed that the United States both should and could remain aloof from the conflict in Europe.

But many factors pulled the United States into the conflict that later became known as World War I. America's economic prosperity to a large extent rested on commercial ties with Europe. U.S. trade with the Allies (England, France, Russia) exceeded $800 million in 1914, whereas trade with the Central Powers (Germany, Austria, Turkey) stood at approximately $170 million in that same year. Much of the trade with Great Britain and France was financed through loans from American banks, something President Wilson and Secretary of State William Jennings Bryan openly discouraged because both men believed that those economic interests might eventually draw the United States into the conflict. Indeed, Wilson and Bryan probably were correct. Nevertheless, American economic interests were closely tied to those of Great Britain and France. Thus a victory by the Central Powers might damage U.S. trade. As Wilson drifted to an acceptance of this fact, Bryan had to back down.

A second factor pulling the United States into the war was the deep-seated feelings of President Wilson himself. Formerly a constitutional historian (Wilson had been a college professor and university president before entering the political arena as a reform governor of New Jersey), Wilson had long admired the British people and their form of government. Although technically neutral, the president strongly, though privately, favored the Allies and viewed a German victory as unthinkable. Moreover, many of Wilson's key advisers and the people close to him were decidedly pro-British. Such was the opinion of the president's friend and closest adviser, Colonel Edward House, as well as that of Robert Lansing (who replaced Bryan as secretary of state)[1] and Walter Hines Page (ambassador to England). These men and others helped strengthen Wilson's strong political opinions and influence the president's changing position toward the war in Europe. Hence, although Wilson asked Americans to be neutral in thought as well as in deed, in fact he and his principal advisers were neither. More than once, the president chose to ignore British violations of America's neutrality. Finally, when it appeared that the Central Powers might outlast their enemies, Wilson was determined to intercede. It was truly an agonizing decision for the president, who had worked so diligently to keep his nation out of war.

A third factor affecting the United States' neutrality was the strong ethnic ties of many Americans to the Old World. Many Americans had been born in Europe, and an even larger number were the sons and daughters of European immigrants (Tables 1 and 2). Although these people considered

1. Bryan resigned in 1915, in protest over what he considered Wilson's too sharp note to Germany over the sinking of the passenger liner *Lusitania*. Wilson called the act "illegal and inhuman." Bryan sensed that the Wilson administration was tilting away from neutrality.

1. Foreign-Born Population, by Country of Birth*

Country of Birth	Total Foreign Born
England	813,853
Scotland	254,570
Ireland	1,037,234
Germany	1,686,108
Austria	575,627
Hungary	397,283
Russia	1,400,495
Italy[2]	1,610,113

*Both this table and Table 2 were compiled from the U.S. census of 1920, the closest census to America's entrance into World War I (1917). The figures on Ireland include Northern Ireland, and the figures on Russia include the Baltic States.

2. Native-Born Population of Foreign or Mixed Parentage, by Country of Origin

Country of Origin of Parents	Total Native-Born Children
England and Wales	1,864,345
Scotland	514,436
Ireland	3,122,013
Germany	5,346,004
Austria	1,235,097
Hungary	538,518
Russia	1,508,604
Italy	1,751,091

themselves to be, and were, Americans, some retained emotional ties to Europe that they sometimes carried into the political arena—ties that could influence America's foreign policy.

2. Italy entered the war in 1914 on the side of the Central Powers. In March 1915, however, Italy switched sides, declaring war on Austria-Hungary in March 1915 and on Germany the next year.

Finally, as the largest neutral commercial power in the world, the United States soon became caught in the middle of the commercial warfare of the belligerents. With the declaration of war, both Great Britain and Germany threw up naval blockades. Great Britain's blockade was designed to cut the Central Powers off from war materiel. American commercial vessels bound for Germany were stopped, searched, and often seized by the British navy. Wilson protested British policy many times, but to no effect. After all, giving in to Wilson's protests would have deprived Britain of its principal military asset: the British navy.

Germany's blockade was even more dangerous, partly because the vast majority of American trade was with England and France. In addition, however, Germany's chief method of blockading the Allies was the use of the submarine, a comparatively new weapon in 1914. Because of the nature of the submarine (lethal while underwater, not equal to other fighting vessels on the surface), it was difficult for the submarine to remain effective and at the same time adhere to international law, such as the requirement that sufficient warning be given before sinking an enemy ship.[3] In 1915, hoping to terrorize the British into making peace, Germany unleashed its submarines in the Atlantic with orders to sink all ships flying Allied flags. In March, a German submarine sank the

3. International laws governing warfare at sea, as well as neutral shipping during wartime, were written in the mid-eighteenth century, more than one hundred years before the submarine became a potent seagoing weapon.

[135]

CHAPTER 5

HOMOGENIZING
A PLURALISTIC
CULTURE:
PROPAGANDA
DURING WORLD
WAR I

British passenger ship *Falaba*. Then on May 7, 1915, the British liner *Lusitania* was sunk with a loss of more than 1,000 lives, 128 of them American. Although Germany had published warnings in American newspapers specifically cautioning Americans not to travel on the *Lusitania,* and although it was ultimately discovered that the *Lusitania* had gone down so fast (in only eighteen minutes) because the British were shipping ammunition in the hold of the passenger ship, Americans were shocked by the Germans' actions on the high seas. Most Americans, however, continued to believe that the United States should stay out of the war and approved of Wilson's statement, issued three days after the *Lusitania* sank to the bottom, that "there is such a thing as a man being too proud to fight."

Yet a combination of economic interests, German submarine warfare, and other events gradually pushed the United States toward involvement. In early February 1917, Germany announced a policy of unrestricted submarine warfare against all ships—belligerent and neutral alike. Ships would be sunk without warning if found to be in what Germany designated forbidden waters. Later that month, the British intercepted a secret telegram intended for the German minister to Mexico, stationed in Mexico City. In that telegram, German foreign secretary Arthur Zimmermann offered Mexico a deal: Germany would help Mexico retrieve territory lost to the United States in the 1840s if Mexico would make a military alliance with Germany and declare war on the United States in the event that

the United States declared war on Germany. Knowing the impact that such a telegram would have on American public opinion, the British quickly handed the telegram over to Wilson, who released it to the press. From that point on, it was but a matter of time before the United States would become involved in World War I.

On March 20, 1917, President Wilson called his cabinet together at the White House to advise him on how to proceed in the deteriorating situation with Germany. Wilson's cabinet officers unanimously urged the president to call Congress into session immediately and ask for a declaration of war against Germany. When the last cabinet member had finished speaking, Wilson said, "Well, gentlemen, I think there is no doubt as to what your advice is. I thank you," and dismissed the meeting without informing the cabinet of his own intentions.

Yet even though Wilson had labored so arduously to keep the United States out of the war in Europe, by March 20 (or very soon after) his mind was made up: The United States must make war on Germany. Typing out his war message on his own Hammond portable typewriter, Wilson was out of sorts and complained often of headaches. The president, devoted to peace and Progressive reform, was drafting the document he had prayed he would never have to write.

On April 2, 1917, President Wilson appeared in person before a joint session of Congress to deliver his war message. Congress was ready. On April 4, the Senate approved a war declaration (the vote was 82–6). The House of Representatives followed suit two days later (with a vote of 373–50).[4]

At the outset of America's entry into the war, many government officials feared (incorrectly, as it turned out) that large blocs of Americans would not support the war effort. In 1917, the Bureau of the Census had estimated that approximately 4,662,000 people living in the United States had been born in Germany or in one of the other Central Powers.[5] As Tables 1 and 2 show, the United States also contained a large number of Irish Americans, many of whom were vehemently anti-British and hence emotionally sided with the Central Powers. Could this heterogeneous society be persuaded voluntarily to support the war effort? Could Americans of the same ethnic stock as the enemies be rallied to the cause?

Furthermore, there had been no decisive event to prompt the war declaration (some even thought the Zimmermann telegram was a British hoax). Would Americans support such a war with sufficient unanimity? No firing on Fort Sumter or blowing up of the battleship *Maine* had forced America's entrance into World War I. The *Lusitania* sinking had occurred two years before the war declaration. Without the obvious threat of having been attacked, would the American people stand together to defeat the faraway enemy? Could American isolationist and noninterventionist opinion, very strong as late as the presidential election of 1916, be overcome? To solidify the nation behind the war, Wilson created the Committee on Public Information.

THE METHOD

For George Creel and the Committee on Public Information, the purposes of propaganda were very clear:

1. Unite a multiethnic, pluralistic society behind the war effort.

2. Attract a sufficient number of men to the armed services and elicit universal civilian support for those men.

3. Influence civilians to support the war effort by purchasing war bonds or by other actions (such as limiting personal consumption or rolling bandages).

4. Influence civilians to put pressure on other civilians to refrain from antiwar comments, strikes, antidraft activities, unwitting dispersal

4. The fifty-six votes in the Senate and House against the declaration of war essentially came from three separate groups: senators and congressmen with strong German and Austrian constituencies, isolationists who believed the United States should not become involved on either side, and some Progressive reformers who maintained that the war would divert America's attention from political, economic, and social reforms.

5. No census had been taken since 1910, so this was a very rough guess. As shown in Table 1, the bureau's 1917 estimate was much too high, almost double the actual number of

people living in the United States who had been born in Germany or in one of the other Central Powers.

CHAPTER 5

HOMOGENIZING
A PLURALISTIC
CULTURE:
PROPAGANDA
DURING WORLD
WAR I

of information to spies, and other public acts that could hurt the war effort.

To achieve these ends, propaganda techniques had to be used with extreme care. For propaganda to be effective, it would have to contain one or more of the following features:

1. Portrayal of American and Allied servicemen in the best possible light.
2. Portrayal of the enemy in the worst possible light.
3. Portrayal of the American and Allied cause as just and the enemy's cause as unjust.
4. Message to civilians that they were being involved in the war effort in important ways.
5. Communication of a sense of urgency to civilians.

In this chapter, you are given the following six types of World War I propaganda to analyze, some of it produced directly by the Committee on Public Information and some produced privately but examined and approved by the committee:

1. One popular song, perhaps the most famous to come out of World War I, performed in music halls and vaudeville houses. Although the Committee on Public Information did not produce this kind of material, it could—and did—discourage performances of "unpatriotic" popular songs.
2. Four newspaper and magazine advertisements produced directly by the Committee on Public Information.
3. Nine posters either commissioned or approved by the committee and used for recruiting, advertising liberty loans,[6] and other purposes.
4. Two cartoons, one an editorial cartoon and the other the winning cartoon in a contest sponsored by a U.S. Army camp publication.
5. Two excerpts of speeches by Four Minute Men and one poem by a Four Minute Man.
6. Material concerning American-made feature films, including suggestions to theater owners on how to advertise the film *Kultur* (Culture), two film advertisements, and one still photograph to be used in advertising a feature film.

As you examine the evidence, you will see that effective propaganda operates on two levels. On the surface, there is the logical appeal for support to help win the war. On another level, however, certain images and themes are used to excite the emotions of the people for whom the propaganda is designed. As you examine the evidence, ask yourself the following questions:

1. For whom was this piece of propaganda designed?
2. What was this piece of propaganda trying to get people to think? To do?
3. What logical appeal was being made?
4. What emotional appeals were being made?

6. Liberty loans were loans made by U.S. citizens to the government to finance the war effort. They were repaid with interest, and were similar to liberty bonds (see page 159).

5. What might have been the results, positive and negative, of these kinds of appeals?

In songs, speeches, advertisements, and film reviews, are there key words or important images? Where there are illustrations (advertisements, posters, cartoons), what facial expressions and images are used? Finally, are there any common logical and emotional themes running through American propaganda during World War I? How did the United States use propaganda to mobilize public opinion during World War I? What were some of the consequences, positive and negative, of this type of propaganda?

THE EVIDENCE

Source 1 is a popular song by George M. Cohan, 1917.

1. "Over There."

Johnnie, get your gun,
Get your gun, get your gun,
Take it on the run,
On the run, on the run.
Hear them calling you and me,
Every son of liberty.
Hurry right away,
No delay, no delay.
Make your daddy glad
To have had such a lad.
Tell your sweetheart not to pine,
To be proud her boy's in line.

Chorus (repeat chorus twice)
Over there, over there,
Send the word, send the word over there—
That the Yanks are coming,
The Yanks are coming,
The drums rum-tumming
Ev'rywhere.
So prepare, say a pray'r,
Send the word, send the word to beware.
We'll be over, we're coming over,
And we won't come back till it's over
Over there.

CHAPTER 5

HOMOGENIZING
A PLURALISTIC
CULTURE:
PROPAGANDA
DURING WORLD
WAR I

Sources 2 through 5 from James R. Mock and Cedric Larson, *Words That Won the War: The Story of the Committee on Public Information* (Princeton: Princeton University Press, 1939), pp. 64, 169, 98, 184. Photos: The National Archives.

2. Advertisement Urging Americans to Report the Enemy.

Spies *and* Lies

German agents are everywhere, eager to gather scraps of news about our men, our ships, our munitions. It is still possible to get such information through to Germany, where thousands of these fragments—often individually harmless—are patiently pieced together into a whole which spells death to American soldiers and danger to American homes.

But while the enemy is most industrious in trying to collect information, and his systems elaborate, he is *not* superhuman—indeed he is often very stupid, and would fail to get what he wants were it not deliberately handed to him by the carelessness of loyal Americans.

Do not discuss in public, or with strangers, any news of troop and transport movements, or bits of gossip as to our military preparations, which come into your possession.

Do not permit your friends in service to tell you—or write you—"inside" facts about where they are, what they are doing and seeing.

Do not become a tool of the Hun by passing on the malicious, disheartening rumors which he so eagerly sows. Remember he asks no better service than to have you spread his lies of disasters to our soldiers and sailors, gross scandals in the Red Cross, cruelties, neglect and wholesale executions in our camps, drunkenness and vice in the Expeditionary Force, and other tales certain to disturb American patriots and to bring anxiety and grief to American parents.

And do not wait until you catch someone putting a bomb under a factory. Report the man who spreads pessimistic stories, divulges—or seeks—confidential military information, cries for peace, or belittles our efforts to win the war.

Send the names of such persons, even if they are in uniform, to the Department of Justice, Washington. Give all the details you can, with names of witnesses if possible—show the Hun that we can beat him at his own game of collecting scattered information and putting it to work. The fact that you made the report will not become public.

You are in contact with the enemy today, just as truly as if you faced him across No Man's Land. In your hands are two powerful weapons with which to meet him—discretion and vigilance. *Use them.*

COMMITTEE ON PUBLIC INFORMATION

8 JACKSON PLACE, WASHINGTON, D. C.

George Creel, Chairman
The Secretary of State
The Secretary of War
The Secretary of the Navy

Contributed through Division of Advertising  *United States Gov't Comm. on Public Information*

3. Advertisement for Fighting the Enemy by Buying Liberty Bonds.

Bachelor *of* Atrocities

IN the vicious guttural language of Kultur, the degree A. B.
means Bachelor of Atrocities. Are you going to let the Prussian
Python strike at your Alma Mater, as it struck at the University
of Louvain?[7]

The Hohenzollern[8] fang strikes at every element of decency and culture and taste that your college stands for. It leaves a track so terrible that only whispered fragments may be recounted. It has ripped all the world-old romance out of war, and reduced it to the dead, black depths of muck, and hate, and bitterness.

You may soon be called to fight. But you are called upon right now to buy Liberty Bonds. You are called upon to economize in every way. It is sometimes harder to live nobly than to die nobly. The supreme sacrifice of life may come easier than the petty sacrifices of comforts and luxuries. You are called to exercise stern self-discipline. Upon this the Allied Success depends.

Set aside every possible dollar for the purchase of Liberty Bonds. Do it relentlessly. Kill every wasteful impulse, that America may live. Every bond you buy fires point-blank at Prussian Terrorism.

BUY U. S. GOVERNMENT BONDS FOURTH LIBERTY LOAN

Contributed through Division of Advertising

United States Gov't Comm. on Public Information

This space contributed for the Winning of the War by
A. T SKERRY, '84, and CYRILLE CARREAU, '04.

Appeal to the Symbols of Education

Two Graduates of New York University Contributed the Space for This
CPI Advertisement in Their "Alumni News"

7. The University of Louvain, in Belgium, was pillaged and partially destroyed by German troops. Some professors were beaten and others killed, and the library (containing 250,000 books and manuscripts, some irreplaceable) was totally destroyed. The students themselves were home for summer vacation.
8. Hohenzollern was the name of the German royal family since the nation's founding in 1871. It had been the Prussian royal family since 1525.

CHAPTER 5

HOMOGENIZING
A PLURALISTIC
CULTURE:
PROPAGANDA
DURING WORLD
WAR I

4. Advertisement Contrasting the American Idea with the German Idea.

THE GERMAN IDEA

SHALL this war make Germany's word the highest law in the world?
Read what she expects. Here are the words of her own spokesmen.
Then ask yourself where Germany would have the United States
stand after the war.

Shall we bow to Germany's wishes--assist German ambition?

No. The German idea must be so completely crushed that it will
never again rear its venomous head.

It's a fight, as the President said, "to the last dollar, the last drop
of blood."

THE AMERICAN IDEA

The President's Flag Day Speech, With
Evidence of Germany's plans. 32
pages.
The War Message and the Facts Be-
hind It. 32 pages.
The Nation in Arms. 16 pages.
Why We Fight Germany.
War, Labor and Peace.

THE GERMAN IDEA

Conquest and Kultur. 160 pages.
German War Practices. 96 pages.
Treatment of German Militarism and
German Critics.
The German War Code.

COMMITTEE ON PUBLIC INFORMATION
8 JACKSON PLACE, WASHINGTON, D. C.

Contributed through Division of Advertising, United
States Governm't Committee
on Public Information

George Creel, Chairman
The Secretary of State
The Secretary of War
The Secretary of the Navy

This space contributed for the Winning of the War by

The Publisher of

*Advertisement in the "American Magazine." Cities on the Map Bear
Such Names as Heineapolis and Ach Looey. Note the
"American Reservation" in the Southwest*

5. Advertisement Appealing to History Teachers.

The Committee on Public Information
Established by Order of the President, April 4, 1917

Distribute free *except as noted* the following publications :

I.   Red, White and Blue Series :

No. 1.   How the War Came to America (English, German, Polish, Bohemian, Italian, Spanish and Swedish).

No. 2.   National Service Handbook (primarily for libraries, schools, Y. M. C. A.'s, Clubs, fraternal organizations, etc., as a guide and reference work on all forms of war activity, civil, charitable and military).

No. 3.   The Battle Line of Democracy.   Prose and Poetry of the Great War.   Price 25 cent. Special price to teachers.   Proceeds to the Red Cross.   Other issues in preparation.

II.   War Information Series :

No. 1.   The War Message and Facts Behind it.

No. 2.   The Nation in Arms, by Secretaries Lane and Baker.

No. 3.   The Government of Germany, by Prof. Charles D. Hazen.

No. 4.   The Great War from Spectator to Participant.

No. 5.   A War of Self Defense, by Secretary Lansing and Assistant Secretary of Labor Louis F. Post.

No. 6.   American Loyalty by Citizens of German Descent.

No. 7.   Amerikanische Bürgertreue, a translation of No. 6.

Other issues will appear shortly.

III.   Official Bulletin :

Accurate daily statement of what all agencies of government are doing in war times.   Sent free to newspapers and postmasters (to be put on bulletin boards).   Subscription price $5.00 per year.

Address Requests to

Committee on Public Information, Washington, D. C.

What Can History Teachers Do Now?

You can help the community realize what history should mean to it.

You can confute those who by selecting a few historic facts seek to establish some simple cure-all for humanity.

You can confute those who urge that mankind can wipe the past off the slate and lay new foundations for civilization.

You can encourage the sane use of experience in discussions of public questions.

You can help people understand what democracy is by pointing out the common principle in the ideas of Plato, Cromwell, Rousseau, Jefferson, Jackson and Washington.

You can help people understand what German autocracy has in common with the autocracy of the Grand Mogul.

You can help people understand that democracy is not inconsistent with law and efficient government.

You can help people understand that failure of the past to make the world safe for democracy does not mean that it can not be made safe in the future.

You can so teach your students that they will acquire "historical mindedness" and realize the connection of the past with the present.

You can not do these things unless you inform your self, and think over your information.

You can help yourself by reading the following :
"History and the Great War" bulletin of Bureau of Education.
A series of articles published throughout the year in THE HISTORY TEACHER'S MAGAZINE.

You can obtain aid and advice by writing to
The National Board for Historical Service, 1133 Woodward Building, Washington, D. C.
United States Bureau of Education, Division of Civic Education, Washington, D. C.
Committee on Public Information, Division of Educational Co-operation, 10 Jackson Place, Washington, D. C.
The Committee on Patriotism through Education of the National Security League, 31 Pine Street, New York City.
Carnegie Endowment for International Peace, 2 Jackson Place, Washington, D. C.
National Committee of Patriotic and Defense Societies, Southern Building, Washington, D. C.
The World Peace Foundation, 40 Mount Vernon St., Boston, Mass.
American Association for International Conciliation, 407 West 117th Street, New York City.
The American Society for Judicial Settlement of International Disputes, Baltimore, Md.
The Editor, THE HISTORY TEACHER'S MAGAZINE, Philadelphia.

CHAPTER 5

HOMOGENIZING
A PLURALISTIC
CULTURE:
PROPAGANDA
DURING WORLD
WAR I

Source 6 from *The James Montgomery Flagg Poster Book,* introduction by Susan E. Meyer (New York: Watson-Guptill Publications, 1975). Courtesy of the Library of Congress.

6. The Famous Uncle Sam Poster.

Source 7 from Peter Stanley, *What Did You Do in the War, Daddy?* (Melbourne: Oxford University Press, 1983), p. 55. Photo: Imperial War Museum.

7. Poster Portraying Germany as a Raging Beast.

Sources 8 through 10 from *The James Montgomery Flagg Poster Book*.

8. Recruiting Poster.

9. Poster Depicting U.S. Relationship with England.

Source 10: Hoover Institution, Stanford University.

10. Poster Urging Americans to Buy Liberty Bonds.

CHAPTER 5

HOMOGENIZING
A PLURALISTIC
CULTURE:
PROPAGANDA
DURING WORLD
WAR I

Source 11 from Stanley, *What Did You Do in the War, Daddy?* p. 65.

11. Poster for the Fourth Liberty Bond Campaign.

Source 12 from Joseph Darracott, ed., *The First World War in Posters* (New York: Dover Publications, 1974), p. 30.

12. Poster with Boy Scout Motto Promoting Liberty Bonds.

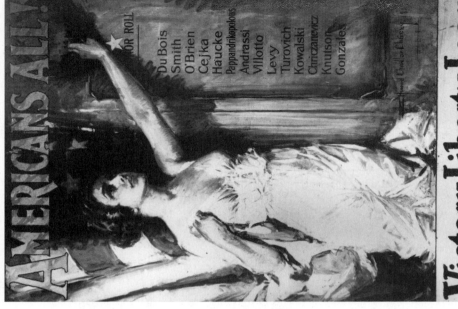

Source 14 from Walton Rawls, *Wake Up, America! World War I and the American Poster* (New York: Abbeville Press, 1988), p. 232.

14. Americans All!

Source 13 from Anthony Crawford, *Posters in the George C. Marshall Research Foundation* (Charlottesville: University of Virginia Press, 1939), p. 30. Photo: Culver Pictures.

13. Poster Targeting American Women.

Source 15 from John Higham, *Strangers in the Land: Patterns of American Nativism,* 1860–1925 (New Brunswick, N.J.: Rutgers University Press, 1955), p. 210.

15. Editorial Cartoon. German American Dr. Karl Muck, Conductor of the Boston Symphony Orchestra, Needed a Police Escort When He Conducted a Concert in March 1918 in New York City.

Source 16 from *New York Times,* January 6, 1918.

16. Prize-Winning Cartoon in *Trench and Camp* Cartoon Contest.[9]

9. *Trench and Camp* was a weekly publication of the U.S. Army for its thirty-two training centers in the United States. For his winning cartoon, Hines won a wristwatch. In the cartoon, the American soldier is holding a *pickelhaube,* a German spiked helmet.

Sources 17 through 19 from Cornbise, *War as Advertised: The Four Minute Men and America's Crusade,* pp. 72–73, 122, 60.

17. Excerpt of a Speech by a Four Minute Man.

Ladies and Gentlemen:

I have just received the information that there is a German spy among us—a German spy watching *us.*

He is around here somewhere, reporting upon you and me—sending reports about us to Berlin and telling the Germans just what we are doing with the Liberty Loan. From every section of the country these spies have been getting reports over to Potsdam[10]—not general reports but details— where the loan is going well and where its success seems weak, and what people are saying in each community.

For the German government is worried about our great loan. Those Junkers[11] fear its effect upon the German *morale.* They're raising a loan this month, too.

If the American people lend their billions now, one and all with a hip-hip-hurrah, it means that America is united and strong. While, if we lend our money half-heartedly, America seems weak and autocracy remains strong.

Money means everything now; it means quicker victory and therefore less bloodshed. We are *in* the war, and now Americans can have but *one* opinion, only *one* wish in the Liberty Loan.

Well, I hope these spies are getting their messages straight, letting Potsdam know that America is *hurling back* to the autocrats these answers:

For treachery here, attempted treachery in Mexico, treachery everywhere—*one billion.*

For murder of American women and children—*one billion more.*

For broken faith and promise to murder more Americans—*billions and billions more.*

And then we will add:

In the world fight for Liberty, our share—*billions and billions and billions and endless billions.*

Do not let the German spy hear and report that *you* are a slacker.

10. Potsdam (a suburb of Berlin) was where the Kaiser lived.
11. Junkers were the Prussian nobility.

CHAPTER 5

HOMOGENIZING
A PLURALISTIC
CULTURE:
PROPAGANDA
DURING WORLD
WAR I

18. Part of a Speech by a Four Minute Man.

German agents are telling the people of this . . . race[12] through the South
that if they will not oppose the German Government, or help our Government, they will be rewarded with Ford automobiles when Germany is in
control here. They are told that 10 negroes are being conscripted to 1 white
man in order that the Negro race may be killed off; and that the reason
Germany went into Belgium was to punish the people of that country for
the cruel treatment of the negroes in the Congo.

19. Poem Read by Four Minute Men: "It's Duty Boy."

My boy must never bring disgrace to his immortal sires—
At Valley Forge and Lexington they kindled freedom's fires,
John's father died at Gettysburg, mine fell at Chancellorsville;
While John himself was with the boys who charged up San Juan Hill.
And John, if he was living now, would surely say with me,
"No son of ours shall e'er disgrace our grand old family tree
By turning out a slacker when his country needs his aid."
It is not of such timber that America was made.
I'd rather you had died at birth or not been born at all,
Than know that I had raised a son who cannot hear the call
That freedom has sent round the world, its precious rights to save—
This call is meant for you, my boy, and I would have you brave;
And though my heart is breaking, boy, I bid you do your part,
And show the world no son of mine is cursed with craven heart;
And if, perchance, you ne'er return, my later days to cheer,
And I have only memories of my brave boy, so dear,
I'd rather have it so, my boy, and know you bravely died
Than have a living coward sit supinely by my side.
To save the world from sin, my boy, God gave his only son—
He's asking for MY boy, to-day, and may His will be done.

12. At the front lines in France, Germans barraged America's African American soldiers with
leaflets urging them to desert (none did). One of those propaganda leaflets said, in part, "Do
you enjoy the same rights as the white people do in America . . . or are you rather not treated
over there as second-class citizens?" As to the charge of discrimination against African Americans by draft boards, there were numerous complaints that African Americans found it almost
impossible to get exemptions from military service. In the end, about 31 percent of the African
Americans who registered were called into service, as opposed to 26 percent of the registered
whites. To counteract German propaganda, prominent African Americans were sent to France
to lecture to the African American troops.

Source 20 from *The Moving Picture World,* September 28, 1918.

20. Promotional Tips to Theater Managers.

ADVERTISING AIDS FOR BUSY MANAGERS

"KULTUR."

William Fox Presents Gladys Brockwell in a Typical Example of the Brutality of the Wilhelmstrasse to Its Spy-slaves.

Cast.

Countess Griselda Von Arenburg,
Gladys Brockwell
Eliska ....Georgia Woodthorpe
René de Bornay.................William Scott
Baron von Zeller ....Willard Louis
Archduke Franz Ferdinand ....Charles Clary
Danilo ....Nigel de Brullier
The Kaiser ....William Burress
Emperor Franz Josef.........Alfred Fremont

Directed by Edward J. Le Saint.

The Story: The Kaiser decides that the time is ripe for a declaration of war, and sends word to his vassal monarch of Austria. René de Bornay is sent by France to discover what is being planned. He meets the Countess, who falls in love with him. She sickens of the spy system and declares that she is done with it, but is warned that she cannot withdraw. She is told to secure René's undoing, but instead procures his escape and in her own boudoir is stood against the wall and shot for saving the man whom she loves better than her life.

Feature Gladys Brockwell as Countess Griselda Von Arenburg and William Scott as René de Bornay.

Program and Advertising Phrases: Gladys Brockwell, Star of Latest Picture, Exposing Hun Brutality and Satanic Intrigue.
How An Austrian Countess Gave Her All for Democracy.
She Was an Emperor's Favorite Yet She Died for World Freedom.
Story of an Emperor's Mistress and a Crime That Rocked the World.
Daring Exposure of Scandals and Crimes in Hun Court Circles.
Astonishing Revelations of Hun Plots to Rape Democracy.

Advertising Angles: Do not offer this as a propaganda story, but tell that it is one of the angles of the merciless Prussian spy system about which has been woven a real romance. Play up the spy angle heavily both in your newspaper work and through window cards with such lines as "even the spies themselves hate their degradation." Miss Brockwell wears some stunning and daring gowns in this play, and with these special appeal can be made to the women.

21. Advertisement for the Feature Film *The Kaiser, the Beast of Berlin,* Described by Some as the Most Famous "Hate Picture."

Source 22: The Everett Collection.

22. Still Photograph Used for Advertising from *The Kaiser, the Beast of Berlin.*

CHAPTER 5

HOMOGENIZING
A PLURALISTIC
CULTURE:
PROPAGANDA
DURING WORLD
WAR I

Source 23: Fox Film Corporation, 1918.

23. Advertising Poster for *The Prussian Cur.*

QUESTIONS TO CONSIDER

Source 1, George M. Cohan's enormously popular song, "Over There," was familiar to almost every American in 1917–1918 and has been since. What was the song urging young men to do? What emotions were the song's lyrics trying to arouse? How would you interpret the lines, "Make your daddy glad" and (speaking of sweethearts) "To be proud her boy's in line"? Tapes and records of the song "Over There" are readily available. As you listen to the song, how does it make you feel?

The next pieces of evidence (Sources 2 through 5) were produced by the Committee on Public Information. How are the Germans portrayed in "Spies and Lies" (Source 2)? In "Bachelor of Atrocities" (Source 3)? In "The German Idea" (Source 4)? Source 5 is an appeal to history teachers. Did the Committee on Public Information ask history teachers to "tilt" their treatments of the past? If so, how? Were there any dangers inherent in the kinds of activities the committee was urging on patriotic Americans?

In some ways, poster art (Sources 6 through 14) is similar to editorial cartoons, principally because the artist has only one canvas or frame on which to tell his or her story. Yet the poster must be more arresting than the cartoon, must convey its message rapidly, and must avoid ambiguities and confusion. Posters, commissioned or approved by the Committee on Public Information, were an extremely popular form of propaganda during World War I. Indeed, so popular were the posters of James Montgomery Flagg (1877–1960) that he helped sell $1,000 of liberty bonds by performing (in his case, painting posters) in front of the New York Public Library.

Source 6, by Flagg, probably is the most famous poster ever created. The idea was taken from a British poster by Alfred Leete, and Flagg was his own model for Uncle Sam. The poster is still used by the U.S. Army. What feeling did the poster seek to elicit?

Sources 7, 8, 10, and 11 urged enlistment and the purchase of liberty bonds. What innuendos are common to all four posters? What feelings were these posters intended to elicit? How are Germans portrayed?

Source 9 ("Side by Side") makes a dramatically different appeal. What is that appeal? Why did the committee think that appeal was necessary?

Sources 12 and 13 focus on women. How are women portrayed? What appeals are contained in these posters? Also, in Source 12, there is a role for boys. What is the relationship between the boy and the very strong Miss Liberty?

Source 14 is a most interesting poster, given the role assigned to the Committee on Public Information and the government's fears. What emotion did this extraordinary work attempt to elicit? How does that poster appear to address the government's fears?

Speaking of cartoons, nineteenth-century New York political boss William Marcy ("Boss") Tweed once exclaimed, "Let's stop these damn pictures. I don't care so much what the papers say about me—my constituents

CHAPTER 5

HOMOGENIZING
A PLURALISTIC
CULTURE:
PROPAGANDA
DURING WORLD
WAR I

can't read; but damn it, they can see the pictures!" The editorial cartoon from the *New York Herald* (Source 15) is fairly self-explanatory. What emotions does the cartoon seek to elicit? What actions, intended or unintended, might have resulted from those emotions? Muck, incidentally, was deported. Frank Hines's prize-winning cartoon (Source 16) seeks to elicit very different emotions. Compare this cartoon with George M. Cohan's lyrics (Source 1).

Sources 17 through 19, by the Four Minute Men, are from the Committee on Public Information's *Bulletin,* which was distributed to all volunteer speakers. Several of the "Four Minute Men" were women. Speakers received certificates from President Wilson after the war. What appeals are made in Source 17? How are appeals to African Americans (Source 18) the same or different? Source 19 (the poem) is particularly painful to read. Why is that so? How can this poem be compared with Sources 1 and 16?

In 1917–1918, the American film industry and the Committee on Public Information produced over 180 feature films, 6 serials, 72 short subjects, 112 documentaries, 44 cartoons, and 37 liberty loan special films. Unfortunately, the vast majority of those motion pictures no longer are available, principally because the nitrate film stock on which these films were printed was extremely flammable and subject to decomposition.[13]

No sound films were produced in the United States before 1927. Until that time, a small orchestra or (more prevalent) a piano accompanied a film's showing. What dialogue there was—and there was not much—was given in subtitles.

The advertising aids for the film *Kultur* (Source 20) suggest a number of phrases and angles designed to attract audiences. What are the strongest appeals suggested to theater owners? Do those same appeals also appear in songs, advertisements, posters, cartoons, and speeches?

Sources 21 through 23 are advertisements for two films produced in 1918, *The Kaiser, the Beast of Berlin* (Sources 21 and 22) and *The Prussian Cur* (Source 23). What appeal is made to prospective viewers in Source 21? How are Germans depicted in Source 22? How can Source 22 be compared with Sources 7, 8, 10, and 11? How can Source 23 be compared with those sources as well?

You must now summarize your findings and return to the central questions: How did the United States use propaganda to mobilize public opinion in support of our participation in World War I? What were the consequences, positive and negative, of the mobilization of public opinion?

13. In 1949, an improved safety-based stock was introduced. Those films that do survive, except in private collections, are in the Library of Congress; the American Film Institute Library in Beverly Hills, California; the Academy of Motion Picture Arts and Sciences in Los Angeles; the Museum of Modern Art in New York; the National Archives in Washington, D.C.; the New York Public Library; and the Wisconsin Center for Theater Research in Madison.

⌒ EPILOGUE ⌒

The creation of the Committee on Public Information and its subsequent work show that the Wilson administration had serious doubts concerning whether the American people, multiethnic and pluralistic as they were, would support the war effort with unanimity. And, to be sure, there was opposition to American involvement in the war, not only from socialist Eugene Debs and the left but also from reformers Robert La Follette, Jane Addams, and others. As it turned out, however, the Wilson administration's worst fears proved groundless. Americans of all ethnic backgrounds overwhelmingly supported the war effort, sometimes rivaling each other in patriotic ardor. How much of this unanimity can be attributed to patriotism and how much to the propaganda efforts of the Committee on Public Information will never really be known. Yet, for whatever reason, it can be said that the war had a kind of unifying effect on the American people. Women sold liberty bonds, worked for agencies such as the Red Cross, rolled bandages, and cooperated in the government's effort to conserve food and fuel. Indeed, even African Americans sprang to the colors, reasoning, as did the president of Howard University, that service in the war might help them achieve long-withheld civil and political rights.

However, this homogenization was not without its price. Propaganda was so effective that it created a kind of national hysteria, sometimes with terrible results. Vigilante-type groups often shamefully persecuted German Americans, lynching one German American man of draft age for not being in uniform (the man was physically ineligible, having only one eye) and badgering German American children in and out of school. Many states forbade the teaching of German in schools, and a host of German words were purged from the language (sauerkraut became liberty cabbage, German measles became liberty measles, hamburgers became liberty steaks, frankfurters became hot dogs). The city of Cincinnati even banned pretzels from saloons. In such an atmosphere, many Americans lived in genuine fear of being accused of spying or of becoming victims of intimidation or violence. In a society intent upon homogenization, being different could be dangerous.

During such hysteria, one would expect the federal government in general and the Committee on Public Information in particular to have attempted to dampen the more extreme forms of vigilantism. However, it seemed as if the government had become the victim of its own propaganda. The postmaster general (Albert Burleson), empowered to censor the mail, looking for examples of treason, insurrection, or forcible resistance to laws, used his power to suppress all socialist publications, all anti-British and pro-Irish mail, and anything that he believed threatened the war effort. One movie producer, Robert Goldstein, was sentenced to ten years in prison for releasing his film *The Spirit of '76* (about the American Revolution) because it por-

CHAPTER 5

HOMOGENIZING
A PLURALISTIC
CULTURE:
PROPAGANDA
DURING WORLD
WAR I

trayed the British in an unfavorable light.[14] Socialist party leader Eugene Debs was given a similar sentence for criticizing the war in a speech in Canton, Ohio.[15] The left-wing Industrial Workers of the World (IWW) was broken. Freedom of speech, press, and assembly were violated countless times, and numerous lynchings, whippings, and tar-and-featherings occurred. Excesses by both government and private individuals were as effective in *forcing* homogeneity as were the voluntary efforts of American people of all backgrounds.

Once the hysteria had begun, it is doubtful whether even President Wilson could have stopped it. Yet Wilson showed no inclination to do so, even stating that dissent was not appreciated by the government. Without the president to reverse the process, the hysteria continued unabated.

Before the outbreak of World War I, anti-immigrant sentiment had been growing, although most Americans seem to have believed that the solution was to Americanize the immigrants rather than to restrict their entrance. But the drive toward homogenization that accompanied America's war hysteria acted to increase cries for restricting further immigration and to weaken champions of the "melting pot." As restriction advocate Madison Grant wrote in 1922, "The world has seen many such [racial] mixtures and the character of a

mongrel race is only just beginning to be understood at its true value. . . . Whether we like to admit it or not, the result of the mixture of two races . . . gives us a race reverting to the more ancient, generalized and lower type." Labor leaders, journalists, and politicians called for immigration restrictions, and a general immigration restriction (called the National Origins Act) became law in 1924.

This insistence on homogenization also resulted in the Red Scare of 1919, during which Attorney General A. Mitchell Palmer violated many people's civil liberties in a series of raids, arrests, and deportations directed largely against recent immigrants. As seen, the efforts to homogenize a pluralistic nation could have an ugly side.

As Americans approached World War II, some called for a revival of the Committee on Public Information. Yet President Franklin Roosevelt rejected this sweeping approach. The Office of War Information was created, but its role was a restricted one. Even so, Japanese Americans were subjected to relocation and humiliation in one of the more shameful episodes of recent American history. And although propaganda techniques were sometimes more subtle, they nevertheless displayed features that would cause Americans to hate their enemies and want to destroy them. Japanese especially were portrayed as barbaric. A good example is Source 24. In general, however, a different spirit pervaded the United States during World War II, a spirit generally more tolerant of American pluralism and less willing to stir Americans into an emotional frenzy.

14. This gave rise to a court case with the improbable title *United States v. The Spirit of '76.*
15. Debs was indicted the day before he made his speech. He spent three years in prison.

And yet the possibility that propaganda will create mass hysteria and thus endanger the civil rights of some Americans is present in every national crisis, especially in wartime. In the "total wars" of the twentieth century, in which civilians played as crucial a role as fighting men (in factories, in training facilities for soldiers, and in shipping soldiers and materiel to the front), the mobilization of the home front was a necessity. But could that kind of mobilization be carried too far?

Source 24: Library of Congress.

24. United States Army Poster from World War II.

CHAPTER

THE "NEW" WOMAN OF THE 1920s:
IMAGE AND REALITY

 THE PROBLEM

With the publication of his novel *Main Street* in 1920, American author Sinclair Lewis produced the first of several best sellers. This novel was especially popular among college students, perhaps because many of them identified with the young protagonist, Carol, a so-called new woman of the early twentieth century: college educated, young, attractive, idealistic, ambitious, and "modern." The novel begins as Carol, who has graduated from a coeducational college in the Midwest and then drifted into library school in Chicago, returns to St. Paul, Minnesota, as a librarian. Bored, lonely, and dissatisfied with her job, she soon meets Dr. Will Kennicott, more than twelve years her senior. After a brief courtship, they marry and return to his hometown of Gopher Prairie.

In the small town of Gopher Prairie, the young bride finds narrow-mindedness, conformity, vicious gossip, and rigid insistence on traditional male and female roles. None of her efforts to improve her situation—town beautification plans, a community theater, a reading and discussion group—is successful. With the birth of a child, Carol feels more trapped and desperate. Finally, determined to find a better life, she separates from her husband and moves to Washington, D.C., with her young son. There she works as a government clerk, rents an apartment, and makes a lively new circle of friends. After a year, her husband comes to visit her, and five months later, pregnant again, she returns to Gopher Prairie for good.

At the end of the novel, Carol Kennicott passionately defends her rebellion and her aspirations for women, crying out that she may have failed, but she tried her best. "Sure. . . . feels like it might snow tomorrow," her husband replies. "Have to be thinking about putting up the storm windows pretty soon."

Was there a "new" woman who came of age in the 1920s? Were young women liberated from outmoded expectations based on gender? In this chapter, the central question asks you to analyze both the images and the realities of the new woman as portrayed in best sellers, nonfiction, and films from the 1920s.

⚬ BACKGROUND ⚬

The 1920s have caught the imaginations of both historians and the general public, who have, nevertheless, found the period difficult and elusive to characterize. Marked at its beginning by the conclusion of the Great War (which we now call World War I) and at its end by the disastrous stock market crash of 1929, this decade seemed special even to those people living at the time. Many of them called it the Jazz Age. It was in some ways an era of incredibly rapid changes, most noticeably in the economic and cultural aspects of American life. Some of these changes raised very real questions about the values and assumptions of an older, more rural way of life. Indeed, one useful way to examine the decade is in terms of the strains and conflicts between pre–World War I attitudes, beliefs, and behaviors and those of twentieth-century modernism.

Economically, after some postwar dislocations in 1920 and 1921, the country seemed to be enjoying enormous prosperity. Mass production of new goods fed consumer demand fueled by seductive advertising, and personal worth increasingly became identified with possessing up-to-date material goods. Business practices and values were widely admired, imitated, and accepted by the general public, as corporate mergers and the development of chain stores standardized and homogenized the goods and services available to customers in all sections of the country. Like Henry Ford, corporate leaders soon came to understand that better-paid workers could buy more products and that more satisfied workers produced more. Management transformed its hostility toward organized labor into "corporate paternalism," an approach to labor relations that reduced labor union membership during the decade. Technological breakthroughs in both pure and applied science, as well as in medicine, seemed to promise better and healthier lives for all Americans. That farming, mining, and a few other sectors of the economy were not sharing in this prosperity did not seem very important.

Continuity rather than change characterized the politics of the decade.

With the exception of the presidential election of 1928, which pitted old stock American, Protestant, "dry," Republican, rural, small-town candidate Herbert Hoover against Democrat Alfred Smith, who seemed to represent the newer, ethnic, Catholic, "wet" immigrants from urban areas, American politics was business as usual. The three conservative Republican presidents—Warren Harding, Calvin Coolidge, and Herbert Hoover—in theory opposed intervening in the economy but in practice were pro-business in their actions. From the scandalous, graft-ridden administration of Warren Harding, the farm bill veto and strikebreaking activities of Calvin Coolidge, and the anti-Progressive decisions of the U.S. Supreme Court, to the short-lived flurry of hope for a new Progressive party under the leadership of Senator Robert La Follette, little positive change was achieved.

What seemed most obvious to the majority of people were the rapid cultural changes taking place in American society. Urbanization, along with the radio and movies, made possible the rise of a truly national mass culture. Radio listeners in all parts of the country could enjoy the new music, especially jazz, and the new spectator sports, such as baseball and football. Even small cities had movie theaters. In Muncie, Indiana (population 35,000 in 1920), there were nine theaters that showed more than twenty different films every week. Because of the rapidity of communication, such varied individuals as baseball player George Herman "Babe" Ruth, aviator Charles Lindbergh, and English Channel swimmer Gertrude Ederle became widely admired national heroes. The proliferation and popularity of mass-circulation magazines for both middle- and working-class readers were paralleled by the success of the new middle-class book clubs, which created instant best sellers, in both fiction and nonfiction. Some serious writers of the Lost Generation[1] left the country; others stayed home and wrote critically of the materialism and values of the era. And in the Harlem Renaissance, a new generation of African American authors found their voice and wrote about the strengths of their heritage.

Perhaps the single most important factor in changing the way Americans lived in this era was the automobile. When asked about changes that had taken place in his lifetime, one long-time Muncie resident replied, "I can tell you what's happening in just four letters: A-U-T-O!" The automobile offered the freedom to live farther away from one's place of work, visit other nearby towns, and go away for a vacation. For young people, access to an automobile meant freedom from chaperons or curious neighbors, as serious courtship was replaced by casual dating. By the 1920s, the automobile also had become an important status symbol for both youths and their parents.

Such sweeping changes were not without opposition, and the twenties witnessed a series of reactions against the forces of modernism. Feeling overwhelmed by the late nineteenth- and

1. Writers such as Ernest Hemingway and Sinclair Lewis who had been disillusioned by World War I and whose work questioned the old prewar values.

early twentieth-century influx of poorer immigrants from southern and eastern Europe, Congress established a temporary and then a permanent quota system to bar them. These laws marked the abandonment of the traditional American policy of welcoming those who immigrated for economic opportunity.

The twenties also saw the rise of a new Ku Klux Klan, for the first time popular in urban areas and outside the South, dedicated to "100 percent Americanism" and devoted to enforcing the values of a nineteenth-century rural America. Two famous trials of the decade, the Sacco and Vanzetti case against Italian anarchists convicted of committing a murder during a payroll robbery and the Scopes case, in which a teacher was found guilty of breaking Tennessee law by teaching about evolution, highlighted the social and cultural strains inherent in the conflict between the older values of rural, small-town America and modernism.

Perhaps nowhere were these strains more evident than in the heated debates of the decade about the proper place and roles of women. There was no doubt in the minds of contemporary observers that women's roles were changing. The Nineteenth Amendment, granting women the vote, had been ratified in 1920, setting off wild speculations about the impact women voters might have on politics. Transforming their organization into the League of Women Voters, the leaders of the National American Woman's Suffrage Association urged citizenship education and took a neutral, bipartisan position on candidates. Thus vot-

ing patterns did not change much. Social feminists did successfully lobby for the Sheppard-Towner maternal and infant health care bill, although their efforts to ratify the child labor amendment met with defeat. The more radical feminists of the National Woman's Party surveyed the remaining legal discriminations against women and, in 1923, proposed an equal rights amendment (ERA), which would have required that all laws apply equally to men and women. Those women who favored protective labor laws for women opposed the ERA, however, and feminists, all of whom wanted to expand women's opportunities and choices, were once again divided over goals and strategies.

Economically, women continued to enter the work force but were clustered in "women's jobs." Approximately one in four women worked for pay. Most women workers were young and unmarried, although more married women were taking paid employment during the twenties. Openings for women in the service sector expanded, as did clerical jobs and a limited number of professional positions. But women in general were not taken seriously as workers. Employers believed that they worked only to earn "pin money" for unnecessary purchases and that they would quit their jobs as soon as they could. Married women who worked carried the double burden of paid employment and unpaid housework and often faced public disapproval as well. In spite of unequal pay and limited employment opportunities, many "new" women of the twenties worked diligently and expected to rise to higher positions on the basis of their merit. This was especially true of women with high school and college educations.

Culturally, there were noticeable changes in the appearance and behavior of younger women. The new woman had begun to emerge well before World War I, but in the 1920s, popularized by the media and the cartoons of John Held, Jr., a single stereotype began to dominate: the flapper. The flapper, so called because of the short-lived fad of wearing unbuckled galoshes that flapped when she walked, had short "bobbed" hair and wore cosmetics, short skirts, and dangling beads. She often smoked and even drank in public, and she presented herself as a "good sport" and "pal" to men of her own age. Flirting with and dating many different young men, she often seemed to care only about dancing and having fun. Older Americans were appalled by the appearance and outraged by the behavior of this 1920s woman. Worried and upset about the practice of "petting" (engaging in sexual intimacies that usually stopped just short of sexual intercourse), Americans complained that the new woman was completely immoral.

Of course, as historian Paul Carter has pointed out, there was another side to the twenties, and only a small minority of women were flappers. Nevertheless, fashion responded to the flapper style, middle-aged married women adopted variations of it, and even mail-order catalogues intended for rural and small-town consumers featured models with short hair and skimpy skirts. Films, novels, nonfiction, mass-circulation magazines, and advertisements all portrayed the new woman, investigated the dilemmas she faced, and reached conclusions about her life based on their own presuppositions and value judgments.

In this chapter, you will be analyzing both best-selling fiction and some selected nonfiction, as well as the images presented by two popular film stars, to determine the degree to which there was a new woman who came of age in the 1920s. To do so, you will need to compare the image of the new woman with some of the realities of her life.

⊂◯⊃ THE METHOD ⊂◯⊃

Historians must always be aware of the possibility that an *image*—how a person or a particular time appeared—may be quite different from its historical *reality*—how that person or era actually was. The independent ethical cowboy, the docile and happy slave, and the passive, oppressed Victorian wife and mother are all examples of historically inaccurate images. Such images are usually culturally constructed. Sometimes, as in the case of the new woman of the 1920s, the image is created by contemporaries who are attempting to understand their own times. The image may also be created at a later time. For example, the story of George Washington, who was so honest that he would not lie about chopping down his father's cherry tree, is a consciously developed and accepted image created by Americans who were seeking national heroes in an uncertain and difficult period of history.

The image of the new woman of the 1920s came from many sources, including journalism, films, and advertising. In this chapter, you will primarily be using fiction and nonfiction to determine both the image of the new woman—how she was portrayed—and the reality—how different from previous women she actually was. You will be supplementing your analysis of the image of the new woman with some visual evidence, photographs of two popular female film stars.

Since the nineteenth century, women have provided the bulk of the readership for popular novels, often those written by other women. In the 1920s, book clubs patronized by middle-class subscribers chose book-of-the-month selections on the basis of their potential appeal to club members and, in the process, helped to create widely read and discussed best sellers. Another phenomenon of the 1920s was the influx of students on college campuses. Certain books became fads, and most students read them. The excerpts from the novels that you will be analyzing here are examples of these kinds of popular fiction. Describe the image of the new woman portrayed in each novel: How does she look? What do others think about her? How does she feel about herself? What does she do? What happens to her?

When a resident of Muncie submitted a story to *Live Stories,* the magazine rejected it, stating that "stories should embody picturesque settings for action; they should also present situations of high emotional character, rich in sentiment. A moral conclusion is essential." Although our own modern fiction often does not contain a "moral conclusion" or message, popular fiction in the 1920s almost always did. When you analyze the excerpts from the best-selling novels of the twenties, also ask yourself questions about the conclusions: Who wins? Who loses? Why?

It would be a mistake, however, to depend solely on fiction to understand the past. In this chapter, you will also be reading three nonfiction excerpts from two books and an article. Reformers, especially Progressives of the late nineteenth and early twentieth centuries, used nonfiction and documentary photographs extensively to educate the public about problems created by rapid industrialization and urbanization. By the 1920s, there was a large middle-class audience for nonfiction. Serious books such as H. G. Wells's *Outline of History* and Will Durant's *The Story of Philosophy* each sold over a million copies. These books were obviously educational. Other nonfiction, such as *Woman and the New Race,* tried to persuade readers to support a particular course of action. *Middletown* documented conditions and attitudes through direct field research, and "Feminist—New Style" sought to explain the times in which its readers were living. Nonfiction should be both compared to and contrasted with fiction from the same historical period to provide a more complete understanding of U.S. history.

Finally, you will compare and contrast the public images of movie stars Mary Pickford and Clara Bow. Nicknamed "America's Sweetheart," Pickford was born in 1893 and began making films as a teenager. She was extremely popular among Americans of all ages and socioeconomic classes in the years immediately preceding and following World War I. A shrewd businesswoman, Pickford married the handsome and famous film star Douglas Fairbanks and continued to make films during the 1920s. But she was narrowly typecast, often playing young or teenage "girl" roles even when she was in her thirties, in wholesome, family-oriented movies.

Born in 1905, Clara Bow was a red-haired, seventeen-year-old beauty contest winner who was discovered by Hollywood. She got her start in films in 1923, playing a series of "ordinary girls" such as waitresses, theater usherettes, salesgirls, and manicurists. In all these films, she portrayed a modern working "girl," a flapper who loves dancing, wild parties, and flirting with men. Her real fame came after she was chosen by the English romance writer Elinor Glyn to star in the film adaptation of *IT.* As a result, Clara Bow became the "It Girl" and a role model for thousands of young, female moviegoers. Offstage, her life was very much like that of the flappers she portrayed.

∽ THE EVIDENCE ∽

FICTION

Source 1 from E. M. Hull, *The Sheik* (Boston: Small, Maynard and Company, 1921), pp. 1–2, 4, 10–11, 35, 259, 272–273, 275.

1. Excerpts from E. M. Hull's *The Sheik.*

[*The novel begins at a hotel in French Africa, where a farewell dance is being held for the young Diana Mayo, a "new" woman who is about to leave on a month-long trip through the desert. Lady Conway is talking with a young man about Diana's proposed trip.*]

. . . "I thoroughly disapprove of the expedition of which this dance is the inauguration. I consider that even by contemplating such a tour alone into the desert with no chaperon or attendant of her own sex, with only native camel drivers and servants, Diana Mayo is behaving with a recklessness and impropriety that is calculated to cast a slur not only on her own reputation, but also on the prestige of her country. I blush to think of it. . . . The girl herself seemed, frankly, not to understand the seriousness of her position, and was very flippant and not a little rude. I wash my hands of the whole affair. . . ."

[*Diana, who has a reputation for arrogance, is there with her older brother, who looks bored.*]

. . . By contrast, the girl at his side appeared vividly alive. She was only of medium height and very slender, standing erect with the easy, vigorous carriage of an athletic boy, her small head poised proudly. Her scornful mouth and firm chin showed plainly an obstinate determination, and her deep blue eyes were unusually clear and steady. The long, curling black lashes that shaded her eyes and the dark eyebrows were a foil to the thick crop of loose, red-gold curls that she wore short, clubbed about her ears. . . .

[*At the dance, one of Diana's admirers begs her not to take the trip, confessing that he is in love with her and worried about her safety because she is so beautiful. When he tries to hold her hand, she pulls away.*]

. . . "Please stop. I am sorry. We have been good friends, and it has never occurred to me that there could be anything beyond that. I never thought that you might love me. I never thought of you in that way at all. . . . I am very content with my life as it is. Marriage for a woman means the end of independence, that is marriage with a man who is a man, in spite of all that the most modern woman may say. I have never obeyed any one in my life; I do not wish to try the experiment. I am very sorry to have hurt you. You've been a splendid pal, but that side of life does not exist for me. . . . A man to me is just a companion with whom I ride or shoot or fish; a pal, a comrade, and that's just all there is to it." . . .

[*In spite of everyone's objections, Diana sets off on horseback with an Arab guide and servants she has hired. Before they have gone very far, a large caravan passes them.*]

. . . One of two of the camels carried huddled figures, swathed and shapeless with a multitude of coverings, that Diana knew must be women. The contrast between them and herself was almost ridiculous. It made her feel stifled even to look at them. . . . The thought of those lives filled her with aversion. . . .

[*When night falls, Diana's party is attacked by a group of Arabs, and she is kidnapped and taken to their camp, where Sheik Ahmed Ben Hassan, who masterminded the kidnapping, has sex with her against her will. In spite of herself, she gradually falls in love with him during the next two months. But she pretends to be cold and uncaring for fear he will get tired of her and leave her. Out for a ride with a servant, she is captured by the Sheik's enemy, and when the Sheik tries to rescue her, he is badly wounded. While the Sheik is still unconscious, Diana learns that he*] *is not really an Arab but the son of an English aristocrat and a Spanish noble-woman, adopted by the Arabs after his mother died in the desert.*]

. . . He must live, even if his life meant death to her hopes of happiness; that was nothing compared with his life. She loved him well enough to sacrifice anything for him. If he only lived she could even bear to be put out of his life. It was only he that mattered, his life was everything. . . . If she could only die for him. . . .

[*The Sheik recovers. Convinced that he has grown tired of her, Diana gives in to depression.*]

She wondered numbly what would become of her. It did not seem to matter much. Nothing mattered now that he did not want her any more. The old life was far away, in another world. She could never go back to it. She did not care. It was nothing to her. It was only here in the desert, in Ahmed Ben Hassan's arms, that she had become alive, that she had learned what life really meant, that she had waked both to happiness and sorrow. . . . If she could have had the promise of a child. . . . A child that would be his and hers, a child—a boy with the same passionate dark eyes, the same crisp brown hair, the same graceful body, who would grow up as tall and strong, as brave and fearless as his father. Surely he must love her then. . . . Beside her love, everything dwindled into nothingness. He was her life, he filled her horizon. Honour itself was lost in the absorbing passion of her love. He had stripped it from her and she was content that it should lie at his feet. He had made her nothing, she was his toy, his plaything, waiting to be thrown aside. . . .

[*At the end of the novel, after Diana tries to kill herself rather than be sent back, the Sheik admits that he loves her.*]

Source 2 from Percy Marks, *The Plastic Age* (New York: The Century Company, 1924), pp. 157, 174, 212–213, 216–217, 223–224, 244–245, 248–249, 265, 288, 320, 322.

2. Excerpts from Percy Marks's *The Plastic Age.*

[*The novel begins as Hugh Carver, a high school track star and likable, clean-cut young man, arrives for his freshman year at the all-male college of Sanford. He pledges the same fraternity to which his father belonged, studies just enough to get by with average grades, and spends endless hours discussing life and "girls" with his friends. When one of the upperclassmen suggests that if they went out with "cheap women" it would take their minds off sex, another student disagrees.*]

. . . "The old single standard fight," he said, propping his head on his hand. "I don't see any sense in scrapping about that any more. We've got a single standard now. The girls go just as fast as the fellows."

"Oh, that's not so," Hugh exclaimed. "Girls don't go as far as fellows."

Ferguson smiled pleasantly at Hugh and drawled; "Shut up, innocent; you don't know anything about it. I tell you the old double standard has gone all to hell." . . .

[*In his sophomore year, Hugh—who has just started drinking alcohol—and his roommate, Carl, get drunk and go into town, where two prostitutes try to pick them up.*]

. . . They were crude specimens, revealing their profession to the most casual observer. If Hugh had been sober they would have sickened him, but he wasn't sober; he was joyously drunk and the girls looked very desirable. . . .

[*A football player prevents Hugh from going with the prostitutes, but Carl goes anyway. A few weeks later, Carl and seven others are diagnosed with venereal disease and expelled from Sanford. Hugh's next adventure takes place at a fraternity dance. He doesn't have a date, but he sees a young woman, Hester, whom he has met before. He dances with her.*]

"Hot stuff, isn't it?" she asked lazily.

Hugh was startled. Her breath was redolent of whisky. . . .

As the evening wore on he danced with a good many girls who had whisky breaths. One girl clung to him as they danced and whispered, "Hold me up, kid; I'm ginned." He had to rush a third, a dainty blond child, to the porch railing. She wasn't a pretty sight as she vomited into the garden; nor did Hugh find her gasped comment, "The seas are rough to-night," amusing. Another girl went sound asleep in a chair and had to be carried up-stairs and put to bed. . . .

[*Later that evening, Hester drags Hugh into the darkened dining room of the fraternity house and tells him she wants to pet. Going to get one of the chaperon's coats, he walks in on a couple in bed. Disgusted, he leaves the dance.*]

He thought of Hester Sheville, of her whisky breath, her lascivious pawing—and his hands clenched. "Filthy little rat," he said aloud, "the stinkin', rotten rat."

Then he remembered that there had been girls there who hadn't drunk anything, girls who somehow managed to move through the whole orgy calm and sweet. His anger mounted. It was a hell of a way to treat a decent girl, to ask her to a dance with a lot of drunkards and soused rats.

[*The summer of his junior year, Hugh visits his friend Norry Parker, whose family has a cottage on Long Island. There Hugh meets lots of "new" women.*]

. . . They flirted with him, perfected his "petting" technique, occasionally treated him to a drink, and made no pretense of hiding his attraction for them.

At first Hugh was startled and a little repelled, but he soon grew to like the frankness, the petting, and the liquor; and he was having a much too exciting time to pause often for criticism of himself or anybody else. . . .

[*Just before he leaves, Hugh meets Cynthia Day and falls in love with her.*]

. . . Suddenly Hugh was attracted by a girl he had never seen before. She wore a red one-piece bathing-suit that revealed every curve of her slender, boyish figure. . . . Her hair was concealed by a red bathing-cap, but Hugh guessed that it was brown; at any rate, her eyes were brown and very large. She had an impudent little nose and full red lips. . . .

[*After returning to college that fall, Hugh and Cynthia write to each other regularly, and she accepts his invitation to come to Sanford for prom week.*]

When Hugh eventually saw Cynthia standing on a car platform near him, he shouted to her and held his hand high in greeting. She saw him and waved back, at the same time starting down the steps.

She had a little scarlet hat pulled down over her curly brown hair, and she wore a simple blue traveling-suit that set off her slender figure perfectly. Her eyes seemed bigger and browner than ever, her nose more impudently tilted, her mouth more supremely irresistible. Her cheeks were daintily rouged, her eyebrows plucked into a thin arch. She was New York from her small pumps to the expensively simple scarlet hat. . . .

[*Later, Norry Parker has a talk with Hugh.*]

"I never expected you to fall in love with Cynthia, Hugh," he said in his gentle way. "I'm awfully surprised. . . ."

Hugh paused in taking off his socks. "Why not?" he demanded. "She's wonderful."

"You're so different."

"How different? . . ."

Norry was troubled. "I don't think I can explain exactly," he said slowly. "Cynthia runs with a fast crowd, and she smokes and drinks—and you're —well, you're idealistic."

Hugh pulled off his underclothes and laughed as he stuck his feet into slippers and drew on a bathrobe. "Of course, she does. All the girls do now. She's just as idealistic as I am." . . .

[*That night at the prom, Hugh and Cynthia dance to a "hot" jazz band, get drunk, and go back to Norry's dorm room. Just as they are about to make love, Norry comes in and escorts Cynthia back to her room. Hugh is ashamed and hungover the next morning; Cynthia decides to return to New York. When she asks if he loves her, Hugh says yes, but she knows that he's lying.*]

"I'm twenty and lots wiser about some things than you are. I've been crazy about you—I guess I am kinda yet—and I know that you thought you were in love with me. I wanted you to have hold of me all this time. That's all that mattered. It was—was your body, Hugh. You're sweet and fine, and I respect you, but I'm not the kid for you to run around with. I'm too fast. I woke up early this morning, and I've done a lot of thinking since. You know what we came near doing last night? Well, that's all we want each other for. We're not in love." . . .

[*After prom week, Hugh goes into training for a big track meet and applies himself to his studies. Elected to the prestigious senior council, Hugh begins to plan for his future: graduate school at Harvard and teaching. When Norry returns from Christmas holidays, he tells Hugh that he saw Cynthia and that she looked terrible.*]

. . . "What's the matter? Is she sick?"

Norry shook his head. "No, I don't think she is exactly sick," he said gravely, "but something is the matter with her. You know, she has been going an awful pace, tearing around like crazy. I told you that, I know, when I came back in the fall. Well, she's kept it up, and I guess she's about all in. I couldn't understand it. Cynthia's always run with a fast bunch, but she's never had a bad name. She's beginning to get one now." . . .

[*After this conversation, Hugh writes a brief note to Cynthia asking what's wrong. She replies that she loves him and had tried to give him up because she knew she was bad for him. Confused, Hugh continues to correspond with her and just before graduation asks her to meet him in New York. He can stay only two hours, so they go to a coffee shop to talk. Hugh asks her to marry him, then changes his mind.*]

They discuss prom night, and Hugh tells Cynthia that he has not been drunk at all since then and has regained his self-respect. Cynthia thinks about her own partying.]

She did not say that she knew that he did not love her; she did not tell him how much his quixotic chivalry moved her. Nor did she tell him that she knew only too well that she could lead him to hell, as he said, but that that was the only place she could lead him. . . .

[*Again, Hugh asks her to marry him after he has completed his graduate education and become established. She refuses his offer, lying and saying that she does not love him. She also points out that he shouldn't marry her if he doesn't love her.*]

"Of course not." He looked down in earnest thought and then said softly, his eyes on the table, "I'm glad that you feel that way, Cynthia." She bit her lip and trembled slightly. "I'll confess now that I don't think that I love you either. You sweep me clean off my feet when I'm with you, but when I'm away from you I don't feel that way. I think love must be something more than we feel for each other." He looked up and smiled boyishly. "We'll go on being friends anyhow, won't we?"

Somehow she managed to smile back at him. "Of course," she whispered, and then after a brief pause added: "We had better go now. Your train will be leaving pretty soon." . . .

NONFICTION

Source 3 from Margaret Sanger, *Woman and the New Race* (New York: Brentano's, 1920), pp. 93–95.

3. Excerpt from Margaret Sanger's *Woman and the New Race.*

The problem of birth control has arisen directly from the effort of the feminine spirit to free itself from bondage. Woman herself has wrought that bondage through her reproductive powers and while enslaving herself has enslaved the world. The physical suffering to be relieved is chiefly woman's. Hers, too, is the love life that dies first under the blight of too prolific breeding. Within her is wrapped up the future of the race—it is hers to make or mar. All of these considerations point unmistakably to one fact—it is woman's duty as well as her privilege to lay hold of the means of freedom. Whatever men may do, she cannot escape the responsibility. For ages she has been deprived of the opportunity to meet this obligation. She is now emerging from her helplessness. Even as no one can share the suffering of the overburdened mother, so no one can do this work for her. Others may help, but she and she alone can free herself.

The basic freedom of the world is woman's freedom. A free race cannot be born of slave mothers. A woman enchained cannot choose but give a measure of that bondage to her sons and daughters. No woman can call herself free who does not own and control her body. No woman can call herself free until she can choose consciously whether she will or will not be a mother.

It does not greatly alter the case that some women call themselves free because they earn their own livings, while others profess freedom because they defy the conventions of sex relationship. She who earns her own living gains a sort of freedom that is not to be undervalued, but in quality and in quantity it is of little account beside the untrammeled choice of mating or not mating, of being a mother or not being a mother. She gains food and clothing and shelter, at least, without submitting to the charity of her companion, but the earning of her own living does not give her the development of her inner sex urge, far deeper and more powerful in its outworkings than any of these externals. In order to have that development, she must still meet and solve the problem of motherhood.

Source 4 from Robert S. Lynd and Helen M. Lynd, *Middletown: A Study in American Culture* (New York: Harcourt, Brace and Company, 1929), pp. 256–257, 112, 114–117, 120–121, 123, 131, 241, 266–267.

4. Excerpts from Robert S. and Helen M. Lynd's *Middletown.*

The general attitude reflected in such characteristic school graduation essays of the 1890 period as "Woman Is Most Perfect When Most Womanly" and "Cooking, the Highest Art of Woman" contrasts sharply with the idea of getting one's own living current among the Middletown high school girls of today: 89 per cent. of 446 girls in the three upper classes in 1924 stated that they were planning to work after graduation, and 2 per cent. more were "undecided"; only 3 per cent. said definitely that they did not expect to work. . . .

[*The Lynds reported that married working women were not as accepted as readily as single working women. Nevertheless, they noted that the 1920 census had shown that 28 percent of the working women of Middletown were married.*]

A heavy taboo, supported by law and by both religious and popular sanctions, rests upon sexual relationships between persons who are not married. There appears to be some tentative relaxing of this taboo among the younger generation, but in general it is as strong today as in the county-seat of forty years ago. There is some evidence that in the smaller community of the eighties [1880s] in which everybody knew everybody else, the group prohibition was outwardly more scrupulously observed than today. A man who was a young buck about town in the eighties says, "The fellows nowadays don't seem to mind being seen on the street with a fast woman, but you bet we did then!" . . .

. . . Theoretically, it is the mysterious attraction of two young people for each other and that alone that brings about a marriage, and actually most of Middletown stumbles upon its partners in marriage guided chiefly by "romance." Middletown adults appear to regard romance in marriage as something which, like their religion, must be believed in to hold society together. Children are assured by their elders that "love" is an unanalyzable mystery that "just happens"—"You'll know when the right one comes along," they are told with a knowing smile. . . .

And yet, although theoretically this "thrill" is all-sufficient to insure permanent happiness, actually talks with mothers revealed constantly that, particularly among the business group, they were concerned with certain other factors; the exclusive emphasis upon romantic love makes way as adolescence recedes for a pragmatic calculus. Mothers of the business group give much consideration to encouraging in their children friendships with the "right" people of the other sex, membership in the "right" clubs, deftly warding off the attentions of boys whom they regard it as undesirable for their daughters to "see too much of," and in other ways interfering with and directing the course of true love.

[*Mothers generally looked for "good providers" as husbands for their daughters, and young women who not only could keep house but could be a social asset as wives for their sons, the Lynds found.*]

Not unrelated to this social skill desired in a wife is the importance of good looks and dress for a woman. In one of Marion Harland's *Talks*,[2] so popular in Middletown in the nineties, one reads, "Who would banish from our midst the matronly figures so suggestive of home, comfort, and motherly love?" Today one cannot pick up a magazine in Middletown without seeing in advertisements of everything from gluten bread to reducing tablets' instructions for banishing the matronly figure and restoring "youthful

2. Popular advice essays aimed at women.

beauty." "Beauty parlors" were unknown in the county-seat of the nineties; there are seven in Middletown today.

"Good looks are a girl's trump card," says Dorothy Dix, though she is quick to add that much can be done without natural beauty if you "dress well and thereby appear 50 per cent. better-looking than you are . . . make yourself charming," and "cultivate bridge and dancing, the ability to play jazz and a few outdoor sports."

[*In general, the Lynds noted, Middletown men did not value "brains" in women, believing that although women were purer and more moral than men, they were not as intelligent. Most Middletown citizens were concerned about the striking increase in the divorce rate.*]

The frequency of divorces and the speed with which they are rushed through have become commonplaces in Middletown. "Anybody with $25 can get a divorce" is a commonly heard remark. Or as one recently divorced man phrased it, "Any one with $10 can get a divorce in ten minutes if it isn't contested. All you got to do is to show non-support or cruelty and it's a cinch." . . .

[*The Lynds reported that middle-class women were more likely to use some form of birth control than working-class women.*]

Child-bearing and child-rearing are regarded by Middletown as essential functions of the family. Although the traditional religious sanction upon "fruitfulness" has been somewhat relaxed since the nineties, and families of six to fourteen children, upon which the grandparents of the present generation prided themselves, are considered as somehow not as "nice" as families of two, three, or four children, child-bearing is nevertheless to Middletown a moral obligation. Indeed, in this urban life of alluring alternate choices, in which children are mouths instead of productive hands, there is perhaps a more self-conscious weighting of the question with moral emphasis; the prevailing sentiment is expressed in the editorial dictum by the leading paper in 1925 that "married persons who deliberately refuse to take the responsibility of children are reasonable targets for popular opprobrium." But with increasing regulation of the size of the family, emphasis has shifted somewhat from child-bearing to child-rearing. The remark of the wife of a prosperous merchant, "You just can't have so many children now if you want to do for them. We never thought of going to college. Our children never thought of anything else," represents an attitude almost universal today among business class families and apparently spreading rapidly to the working class.

Although, according to the city librarian, increased interest in business and technical journals has been marked, as in its reading of books Middletown appears to read magazines primarily for the vicarious living in fictional form they contain. Such reading centers about the idea of romance underlying the institution of marriage; since 1890 there has been a trend toward franker "sex adventure" fiction. It is noteworthy that a culture which traditionally taboos any discussion of sex in its systems of both religious and secular training and even until recently in the home training of children should be receiving such heavy diffusion of this material through its periodical reading matter. The aim of these sex adventure magazines, diffusing roughly 3,500 to 4,000 copies monthly throughout the city, is succinctly stated. . . .

. . . "Middletown is amusement hungry," says the opening sentence in a local editorial; at the comedies Middletown lives for an hour in a happy sophisticated make-believe world that leaves it, according to the advertisement of one film, "happy convinced that Life is very well worth living."

Next largest are the crowds which come to see the sensational society films. The kind of vicarious living brought to Middletown by these films may be inferred from such titles as: "*Alimony*—brilliant men, beautiful jazz babies, champagne baths, midnight revels, petting parties in the purple dawn, all ending in one terrific smashing climax that makes you gasp"; "*Married Flirts—Husbands:* Do you flirt? Does your wife always know where you are? Are you faithful to your vows? *Wives:* What's your hubby doing? Do you know? Do you worry? Watch out for *Married Flirts.*" So fast do these flow across the silver screen that, e.g., at one time *The Daring Years, Sinners in Silk, Women Who Give,* and *The Price She Paid* were all running synchronously, and at another "*Name the Man*—a story of betrayed womanhood" *Rouged Lips,* and *The Queen of Sin.* While Western "action" films and a million-dollar spectacle like *The Covered Wagon* or *The Hunchback of Notre Dame* draw heavy houses, and while managers lament that there are too few of the popular comedy films, it is the film with burning "heart interest" that packs Middletown's motion picture houses week after week. Young Middletown enters eagerly into the vivid experience of *Flaming Youth:* "neckers, petters, white kisses, red kisses, pleasure-mad daughters, sensation-craving mothers, by an author who didn't dare sign his name; the truth bold, naked, sensational"—so ran the press advertisement—under the spell of the powerful conditioning medium of pictures presented with music and all possible heightening of the emotional content, and the added factor of sharing this experience with a "date" in a darkened room. Meanwhile, *Down to the Sea in Ships,* a costly spectacle of whaling adventure, failed at the leading theater "because," the exhibitor explained, "the whale is really the hero in the film and there wasn't enough 'heart interest' for the women."

Source 5 from Dorothy Dunbar Bromley, "Feminist—New Style," *Harper's Monthly* (October 1927), pp. 552, 554–556, 558–559.

5. Excerpts from Dorothy Dunbar Bromley's "Feminist—New Style."

Is it not high time that we laid the ghost of the so-called feminist?

"Feminism" has become a term of opprobrium to the modern young woman. For the word suggests either the old school of fighting feminists who wore flat heels and had very little feminine charm, or the current species who antagonize men with their constant clamor about maiden names, equal rights, woman's place in the world, and many another cause . . . *ad infinitum.* Indeed, if a blundering male assumes that a young woman is a feminist simply because she happens to have a job or a profession of her own, she will be highly—and quite justifiably—insulted: for the word evokes the antithesis of what she flatters herself to be. . . .

. . . Why, then, does the modern woman care about a career or a job if she doubts the quality and scope of women's achievement to date? There are three good reasons why she cares immensely: first, she may be of that rare and fortunate breed of persons who find a certain art, science, or profession as inevitable a part of their lives as breathing; second, she may feel the need of a satisfying outlet for her energy whether or no she possesses creative ability; third, she may have no other means of securing her economic independence. And the latter she prizes above all else, for it spells her freedom as an individual, enabling her to marry or not to marry, as she chooses—to terminate a marriage that has become unbearable, and to support and educate her children if necessary. . . .

But even though Feminist—New Style may not see her own course so clearly marked out before her, and even if she should happen to have an income, she will make a determined effort to fit her abilities to some kind of work. For she has observed that it is only the rare American of either sex who can resist the mentally demoralizing effect of idleness. She has seen too many women who have let what minds they have go to seed, so that by the time they are forty or forty-five they are profoundly uninteresting to their husbands, their children, and themselves. . . .

. . . Nor has she become hostile to the other sex in the course of her struggle to orient herself. On the contrary, she frankly likes men and is grateful to more than a few for the encouragement and help they have given her. . . .

When she meets men socially she is not inclined to air her knowledge and argue about woman's right to a place in the sun. On the contrary, she either talks with a man because he has ideas that interest her or because she finds it amusing to flirt with him—and she will naturally find it doubly amusing if the flirtation involves the swift interplay of wits. She will not waste many engagements on a dull-witted man, although it must be admitted that she finds fewer men with stagnant minds than she does women. . . .

. . . As for "free love," she thinks that it is impractical rather than immoral. With society organized as it is, the average man and woman cannot carry on a free union with any degree of tranquillity.

Incidentally, she is sick of hearing that modern young women are cheapening themselves by their laxity of morals. As a matter of fact, all those who have done any thinking, and who have any innate refinement, live by an aesthetic standard of morals which would make promiscuity inconceivable. . . .

. . . She readily concedes that a husband and children are necessary to the average woman's fullest development, although she knows well enough that women are endowed with varying degrees of passion and of maternal instinct. Some women, for instance, feel the need of a man very intensely, while others want children more than they want a husband, want them so much, in fact, that they vow they would have one or two out of wedlock if it were not for the penalty that society would exact from the child, and if it were not for the fact that a child needs a father as much as a mother.

But no matter how much she may desire the sanction of marriage for the sake of having children, she will not take any man who offers. First of all a man must satisfy her as a lover and a companion. And second, he must have the mental and physical traits which she would like her children to inherit. . . .

. . . But even while she admits that a home and children may be necessary to her complete happiness, she will insist upon *more freedom and honesty within the marriage relation.*

She considers that the ordinary middle-class marriage is stifling in that it allows the wife little chance to know other men, and the husband little chance to know other women—except surreptitiously. It seems vital to her that both should have a certain amount of leisure to use exactly as they see fit, without feeling that they have neglected the other. . . .

Feminist—New Style would consider it a tragedy if she or her husband were to limit the range of each other's lives in any way. Arguing from the fact that she herself can be interested in other men without wanting to exchange them for her husband, she assumes that she has something to give him that he may not find in other women. But if the time should come when it was obvious that he preferred another woman to her or that he preferred to live alone, she would accept the fact courageously, just as she would expect him to accept a similar announcement from her; although she would hope that they would both try to preserve the relationship if it were worth preserving, or if there were children to be considered. But if the marriage should become so inharmonious as to make its continuation a nightmare, she would face the tragedy, and not be submerged by it. For life would still hold many other things—and people—and interests.

6. Still Photographs of Mary Pickford and Clara Bow.

Source 6a: Archive Photos.

6a. Mary Pickford, Photo Portrait.

Source 6b: Archive Photos.

6b. Pickford in *Tess of Storm Country* (1922).

Source 6c: Archive Photos/American Stock.

6c. Clara Bow, Publicity Still.

Source 6d: Museum of Modern Art Film Archive.

6d. Bow in *Mantrap* (1926).

QUESTIONS TO CONSIDER

The first part of the evidence (Sources 1 and 2) consists of excerpts from two best sellers: the enormously popular novel *The Sheik* (1921), which went into fifty printings in the first year of its publication and was later made into an equally popular film starring Rudolph Valentino, and *The Plastic Age* (1924), a novel that became a fad on college campuses across the country. Although both of these sources are fiction, historians often analyze the images portrayed in popular novels and stories for clues to understanding the everyday culture of a society. How are the "new" women in these novels portrayed? What do people think about them? How do they feel about themselves? What happens to them? Are any moral messages contained in the ways these novels conclude?

The second part of the evidence (Sources 3 through 5) is from two nonfiction books widely discussed by middle-class readers and an article by a "new" woman published in the middle-class magazine *Harper's Monthly*. Because of the social purity laws of the late nineteenth and early twentieth centuries, birth control information and devices were illegal in many states. Through women's clinics, pamphlets, and books, Margaret Sanger struggled to make birth control legal and acceptable. What did she want women to do? Why did she believe that access to birth control was so important for women?

In 1925, sociologists Robert and Helen Lynd, along with three female field researchers, conducted in-depth interviews in a medium-size city they called Middletown (Muncie, Indiana). They were interested in the changes that had occurred since the 1890s, particularly the changes in the way people lived and what they believed. These interviews (Source 4) have become a valuable resource for social historians and were of great interest to people living at the time. What trends did the Lynds identify with respect to working women? What did people think about women who worked outside the home? What were the attitudes of the residents toward premarital sex? Marriage? Divorce? Birth control? Child rearing? How did the citizens react to the new emphasis on sex and sexuality in mass culture?

Dorothy Bromley's article (Source 5) is an attempt to describe the young women whom she called "New Style" feminists. According to Bromley, why didn't young women like to be called feminists? In what ways were they independent? What were their attitudes toward men? Toward marriage and children? What were their goals for themselves?

Finally, consider the contrasting film images of Mary Pickford (Sources 6a and 6b), whose popularity began before World War I and continued into the 1920s, and Clara Bow (Sources 6c and 6d), a new star of the 1920s who was called the "It Girl" because of a film in which she had played a flapper with a lot of sex appeal. What impression did each woman give? What sort of traits did each seem to represent? In what ways did the "ideal" type of young woman as portrayed in films seem to change in the 1920s? How can you explain the continuing popularity of Mary Pickford among audiences of all ages in the 1920s?

Now you are ready to summarize what you have found. From the fiction and nonfiction you have read, as well as the photos of the movie stars you have compared, how would you describe the image of the new woman of the 1920s? What were the realities that affected her? What were the limits of her freedom? And finally, to what degree was the young woman of the 1920s actually new or different from young women of the previous generation?

⤬ EPILOGUE ⤬

For all practical purposes, the stock market crash of 1929 and the deep depression that lasted throughout the 1930s ended the fascination with the new woman and replaced it with sympathy and concern for the "forgotten man." Women who worked, especially married women, were perceived as taking jobs away from unemployed men who desperately needed to support their families. In hard times, people clung to traditional male and female roles: Men should be the breadwinners, and women should stay home and take care of the family. Women's fashions changed just as dramatically. Clothing became more feminine, hemlines dropped, and hair styles were no longer short and boyish.

Yet women, including married women, continued to move into paid employment throughout the 1930s, and with the United States' entry into World War II, millions of women who had never held paying jobs before went to work in factories and shipyards, motivated by patriotism and a desire to aid the war effort. By the 1950s, women workers, having been replaced by returning veterans, were once again being urged to stay at home and fulfill their destinies as wives and mothers. Women's educational achievements and age at marriage dropped, while the white middle-class birthrate nearly doubled. Women were still entering the work force, but in feminized clerical and retail jobs and in professions such as elementary school teaching and nursing. Fashions changed from knee-length tailored suits and dresses and "Rosie the Riveter" slacks to puff-sleeved, tiny-waisted, full-skirted, ankle-length dresses.

The problem of image versus reality, so prominent in the 1920s, was also present in the 1960s. By the mid-1960s, another new woman was emerging. Wearing jeans, T-shirts, jewelry, and long hair, young women were dressing like young men. New feminist organizations were founded, a revised version of the ERA was passed by Congress (but not ratified by the states), and millions of women entered universities, paid jobs, and professions. Older Americans expressed a dislike for unisex clothing, were concerned about the easy birth control available with oral contraceptives, and questioned the morality of young women and the popularity of primitive-sounding music. Films, best-selling novels, nonfiction, and advertising all portrayed images of these newest "new" women, but almost never analyzed the realities of their lives.

CHAPTER 7

DOCUMENTING THE DEPRESSION: THE FSA PHOTOGRAPHERS AND RURAL POVERTY

❧ THE PROBLEM ❧

On a cold, rainy afternoon in the spring of 1936, Dorothea Lange was driving home from a month-long field trip to central California. One of several young photographers hired by the Historical Section of the Farm Security Administration (FSA), Lange had been talking with migrant laborers and taking photographs of the migrants' camps.

After passing a hand-lettered road sign that read PEA PICKERS CAMP, Lange drove on another twenty miles. Then she stopped, turned around, and went back to the migrant camp. The pea crop had frozen, and there was no work for the pickers, but several families were still camped there. She ap-

proached a woman and her daughters, talked with them briefly, asked to take a few pictures, and left ten minutes later. The result was one of the most famous images of the Great Depression, "Migrant Mother" (see Source 8). This photograph and others like it moved Americans deeply and helped to create support for New Deal legislation and programs to aid migrant workers, sharecroppers, tenant farmers, and small-scale farmers.

In this chapter, you will be analyzing some of the documentary photographs from the FSA to determine how and why they were so effective in creating support for New Deal legislation.

CHAPTER 7

DOCUMENTING
THE
DEPRESSION:
THE FSA
PHOTOGRAPHERS
AND RURAL
POVERTY

BACKGROUND

In 1930, President Herbert Hoover was at first bewildered and then defensive about the rapid downward spiral of the nation's economy. Hoover, like many other Americans, believed in the basic soundness of capitalism, advocated the values of individualism, and maintained that the role of the federal government should be limited. Nevertheless, Hoover was a compassionate man. As private relief sources dried up, he authorized public works projects and some institutional loans, at the same time vetoing other relief bills and trying to convince the nation that prosperity would return soon. The media, especially newspapers and middle-class magazines, followed Hoover's lead.

Americans turned out at the polls in record numbers for the election of 1932—and voted for the Democratic candidate, Franklin D. Roosevelt, in equally record numbers. As unemployment increased dramatically along with bank and business failures, Congress reacted by rapidly passing an assortment of programs collectively known as the New Deal. Calling together a group of experts (mainly professors and lawyers) to form a "brain trust," the newly elected president acted quickly to try to restore the nation's confidence. In his fireside radio chats, as well as in his other speeches, Roosevelt consistently reassured the American public that the country's economic institutions were sound.

Like her husband, first lady Eleanor Roosevelt was tireless in her efforts to mitigate the effects of the depression.

With boundless energy, she traveled throughout the country, observing conditions firsthand and reporting back to her husband. One of the few New Dealers deeply committed to civil rights for African Americans, she championed both individuals and the civil rights movement whenever she could. Although she was criticized and ridiculed for her nontraditional behavior as first lady, to millions of Americans, Eleanor Roosevelt was the heart of the New Deal. In fact, during the depression, more than 15 million Americans wrote directly to the president and first lady about their personal troubles and economic difficulties.

In an emergency session early in 1933, Congress began the complicated process of providing immediate relief for the needy and legislation for longer-term recovery and reform. Banking, business, the stock market, unemployed workers, farmers, and young people were targets of this early New Deal legislation.

The New Deal administration soon realized that the problems of farmers were going to be especially difficult to alleviate. To meet the unusual European demand for farm products during World War I, many American farmers had overexpanded. They had mortgaged their farms and borrowed money to buy expensive new farm equipment, but most had not shared in the profits of the so-called prosperous decade of the 1920s.

Unfortunately, the New Deal's Agricultural Adjustment Act (AAA) benefited only relatively large, prosperous farmers. Intended to reduce farm production and thus improve the prices farmers received for their goods, the AAA unintentionally encouraged large farmers to accept payment for reducing their crops, use the money to buy machinery, and evict the sharecroppers and tenants who had been farming part of their land. Explaining to Dorothea Lange why his family was traveling to California, one farmer simply said they had been "tractored out." With no land of their own to farm, sharecroppers and tenants packed their few belongings and families into old trucks and cars and took to the road looking for seasonal agricultural work in planting, tending, or picking produce.

In so doing, they joined thousands of other American farm families who lived in the Dust Bowl—the plains and prairie states where unwise agricultural practices and a long drought had combined to create terrifying dust storms that blotted out the sun, blew away the topsoil, and actually buried some farms in dust. These Dust Bowl refugees, along with former tenants and sharecroppers, joined Mexican Americans already working as migrant laborers in California. For those left behind, especially in the poverty-stricken areas of the rural Midwest and South, conditions were almost as terrible as in the migrant camps.

It was to aid these displaced farmers that President Roosevelt created the Resettlement Administration (RA), which two years later became the Farm Security Administration (FSA). The RA was headed by Rexford Tugwell, an economics professor from Columbia University. A former Progressive, Tugwell was an optimist who believed that if the public was educated about social and economic problems, they would support legislation to correct whatever was wrong. To accomplish this task, he hired Roy Stryker, a former graduate student of his, to direct the Historical Section of the agency.

Stryker in turn hired a small group of photographers to travel around the country and take photos illustrating the difficulties faced by small farmers, tenants, and sharecroppers and, to a lesser extent, the FSA projects intended to ameliorate these problems. Hoping to mobilize public opinion in support of FSA-funded projects such as model migrant camps, rural cooperatives, health clinics, and federal relief for the poorest families, Stryker made the photographs widely available to national middle-class magazines and local newspapers. The Historical Section also organized traveling exhibits and encouraged authors to use the photographs in their books.

How did Americans feel when they saw these images? What qualities did the photographs portray? Why were they so effective in creating support for New Deal legislation?

CHAPTER 7

DOCUMENTING
THE
DEPRESSION:
THE FSA
PHOTOGRAPHERS
AND RURAL
POVERTY

THE METHOD

By the end of the nineteenth century, technological advances had made using cameras and developing photographs easier, but both the equipment and the developing methods were still cumbersome and primitive by today's standards. Nevertheless, people were fascinated by photography, and many talented amateurs, such as E. Alice Austen, spent hours taking pictures of their families, friends, and homes. Indeed, these photographs are an important source of evidence for social historians trying to reconstruct how Americans lived in the past.

Documentary photography, however, has a different purpose: reform. During the Progressive era of the late nineteenth and early twentieth centuries, middle-class Americans increasingly became concerned about the growing number of poor families who depended on the labor of their children to supplement their meager standard of living. First Jacob Riis, the author of *How the Other Half Lives* (1890), and then Lewis Hine, in his work for the National Child Labor Committee, photographed the living and working conditions of young children and documented the ill effects of child labor. These photographs were used to persuade the public to support the abolition of child labor. In states that were unwilling to end child labor completely, the pictures were used to convince people to support the strict regulation of young people's work. Although this effort was successful in some states, it failed on the national level when the U.S. Supreme Court struck down a federal law regulating child labor in 1919 (*Hammer v. Dagenhart*).

Roy Stryker was impressed by the power of such photographs and had used many of Hine's images to illustrate Rexford Tugwell's reform-oriented economics textbook in the 1920s. The dozen or so talented photographers whom Stryker hired to work for the Historical Section of the FSA were relatively young (most were in their twenties or thirties) and came from a variety of backgrounds. Most, like Dorothea Lange, Walker Evans, Jack Delano, Carl Mydans, John Collier, Marion Post (Wolcott), and Theodor Jung, were already either established professionals or serious amateurs. Others took their first professional photographs for the Historical Section: Ben Shahn and Russell Lee had been painters, and Arthur Rothstein and John Vachon were unemployed college students. All the photographers were white, except Gordon Parks, a twenty-nine-year-old African American fashion photographer who joined the Historical Section in 1941. Parks never photographed farmers while at the FSA; instead, he sensitively documented the lives of African Americans and racial discrimination in Washington, D.C.

Although the Progressive photographers such as Lewis Hine often posed their subjects or emphasized their dirt and poverty, the FSA photographers generally did not. Working in the field, they relied on taking vast quantities of photographs and sending them to

Stryker, who selected what he wanted for the files. Walker Evans, who worked briefly for the FSA, was an exception, however. When he and James Agee were in Alabama photographing tenant farmers for their book *Let Us Now Praise Famous Men* (1941), Evans rearranged furniture, posed and reposed people, and cleaned up what he thought was clutter. Working with a huge eight-by-ten view camera, Evans considered himself an artist who saw the potential for beauty in the poverty and hard lives of the tenant farmers. According to historian James Curtis, Evans also thought middle-class viewers would react more sympathetically to his vision of the rural poor than to the actual realities of their poverty.

Stryker himself was not a photographer but an able administrator who planned the field trips, developed background reading lists for the photographers, and wrote "shooting scripts" to guide them once they were in the field. "As you are driving through the agricultural areas . . . ," Stryker wrote to Dorothea Lange in California, "would you take a few shots of various types of farm activities such as your picture showing the lettuce workers?" But beyond these kinds of general suggestions, Stryker gave his photographers remarkable freedom while he concentrated on coordinating their activities, promoting the wide use of their photos, and defending the Historical Section against congressional criticism and budget cuts.

When analyzing these pictures, you must remember that documentary photographs are not intended to present a balanced or an unbiased view. Instead, these photographs are intended to appeal to viewers' emotions and motivate viewers to work for and support change. As a student looking at these photographs, you will need to be specific about *what* you feel and then try to determine *why* the photograph makes you feel that way. Finally, try to make some connections between the photographs and the federal programs sponsored by the RA and the FSA.

CHAPTER 7

DOCUMENTING
THE
DEPRESSION:
THE FSA
PHOTOGRAPHERS
AND RURAL
POVERTY

⟨⟨ THE EVIDENCE ⟩⟩

Sources 1 through 17 from United States Farm Security Administration, Historical Division, Library of Congress, Washington, D.C.

1. Abandoned Farm Home, Ward County, North Dakota, 1940 (John Vachon).

2. "Tractored-Out" Farm, Hall County, Texas, 1938 (Dorothea Lange).

3. Skull, South Dakota Badlands, 1936 (Arthur Rothstein).

CHAPTER 7

DOCUMENTING
THE
DEPRESSION:
THE FSA
PHOTOGRAPHERS
AND RURAL
POVERTY

4. Farmer and Sons in Dust Storm, Cimarron County, Oklahoma, 1936 (Arthur Rothstein).

5. Family Moving to Krebs, Oklahoma, from Idabel, Oklahoma, 1939 (Dorothea Lange).

6. Migrant Family Living in a Shack Built on an Abandoned Truck Bed, Highway 70, Tennessee, 1936 (Carl Mydans).

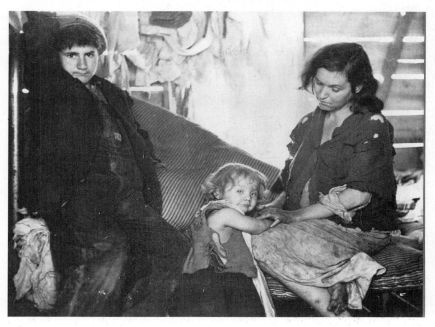

7. Migrants from Oklahoma, Blyth, California, 1936 (Dorothea Lange).

CHAPTER 7

DOCUMENTING
THE
DEPRESSION:
THE FSA
PHOTOGRAPHERS
AND RURAL
POVERTY

8. **Migrant Mother, Nipomo, California, 1936 (Dorothea Lange).**

9. **Mexican Migrant Worker's Home, Imperial Valley, California, 1937 (Dorothea Lange).**

10. Living Quarters of Fruit-Packing House Workers, Berrien, Michigan, 1940 (John Vachon).

11. Plantation Owner and Field Hands, Clarksdale, Mississippi, 1936 (Dorothea Lange).

CHAPTER 7

DOCUMENTING
THE
DEPRESSION:
THE FSA
PHOTOGRAPHERS
AND RURAL
POVERTY

12. Cotton Pickers, Pulaski County, Arkansas, 1935 (Ben Shahn).

13. Owner of the General Store, Bank, and Cotton Gin, Wendell, North Carolina, 1939 (Marion Post Wolcott).

14. **FSA Client and His Family, Beaufort, South Carolina, 1936 (Carl Mydans).**

15. **Mule Dealer, Creedmoor, North Carolina, 1940 (Arthur Rothstein).**

CHAPTER 7

DOCUMENTING
THE
DEPRESSION:
THE FSA
PHOTOGRAPHERS
AND RURAL
POVERTY

16. Bud Fields and His Family, Tenant Farmers, Hale County, Alabama, 1936 (Walker Evans).

17. Christmas Dinner, Tenant Farmer's Home, Southeastern Iowa, 1936 (Russell Lee).

∽ QUESTIONS TO CONSIDER ∽

Sources 1 through 4 are photographs taken to illustrate what had happened to the once-fertile farmlands of the plains and prairies. How would you describe these pictures to someone who could not see them? What had happened to the land? How do these photos make you feel?

Sources 5 through 8 are photographs of farm families who were on the road. They had left or been evicted from the farms where they had lived and were looking for jobs as migrant workers. How would middle-class Americans have felt when they saw these pictures? Which photograph do you think is the most effective? Why?

Sources 9, 10, 12, 14, 16, and 17 show the living and working conditions at migrant camps and for the tenant and sharecropper families who did not leave their homes. What do you notice most when you look at these photographs? How do these pictures make you feel? Why? In contrast, Sources 11, 13, and 15 are of men who were relatively well off during the depression. How are they portrayed? How do you feel about these men? Why?

Finally, think about the photographs as a whole. What messages did they send to the middle-class Americans who saw them in newspapers, magazines, books, or traveling exhibits? What major problems did the photographs portray, and what kinds of programs did the FSA propose to try to aid the poorer farmers? Why do you think these documentary photographs were so effective in creating sympathy and support for aid to these farmers?

∽ EPILOGUE ∽

By 1941, the FSA photographs were well known to millions of Americans, and the Historical Section had justified its existence. That year also saw the publication of the classic book *Let Us Now Praise Famous Men: Three Tenant Families,* written by James Agee and illustrated with photos by FSA photographer Walker Evans. After the Japanese attack on Pearl Harbor in December 1941 and the United States' subsequent entry into World War II, the direction of the Historical Section changed. The buildup of defense industries and the effects of the war on everyday Ameri-cans dominated the photographers' assignments. Eventually, the Historical Section was moved to the Office of War Information, and in 1943, after transferring more than 130,000 FSA photographs to the Library of Congress, Roy Stryker resigned from government service.

America's participation in World War II finally brought an end to the Great Depression—and an end to the New Deal as well. Stryker spent the next decade working for Standard Oil of New Jersey, and most of the former FSA photographers did freelance work, taught courses, or found perma-

CHAPTER 7

DOCUMENTING
THE
DEPRESSION:
THE FSA
PHOTOGRAPHERS
AND RURAL
POVERTY

nent jobs in photojournalism with magazines such as *Life* and *Look*. Ben Shahn went back to his first love, painting, and became a well-known artist. Marion Post (Wolcott) got married and raised a family, returning to photography only when she was in her sixties. The plight of the rural poor was once again forgotten, and middle-class materialism and conformity dominated the cold war years of the 1950s.

Yet a whole new generation was soon to rediscover the work of the FSA photographers. In 1962, Edward Steichen, head of the photography department at the New York Museum of Modern Art and a photographer himself, mounted a major exhibition of the FSA images called "The Bitter Years, 1935–1941." By the end of the 1960s, young Americans also had rediscovered some of the same problems the New Deal photographers had captured in their pictures: rural poverty, racial discrimination, and social injustice. Once again, Americans demanded reform, especially during the presidencies of John F. Kennedy and Lyndon Johnson.

CHAPTER 8

PRESIDENTIAL LEADERSHIP, PUBLIC OPINION, AND THE COMING OF WORLD WAR II: THE USS *GREER* INCIDENT, SEPTEMBER 4, 1941

⧜ THE PROBLEM ⧜

At 11:50 A.M. on Thursday, September 4, 1941, crewmen aboard the destroyer USS *Greer* sighted the track of a torpedo that had been fired at the ship, ultimately passing about two hundred yards astern of the U.S. naval vessel. The *Greer* counterattacked, dropping eight depth charges in an effort to destroy the submarine. At 11:58, a second torpedo track was sighted; this torpedo also missed the ship. For the next six hours, the *Greer* chased the submarine, dropping eleven more depth charges, apparently to no effect. At 6:40 P.M., the American destroyer gave up the search and proceeded to Iceland, its original destination.[1]

On September 11, President Franklin D. Roosevelt went on the radio in one of his famous "fireside chats."[2] Characterizing Germany's submarines as the "rattlesnakes of the Atlantic," the president told listeners that the *Greer* had been attacked without warning while the destroyer was "proceeding on a legitimate mission" and said that thenceforth he would or-

---

1. The USS *Greer* was approximately 125 miles southwest of Reykjavik, Iceland, when

the incident took place. The ship was carrying mail to U.S. Marines stationed in Iceland. The ship, built in 1918, was relegated to the "bone yard" of the Philadelphia Navy Yard sometime after World War I but was recommissioned in 1940. It was named for Rear Admiral James A. Greer (1833–1904), a Civil War veteran (Union) and commander of the European Squadron from 1887 to 1889.

2. The fireside chat was scheduled to be delivered earlier but was postponed when the president's mother died over the weekend.

CHAPTER 8

PRESIDENTIAL
LEADERSHIP,
PUBLIC OPINION,
AND THE
COMING OF
WORLD WAR II:
THE USS *GREER*
INCIDENT,
SEPTEMBER 4,
1941

der American ships to shoot on sight any German submarines; moreover, American ships would protect merchant ships of all nations that were carrying cargoes to Germany's enemies. At the end of Roosevelt's address, the radio network played a recording of the national anthem, and everyone in the diplomatic reception room of the White House (except the president) rose emotionally to their feet.

About two weeks later, a Gallup public opinion poll showed that 56 percent of those surveyed agreed with Roosevelt's "shoot on sight" order,[3] even though it seemed clear that such a step would make war with Germany almost unavoidable. This result was in marked contrast to an October 26–31, 1939, poll, which reported that 96 percent of Americans opposed war against Germany. Yet whether President Roosevelt was using his powers to shape public opinion toward a more belligerent stand against the Axis Powers (Germany, Italy, and Japan) or whether the president carefully followed public opinion as he moved the United States closer to war is a question that still elicits considerable debate.

This chapter concentrates on one incident, the attack on the USS *Greer* by

a German submarine on September 4, 1941. Your task in this chapter is twofold. To begin, you must arrange the evidence. Unlike other chapters in this book, the evidence has not been arranged for you but instead has been set down in no particular order—the way in which historians actually find evidence. Arrange the evidence in order to answer the following two questions (the second part of the task): (1) What *actually happened* in the *Greer* incident? (2) Was President Roosevelt shaping public opinion or following it (or a combination of both)?

The causes of the United States' involvement in World War II are exceedingly complex and would require analyses of literally hundreds of events that took place between the mid-1930s and December 7, 1941, the date of the Japanese attack on Pearl Harbor, which brought the United States into the war in both Europe and the Pacific. You will not be able to determine those causes through an examination and analysis of one single event, albeit a pivotal one. You will, however, be able to gain some important clues regarding President Franklin Roosevelt's attitudes and behavior and their relation to American public opinion.

❧ BACKGROUND ❧

On September 1, 1939, German chancellor Adolf Hitler's armies attacked

Poland. Two days later, France and Great Britain declared war on Germany. Ever since March 1935, when

---

3. The poll was taken between September 19 and 24. Of those surveyed, 34 percent disagreed with Roosevelt's policy, and 10 percent expressed no opinion. See George H. Gallup,

The Gallup Poll: Public Opinion, 1935–1971 (New York: Random House, 1972), Vol. I, p. 299.

Hitler announced that he would defy the Treaty of Versailles and rearm Germany, France and Great Britain had watched with increasing alarm as Germany reoccupied the Rhineland in March 1936, seized and annexed Austria in March 1938, and demanded the Sudetenland (the German-speaking part of Czechoslovakia). At a conference in Munich that took place on September 29–30, 1938, Hitler promised that the Sudetenland was "the last territorial claim which I have to make in Europe." Naively believing that Hitler's appetite had been satiated, Britain's prime minister, Neville Chamberlain, announced that the Munich Conference had brought "peace in our time." But in March 1939 Hitler absorbed the rest of Czechoslovakia. Realizing their error, France and Great Britain declared war when Germany invaded Poland.

Less than two weeks after the attack on Poland, President Roosevelt called Congress into special session to lift the United States' embargo on arms trade with countries at war. The Neutrality Act of 1939 lifted the embargo but mandated that such trade could be carried out only on a "cash and carry" basis (thereby prohibiting any loans to the belligerents, believing that such loans had been a principal cause of America's involvement in World War I)[4] and forbid American troops to enter danger zones in the Atlantic.

The outbreak of war in Europe presented the American people with a di-lemma. On one hand, an overwhelming majority wanted the United States to stay out of the war. Disillusioned by the dashing of their World War I idealism, both the American people and their government had been staunchly isolationist throughout the 1920s and much of the 1930s. On the other hand, most Americans were decidedly unneutral, hoping that the Allied Powers would be able to defeat Germany, Italy, and the Soviet Union.[5] This was especially true after the German blitzkrieg (lightning war) in the spring of 1940. In six weeks, German armies overran Denmark, Norway, Belgium, the Netherlands, Luxembourg, and France (which capitulated on June 22, 1940), leaving Great Britain to stand alone against the German military might. In the summer and fall of 1940, Hitler unleashed the Luftwaffe (the German air force) against Britain in hopes that massive bombing of civilian targets would force the British to surrender. Tens of thousands of British civilians were killed or wounded, the city of Coventry was completely destroyed, and large parts of London lay in ruins (with 20,000 killed in that city alone), but the British tenaciously hung on. "We will never surrender," promised Prime Minister Winston Churchill. Gradually the Royal Air Force gained control of the skies over Great Britain.

In late June 1940, 86 percent of Americans surveyed believed the United States should stay out of the

---

4. In late October 1939, 68 percent of Americans surveyed believed that it had been a mistake for the United States to have entered World War I. See *Gallup Poll,* Vol. I, p. 189.

5. Prior to his attack on Poland, Hitler had signed the Non-Aggression Pact with the Soviet Union. While Germany was smashing the Polish army, the Soviet Union gobbled up eastern Poland.

CHAPTER 8

PRESIDENTIAL
LEADERSHIP,
PUBLIC OPINION,
AND THE
COMING OF
WORLD WAR II:
THE USS *GREER*
INCIDENT,
SEPTEMBER 4,
1941

war, but the bombing of Britain had a profound effect on American public opinion. Asked in early September whether it was more important for the United States to keep out of the war or to help England, a bare majority (52 percent) preferred to help England. Taking advantage of that apparent shift in public opinion, Roosevelt concluded an executive agreement with Churchill to trade fifty World War I vintage American destroyers in exchange for leases on British military bases in the Western Hemisphere (especially in Newfoundland, Bermuda, and Trinidad), which the president claimed was for the purpose of bolstering American defenses. In October 1940, Congress authorized the first peacetime draft of men for military service. But when the *New York Daily News* claimed that the United States "has one foot in the war and the other on a banana peel," Roosevelt retorted, "Your president says this country is not going to war."

Having won reelection by defeating Republican challenger Wendell Willkie, in January 1941 Roosevelt proposed to Congress a sweeping revision of the Neutrality Act that would repeal the cash-and-carry provision and authorize the president to lend or lease war material to Great Britain. Although polls showed that 88 percent of Americans still wanted the United States to stay out of war, at the same time, 54 percent favored the Lend-Lease bill. Congress passed the bill in March 1941 by votes of 317–71 in the House of Representatives and 60–31 in the Senate. Interestingly, the bill in the House was numbered HR1776.

Not all Americans were happy with what appeared to be a trend toward greater and greater involvement in the war in Europe. Germany had approximately thirty submarines (U-boats) in the Atlantic, which were inflicting a terrible toll on British shipping. Isolationists warned that the United States ultimately would have to escort vessels carrying Lend-Lease goods or use American ships, either of which would bring Americans into direct conflict with German U-boats and inevitably into war. For his part, columnist Walter Lippmann attacked Roosevelt himself:

> In this tremendous time the American people must look to the President for leadership. They are not getting leadership from the President. They are not being treated as they deserve to be treated and as they have a right to be treated. They are not being treated as men and women but as if they were inquisitive children. They are not being dealt with seriously, truthfully, responsibly, and nobly. They are being dealt with cleverly, indirectly, even condescendingly and nervously.[6]

Although Roosevelt scoffed at the isolationists and insisted that his actions were meant to keep the nation out of war, not enter it, the isolationists had made a telling point. Between January and June 1941, the British lost 756 merchant ships, with an additional 1,450 damaged. With this loss of ships at the rate of 500,000 tons per month, it was obvious that a large proportion of Lend-Lease goods were ending up on the bottom of the Atlantic. Admiral Harold R. Stark wrote, "The

6. Quoted in T. R. Fehrenbach, *F.D.R.'s Undeclared War, 1939 to 1941* (New York: David McKay Co., 1967), p. 218.

situation is obviously critical in the Atlantic. In my opinion it is hopeless except as we take strong measures to save it."[7]

As it had been in the past, public opinion was contradictory. In May 1941, 79 percent of those surveyed believed the United States should stay out of the war, yet in that same poll, 52 percent said that the U.S. Navy should guard ships carrying war materiel to Britain. Prior to the poll's being taken, Roosevelt ordered Admiral Ernest King to patrol waters as far as longitude 25 degrees west and inform British convoys of lurking German submarines.[8] Then in June 1941, Roosevelt ordered Admiral Stark to send U.S. Marines to occupy Iceland, a possession of Denmark that had been occupied by British troops when Denmark was swallowed in Hitler's blitz-

krieg.[9] Thus the U.S. Navy in essence was escorting British convoys to an island well within the war zone. With the navy short of officers, the U.S. Naval Academy had graduated its 1941 class six months early. Lieutenant Commander Laurence H. Frost had been on the USS *Greer* thirty-five days when the incident with the German submarine took place.

As a reminder, your task in this chapter is to arrange the evidence (which has been provided to you randomly) to answer the following two questions:

1. What *actually happened* in the *Greer* incident of September 4, 1941?
2. Was President Roosevelt *shaping* public opinion, *following* it, or a combination of both?

ᔆ THE METHOD ᔆ

In most cases, historians find it best to arrange the evidence at their disposal in chronological order. This is especially true when a historian is combining a series of events to tell a story (narrative history) or is writing a biography of an individual (biographical history). At first glance, then, it would be most appropriate to arrange your evidence chronologically.

And yet, at second glance, certain interesting problems arise. For example, the deck log of the *Greer* (Source 12) was written by U.S. Navy lieutenant T. H. Copeman on the same day on which the incident took place, or very soon after. So also was U-boat 652's report (Source 13). The speech in the Senate by Senator Robert A. Taft (Source 23), however, was delivered on October 28, 1941. And Roosevelt's fireside chat of September 11 (Source 20) and Secretary of the Navy Frank Knox's address to the American Le-

7. Stark to Admiral Husband S. Kimmel, April 4, 1941, quoted in Patrick Abbazia, *Mr. Roosevelt's Navy: The Private War of the U.S. Atlantic Fleet, 1939–1942* (Annapolis: Naval Institute Press, 1975), p. 153.
8. One joke Admiral King's men told about him was that "while [King] did not yet think he was God, God thought that he was Admiral King." Ibid., p. 134.

9. Iceland's prime minister, Hermann Jonasson, was not informed of the United States' impending occupation until the Marines were already at sea.

CHAPTER 8

PRESIDENTIAL
LEADERSHIP,
PUBLIC OPINION,
AND THE
COMING OF
WORLD WAR II:
THE USS *GREER*
INCIDENT,
SEPTEMBER 4,
1941

gion (Source 21) were delivered several days after the *Greer* incident took place. Yet because all of them are dealing with the events of September 4, these pieces of evidence must be placed with the *Greer*'s deck log. Similarly, the Gallup polls (Sources 1 through 11) often were published weeks after they actually were taken. Public opinion can shift very rapidly, so you must use the dates on which those polls *actually were taken,* not the dates on which they were released.

Once having arranged your evidence, you must then subject it to the test of believability. The deck log of the USS *Greer* and the log of U-652 (the German submarine) were reports to superior officers in Washington and Berlin, respectively, of what actually took place. Are these two reports, the only ones written by eyewitnesses, accurate? How accurate are the *New York Times*'s report of the incident (Sources 14 and 15) and the German disclaimer (Source 18)? Similarly, is President Roosevelt's account of the incident in his September 5 news conference (Source 19) and his September 11 fireside chat (Source 20) an accurate one? If not, why do you think this was so? Admiral Stark was invited to report to the U.S. Senate, and he did so in writing, thereby avoiding a face-to-face confrontation (Source 22). How believable is Stark? Finally, the speech by Taft (Source 23) was delivered by a political opponent of Roosevelt. What is his motivation? Is he believable?

Very quickly you will see that certain pieces of evidence will help you in answering one question but will not be relevant in answering the other. For example, the Gallup polls tell you nothing about what really happened off the coast of Iceland on September 4, 1941, but those same polls will be invaluable in determining President Roosevelt's relations to public opinion. Be precise in matching the polls to Roosevelt actions. Was he ahead of public opinion, behind it, or step by step with it? What does that say about the nature of his presidential leadership? FDR clearly did not tell the full story of the *Greer* incident to the American people, in either his press conference (Source 19) or his fireside chat (Source 20). Why do you think this was so?

Because the evidence has not been arranged for you, you will have to take detailed notes on each piece of evidence. You might want to use a separate sheet of paper or note card for each piece, so you can rearrange the evidence as you rearrange your notes. Be sure to write down your impressions of each source as to its accuracy and believability, as well as any reasons you think the particular piece of evidence is or is not accurate or believable.

The Gallup poll results (Sources 1 through 11) are grouped together, but obviously they will have to be inserted in their proper places in the rest of the evidence (speeches, newspaper account, etc.).

⌒ THE EVIDENCE ⌒

Sources 1 through 11 from Gallup, *The Gallup Poll,* Vol. 1, pp. 270, 275–276, 279–280, 291, 296, 299–302.

1. Gallup Poll, Released March 21, 1941.

EUROPEAN WAR

Interviewing Date 3/9–14/41
Survey #232-K

If you were asked to vote on the question of the United States entering the war against Germany and Italy, how would you vote—to go into the war, or to stay out of the war?

Go in	17%
Stay out	83

The Southern states show the highest vote for war, 20%, and the West Central states the lowest, 14%.

2. Gallup Poll, Released April 23, 1941.

EUROPEAN WAR

Interviewing Date 4/10–15/41
Survey #234-K

Should the United States navy be used to guard ships carrying war materials to Britain?

Yes	41%
No	50
No opinion	9

3. Gallup Poll, Released May 16, 1941.

EUROPEAN WAR

Interviewing Date 5/8–13/41
Survey #236-K

If you were asked to vote today on the question of the United States entering the war against Germany and Italy, how would you vote—to go into the war or to stay out of the war?

Go in	21%
Stay out	79

Five per cent expressed no opinion.

CHAPTER 8

PRESIDENTIAL
LEADERSHIP,
PUBLIC OPINION,
AND THE
COMING OF
WORLD WAR II:
THE USS *GREER*
INCIDENT,
SEPTEMBER 4,
1941

By State

	Go In	Stay Out		Go In	Stay Out
Wisconsin	14%	86%	New Mexico	24	76
Minnesota	15	85	Nevada	24	76
Iowa	15	85	Delaware	25	75
Indiana	15	85	Oklahoma	25	75
Ohio	15	85	Louisiana	26	74
Massachusetts	17	83	Tennessee	26	74
New Hampshire	17	83	Montana	26	74
Illinois	17	83	Utah	26	74
Michigan	18	82	Maryland	27	73
Nebraska	18	82	West Virginia	27	73
South Dakota	18	82	Kentucky	27	73
Connecticut	19	81	Idaho	27	73
Kansas	20	80	Oregon	27	73
North Dakota	21	79	Georgia	28	72
Maine	21	79	Arkansas	28	72
Rhode Island	22	78	Virginia	28	72
Pennsylvania	22	78	Mississippi	28	72
Washington	22	78	Colorado	28	72
Vermont	23	77	North Carolina	29	71
New Jersey	23	77	Alabama	29	71
Missouri	23	77	Texas	29	71
South Carolina	23	77	Wyoming	29	71
California	23	77	Arizona	33	67
New York	24	76	Florida	35	65

4. Gallup Poll, Released May 21, 1941.

EUROPEAN WAR

Interviewing Date 5/8–13/41
Survey #236-K

Should the United States navy be used to guard ships carrying war materials to Britain?

Yes	52%
No	41
No opinion	7

5. Gallup Poll, Released July 25, 1941.

ICELAND

Interviewing Date 7/11–16/41
Survey #241-K

Do you approve or disapprove of the Government's action in taking over the defense of Iceland?

Approve	61%
Disapprove	17
No opinion	22

6. Gallup Poll, Released September 23, 1941.

EUROPEAN WAR

Interviewing Date 8/21–26/41
Survey #245-K

Do you think the American navy should be used to convoy ships carrying war materials to England?

Yes	52%
No	39
No opinion	9

7. Gallup Poll, Released September 26, 1941.

EUROPEAN WAR

Interviewing Date 9/19–24/41
Survey #248-K

Do you approve or disapprove of having the United States shoot at German submarines or warships on sight?

Approve	56%
Disapprove	34

CHAPTER 8

PRESIDENTIAL
LEADERSHIP,
PUBLIC OPINION,
AND THE
COMING OF
WORLD WAR II:
THE USS *GREER*
INCIDENT,
SEPTEMBER 4,
1941

8. Gallup Poll, Released October 1, 1941.

NEUTRALITY

Interviewing Date 9/19–24/41
Survey #248-K

Should the Neutrality Act be changed to permit American merchant ships with American crews to carry war materials to Britain?

Yes	46%
No	40
No opinion	14

By Political Affiliation

Democrats

Yes	51%
No	33
No opinion	16

Republicans

Yes	42%
No	48
No opinion	10

9. Gallup Poll, Released October 5, 1941.

EUROPEAN WAR

Interviewing Date 9/19–24/41
Survey #248-K

Which of these two things do you think is the more important—that this country keep out of war or that Germany be defeated?

Keep out of war	30%
Germany be defeated	70

10. Gallup Poll, Released October 8, 1941.

PRESIDENT ROOSEVELT

Interviewing Date 9/19–24/41
Survey #248-K

So far as you personally are concerned, do you think President Roosevelt has gone too far in his policies of helping Britain, or not far enough?

Too far	27%
About right	57
Not far enough	16

11. Gallup Poll, Released October 19, 1941.

NEUTRALITY

Interviewing Date 10/9–14/41
Survey #250-K

Should the Neutrality Act be changed to permit American ships to be armed?

Yes	72%
No	21
No opinion	7

Should the Neutrality Act be changed to permit American merchant ships with American crews to carry war materials to England?

Yes	46%
No	40
No opinion	14

Source 12 from National Archives, Record Group 45, p. 528.

12. Deck Log, USS *Greer,* September 4, 1941.

4 to 8. 0400[10] Changed course to 056 T, 057 PGC, 092 PSC at standard speed 17.5 knots. 0430 Went to General Quarters.[11] 0503 Secured from General Quarters. 0538 Shifted steering control to after steering station.

---

10. The armed services mark the time of day from 0001 hours (1 minute after midnight) to 2359 hours (1 minute until midnight), not repeating the hours (1, 2, 3, etc.) after noon. Therefore, 0400 is 4:00 A.M., and 1535 (below) is 3:35 P.M.
11. General quarters: full battle alert.

CHAPTER 8

PRESIDENTIAL
LEADERSHIP,
PUBLIC OPINION,
AND THE
COMING OF
WORLD WAR II:
THE USS *GREER*
INCIDENT,
SEPTEMBER 4,
1941

0545 Shifted control back to bridge. 0740 Sighted British plane ULA. 0747 Plane reported U-boat had submerged bearing 057 T, distance 10 miles. Commenced zigzagging in accordance with zigzag plan # 1. Went to General Quarters.

8 to 12. Steaming as before on zigzag courses. 0801 Changed course to 045 T. 0815 Changed speed to 10 knots and started sound search. 0820 Made contact with underwater sound gear and maneuvered on various courses and speeds maintaining contact. 0932 British plane ULA attacked submarine releasing four depth charges. 0952 Plane departed. 1030 Heard submarine propellers on sound gear. 1100 Sighted British plane UAK. 1140 Submarine appeared to be changing course to right approaching ship. Changed course to the right. Bearing changed rapidly aft to starboard and distance closed to about 50 yards. Lost sound contact at 150 yards on starboard bow. Track of submarine sighted. 1144 Sighted firingbubble abeam to starboard opposite bridge distant 25 yards. At time of sighting bubble submarine wake indicated she was then on port quarter. CDD 61 ordered attack. Went ahead flank speed and changed course 180 to the right. 1150 Sighted torpedo track broad on starboard beam distance 1000 yards which passed 200 yards astern. 1156 Attacked dropping 8 depth charges. 1158 Sighted torpedo track 10 degrees on starboard bow and changed course to right to avoid torpedo. Torpedo passed about 100 yards on port beam. Recommenced search of area immediately.

12 to 16. Steaming as before on various courses at various speeds conducting sound search for submarine. 1315 Sighted British destroyer I26. 1316 Discontinued search and set course 059 T, 060 PGC, 099 PSC standard speed 15 knots for Reykjavik, Iceland. Secured from General Quarters, set condition III. 1333 On orders from Commander Destroyer Division 61 changed course to 330 T, 329 PGC, 002 PSC to continue search. 1407 Made sound contact with submarine bearing 10 degrees on starboard bow distance 900 yards. Sounded General Quarters and proceeded to attack submarine. 1412 Attacked submarine dropping eleven depth charges. 1413 Changed course to 250 T, at flank speed. 1414 Changed course to 270 T and slowed to 15 knots. 1415 Slowed to 5 knots continuing on sound search. 1431 Changed course to 095 T and went ahead at 10 knots. 1535 Changed course to 090 T, 089 PGC, 059 PSC. Secured from General Quarters and set condition III.

Approved: [signed]   *Examined:* [signed]
L. H. FROST,   T. H. COPEMAN,
Lt. Comdr. U.S. Navy,   Lieutenant.
Commanding.

Source 13 from National Archives, Record Item T1022, Rolls 3387–3388. Translated by Christiane M. Hunley.

13. Report of U-652 (German Submarine), September 4, 1941.[12]

Date and Time	Occurrences
445	Remained Stopped
445–725	Diving Test
909	Diving alert because of aircraft in 80 degrees, has 2 motors, very high, but close
	Because the crew is tired from the night before, and I do not wish to be surprised once again (the Warrant Officer is of the opinion that we are still undiscovered), I remain underwater
1200	I made the mistake and did not go on a different course
1230	I want to go to periscope depth, but when I have reached 28 meters [from the surface] suddenly at 1230 there fall 3 bombs. I
1300	remain at first at a depth of 25 meters and then go to periscope depth. Perhaps I have an oil trace and, therefore, I want to get away as soon as possible.
1322	Without being heard, a destroyer with 4 chimneys lies in a distance of 1200 meters. Position bow to the right 5-10, apparently stopped.
1328	Course 200 degrees, depth 30 meters. Destroyer is of the same type as in the convoy on 8/25 and 8/26/1941, one of the 50 American vessels that are now sailing for England.
1417	Thus, this is in fact the destroyer which released what were in fact [the three] water bombs at 1230.
	However, I still cannot explain its silent approach. I want to distance myself as soon as possible from this sinister companion.
1420	Have gone to periscope depth. Nothing heard on the hydrophone. The enemy should be at the elapsed distance, if he had remained stopped and stayed at his old location. Instead, he is in a position directly behind me. . . . I can now only believe that I can be heard exactly in his hydrophone and that he follows me with the most frugal turns in such a way that I cannot hear him in the aft sector. Even his backup machines cannot be heard. A plane is flying in the lowest altitude over the destroyer, apparently a large plane. I now must assume that the plane did see me this morning and that it has ordered the destroyer to this location. However, I still do not understand his tentative behavior. I must assume that he wants to slowly starve me [of oxygen], because I cannot count on surfacing unnoticed in the clear visibility of night. Also, he probably can keep this distance, if he succeeded so far.

12. At the conclusion of World War II, all German U-boat records fell into Allied hands and were deposited in the National Archives in Washington, D.C.

CHAPTER 8

PRESIDENTIAL
LEADERSHIP,
PUBLIC OPINION,
AND THE
COMING OF
WORLD WAR II:
THE USS *GREER*
INCIDENT,
SEPTEMBER 4,
1941

Date and Time	Occurrences
1425	Since I must assume that I am being pursued and in order to avoid further attacks as well, or feint attacks, I am now changing to an underwater attack. . . . I can clearly see the enemy: no flag, no name or insignia, caps on the 4 chimneys—an old tin can. [Torpedo fired]
1439	*Bad shot.* Course of attack was incorrectly calculated. The enemy's course was mistakenly assumed to be 230 degrees, although before it was clearly 180 degrees. A quick movement at the time of the shot causes us to conclude that opponent's speed was accelerated, which was not recognized in the periscope as the closeness forced us to use the periscope sparingly. The enemy has either seen me while firing, because he knew I was [close], or heard me, because he must have had me exactly on his instrument. But I only thought later about the fact that for these reasons the unnoticed shot was not successful.
	[Second torpedo fired]
1447	I shot with true position from approximately 120 degrees, but did not manage to achieve the calculated course of attack. . . .
1505–1740	Five water bombs [depth charges], still somewhat spread. Damage only in the diesel room (light bulbs). Moving further to the north, turning several times, going to counter course as the destroyer still often comes close.
2050	Moving slowly in the general direction of NW with a depth of 50 meters. In the E-room the bilge is filling because of the leaking portside sternpost bushing, cannot be pulled along. Either the destroyer already has lost me or follows me. . . .
2324	Two airplanes circle in the destroyer's vicinity, one of which comes awfully close to me. . . .
	One water bomb [depth charge], further away. . . .

Source 14 from *New York Times,* September 5, 1941.

14. News Report of *Greer* Incident.

WASHINGTON, Sept. 4—A submarine of undetermined nationality attacked the United States destroyer Greer this morning in the Atlantic on the way to Iceland, the Navy Department stated tonight. Torpedoes were fired at the vessel.

The Greer, which was not damaged, counter-attacked by dropping depth charges, the announcement said.

President Roosevelt, it was learned, was at once apprised of the incident, but there was no immediate comment from the White House. A spokesman for the State Department said that it was a question for the Navy and that he was not authorized to make any statement.

The Navy reported the attack as follows:

"The U. S. S. Destroyer Greer, en route to Iceland with mail, reported this morning that a submarine had attacked her by firing torpedoes which missed their mark.

"The Greer immediately counter-attacked with depth charges. Results are not known."

The attacking submarine was assumed to be German.

The destroyer was operating as a part of the Atlantic patrol which was established by President Roosevelt early in the Summer. At that time the White House stated that the duties of the patrol were to report to the Navy Department the presence of any potentially hostile craft.

In addition to being the first attack on an American warship in the European war the incident is the first of a warlike nature since American forces took over occupation of Iceland at the invitation of the Icelandic government early in the Summer. . . .

Source 15 from *New York Times,* September 6, 1941.

15. Additional News Concerning the *Greer* Incident.

REYKJAVIK, Iceland, Sept. 5—The men of the United States destroyer Greer, which was attacked by a submarine on the way to Iceland, said on their arrival here today that the Greer's depth charges might well have sunk the undersea vessel.

The incident was described here as a German attack.

The Greer's officers and crew expressed the conviction that they had at least damaged the submarine, for their instruments indicated that they were directly above her when they dropped their bombs.

The destroyer was in very deep water at the time, they added, and thus the submarine may have been sunk without trace.

The American warship was assisted in repelling the attack by British aircraft, they said. Those in the vicinity cooperated in reconnaissance. . . .

CHAPTER 8

PRESIDENTIAL
LEADERSHIP,
PUBLIC OPINION,
AND THE
COMING OF
WORLD WAR II:
THE USS *GREER*
INCIDENT,
SEPTEMBER 4,
1941

Sources 16 and 17 from Abbazia, *Mr. Roosevelt's Navy,* pp. 52, 176.

16. Wehrmacht[13] Command Memorandum, September 1939.

The American Neutrality Law is a shackle for the most war-loving of American Presidents, one which presumably cannot be shaken off so long as we do not provide him with the excuse to breach this shackle. . . . Even if we are convinced that, should the war be of long duration, the USA will enter it in any case . . . it must be our object to delay this event so long that American help would come too late.

17. Hitler to Admiral Raeder, Führer Conference, May 22, 1941.

Weapons are not to be used. Even if American vessels conduct themselves in a definitely unneutral manner . . . weapons are to be used *only if US ships fire the first shot.*

Source 18 from *New York Times,* September 7, 1941.

18. German Communiqué, September 6, 1941.

On the fourth of September a German submarine was attacked with depth bombs and continuously pursued in the German blockade zone at a point charted at Lat. 62 degrees 31 minutes N. and Long. 27 degrees 6 minutes W. The German submarine was unable to establish the nationality of the attacking destroyer.

In justified defense against the attack, the submarine thereupon at 14:39 o'clock fired two torpedoes at the destroyer, both of which missed aim. The destroyer continued its pursuit and attacks with depth bombs until midnight, then abandoned them.

If official American quarters, namely the Navy Department, assert the attack was initiated by the German submarine, such charge can only have the purpose of giving the attack of an American destroyer on a German submarine which was undertaken in complete violation of neutrality a semblance of legality. This attack is evidence that President Roosevelt despite his previous assertions to the contrary has commanded American

13. Wehrmacht: the German military.

destroyers not only to report the location of German U-Boats and other German craft as violating neutrality but also to proceed to attack them.

Roosevelt there is endeavoring with all the means at his disposal to provoke incidents for the purpose of baiting the American people into the war.

Source 19 from Samuel I. Rosenman, *The Public Papers and Addresses of Franklin D. Roosevelt* (New York: Harper & Brothers, 1950), Vol. X, pp. 374–377.

19. FDR Press Conference, September 5, 1941.[14]

THE PRESIDENT. You will all be asking about the attack of yesterday, so we
   might as well clear that up first.

   There is nothing to add, except that there was more than one attack,
   and that it occurred in daylight, and it occurred definitely on the
   American side of the ocean. This time there is nothing more to add
   except two thoughts I have. I heard one or two broadcasters this morning, and I read a few things that have been said by people in Washington, which reminded me of a—perhaps we might call it an allegory.

   Once upon a time, at a place where I was living, there were some
   school children living out in the country who were on their way to
   school, and somebody undisclosed fired a number of shots at them from
   the bushes. The father of the children took the position that there
   wasn't anything to do about it—search the bushes, and take any other
   steps—because the children hadn't been hit. I don't think that's a bad
   illustration, in regard to the position of some people this morning.

   The destroyer—it is a very, very fortunate thing that the destroyer
   was not hit in these attacks. And I think that is all that can be said on
   the subject today.

Q. Mr. President, there is one thing that occurred to me, and I wondered if
   you could clear that up: Was the identification of our ship solely by that
   little flag astern, or were there other ships going with this destroyer?
   Were there larger ships that made identification much easier?

THE PRESIDENT. She was alone at the time, clearly marked. Of course an
   identification number was on her, plus the flag. And the fact remains
   that, as I said before, there was more than one attack.

Q. Mr. President, does that mean more than one torpedo, or—

14. Roosevelt delighted in holding press conferences, and this was his 767th since taking office
in March 1933. He averaged about two per week.

CHAPTER 8

PRESIDENTIAL
LEADERSHIP,
PUBLIC OPINION,
AND THE
COMING OF
WORLD WAR II:
THE USS *GREER*
INCIDENT,
SEPTEMBER 4,
1941

THE PRESIDENT. *(interposing)* More than one attack.

Q. On the same ship, Mr. President?

THE PRESIDENT. On the same ship. . . .

Q. What did you say, sir, about being on the—you said on the American side of the ocean?

THE PRESIDENT. Yes.

Q. Plainly on the American side?

THE PRESIDENT. Yes, yes. . . .

Q. Mr. President, how would you class this incident with regard to a shooting war?

THE PRESIDENT. Oh, well, those are hypothetical questions. I said that was all there was to be said about it.

Q. As another landlubber, I would like to ask a question here. Is it possible for a destroyer to be on the American side of the Atlantic, and still be within the zone delineated by Mr. Hitler as a belligerent zone?

THE PRESIDENT. Such a zone—of course, in the first place, we have never been notified of it, and in the second place it was said to be a blockade. Well, of course, everybody knows that a blockade is never recognized unless it is effective. . . .

Source 20 from Russell D. Buhite and David W. Levy, eds., *F.D.R.'s Fireside Chats* (Norman: University of Oklahoma Press, 1992), pp. 189–196.

20. FDR's Fireside Chat, September 11, 1941.

My fellow Americans. The Navy Department of the United States has reported to me that on the morning of September 4, the United States destroyer *Greer*, proceeding in full daylight toward Iceland, had reached a point southeast of Greenland. She was carrying American mail to Iceland. She was flying the American flag. Her identity as an American ship was unmistakable.

She was then and there attacked by a submarine. Germany admits that it was a German submarine. The submarine deliberately fired a torpedo at the *Greer*, followed later by another torpedo attack. In spite of what Hitler's propaganda bureau has invented, and in spite of what any American obstructionist organization may prefer to believe, I tell you the blunt fact that the German submarine fired first upon this American destroyer without warning, and with deliberate design to sink her.

Our destroyer, at the time, was in waters which the government of the United States had declared to be waters of self-defense—surrounding outposts of American protection in the Atlantic.

In the north of the Atlantic, outposts have been established by us in Iceland, in Greenland, in Labrador, and in Newfoundland. Through these waters there pass many ships of many flags. They bear food and other supplies to civilians; and they bear matériel of war, for which the people of the United States are spending billions of dollars, and which, by congressional action, they have declared to be essential for the defense of our own land.

The United States destroyer, when attacked, was proceeding on a legitimate mission.

If the destroyer was visible to the submarine when the torpedo was fired, then the attack was a deliberate attempt by the Nazis to sink a clearly identified American warship. On the other hand, if the submarine was beneath the surface of the sea and, with the aid of its listening devices, fired in the direction of the sound of the American destroyer without even taking the trouble to learn its identity—as the official German communiqué would indicate—then the attack was even more outrageous. For it indicates a policy of indiscriminate violence against any vessel sailing the seas—belligerent or nonbelligerent.

This was piracy—piracy legally and morally. It was not the first nor the last act of piracy which the Nazi government has committed against the American flag in this war. For attack has followed attack. . . .

[*Here Roosevelt listed other attacks and threats, including the sinking of the three U.S. merchant ships, one of them flying the Panamanian flag.*]

In the face of all this, we Americans are keeping our feet on the ground. Our type of democratic civilization has outgrown the thought of feeling compelled to fight some other nation by reason of any single piratical attack on one of our ships. We are not becoming hysterical or losing our sense of proportion. Therefore, what I am thinking and saying tonight does not relate to any isolated episode.

Instead, we Americans are taking a long-range point of view in regard to certain fundamentals, a point of view in regard to a series of events on land and on sea which must be considered as a whole—as a part of a world pattern.

It would be unworthy of a great nation to exaggerate an isolated incident, or to become inflamed by some one act of violence. But it would be inexcusable folly to minimize such incidents in the face of evidence which makes it clear that the incident is not isolated, but is part of a general plan.

The important truth is that these acts of international lawlessness are a manifestation of a design, a design that has been made clear to the American people for a long time. It is the Nazi design to abolish the freedom of

CHAPTER 8

PRESIDENTIAL
LEADERSHIP,
PUBLIC OPINION,
AND THE
COMING OF
WORLD WAR II:
THE USS *GREER*
INCIDENT,
SEPTEMBER 4,
1941

the seas, and to acquire absolute control and domination of these seas for themselves.

For with control of the seas in their own hands, the way can obviously become clear for their next step—domination of the United States, domination of the Western Hemisphere by force of arms. Under Nazi control of the seas, no merchant ship of the United States or of any other American republic would be free to carry on any peaceful commerce, except by the condescending grace of this foreign and tyrannical power. The Atlantic Ocean which has been, and which should always be, a free and friendly highway for us would then become a deadly menace to the commerce of the United States, to the coasts of the United States, and even to the inland cities of the United States.

The Hitler government, in defiance of the laws of the sea, in defiance of the recognized rights of all other nations, has presumed to declare, on paper, that great areas of the seas—even including a vast expanse lying in the Western Hemisphere—are to be closed, and that no ships may enter them for any purpose, except at peril of being sunk. Actually they are sinking ships at will and without warning in widely separated areas both within and far outside of these far-flung pretended zones.

This Nazi attempt to seize control of the oceans is but a counterpart of the Nazi plots now being carried on throughout the Western Hemisphere— all designed toward the same end. For Hitler's advance guards—not only his avowed agents but also, also his dupes among us—have sought to make ready for him footholds, bridgeheads in the New World, to be used as soon as he has gained control of the oceans. . . .

To be ultimately successful in world mastery, Hitler knows that he must get control of the seas. He must first destroy the bridge of ships which we are building across the Atlantic and over which we shall continue to roll the implements of war to help destroy him, to destroy all his works in the end. He must wipe out our patrol on sea and in the air if he is to do it. He must silence the British Navy.

I think it must be explained over and over again to people who like to think of the United States Navy as an invincible protection, that this can be true only if the British Navy survives. And that, my friends, is simple arithmetic.

For if the world outside of the Americas falls under Axis domination, the shipbuilding facilities which the Axis powers would then possess in all of Europe, in the British Isles, and in the Far East would be much greater than all the shipbuilding facilities and potentialities of all of the Americas— not only greater, but two or three times greater—enough to win. Even if the United States threw all its resources into such a situation, seeking to double and even redouble the size of our Navy, the Axis powers, in control of the rest of the world, would have the manpower and the physical resources to outbuild us several times over.

It is time for all Americans, Americans of all the Americas, to stop being deluded by the romantic notion that the Americas can go on living happily and peacefully in a Nazi-dominated world. . . .

The Nazi danger to our Western world has long ceased to be a mere possibility. The danger is here now—not only from a military enemy but from an enemy of all law, all liberty, all morality, all religion.

There has now come a time when you and I must see the cold, inexorable necessity of saying to these inhuman, unrestrained seekers of world conquest and permanent world domination by the sword: "You seek to throw our children and our children's children into your form of terrorism and slavery. You have now attacked our own safety. You shall go no further."

Normal practices of diplomacy—note writing—are of no possible use in dealing with international outlaws who sink our ships and kill our citizens.

One peaceful nation after another has met disaster because each refused to look the Nazi danger squarely in the eye until it had actually had them by the throat.

The United States will not make that fatal mistake.

No act of violence, no act of intimidation will keep us from maintaining intact two bulwarks of American defense: first, our line of supply of material to the enemies of Hitler; and second, the freedom of our shipping on the high seas.

No matter what it takes, no matter what it costs, we will keep open the line of legitimate commerce in these defensive waters of ours.

We have sought no shooting war with Hitler. We do not seek it now. But neither do we want peace so much that we are willing to pay for it by permitting him to attack our naval and merchant ships while they are on legitimate business.

I assume that the German leaders are not deeply concerned, tonight or any other time, by what we Americans or the American government says or publishes about them. We cannot bring about the downfall of Nazism by the use of long-range invective.

But when you see a rattlesnake poised to strike, you do not wait until he has struck before you crush him.

These Nazi submarines and raiders are the rattlesnakes of the Atlantic. They are a menace to the free pathways of the high seas. They are a challenge to our own sovereignty. They hammer at our most precious rights when they attack ships of the American flag—symbols of our independence, our freedom, our very life.

CHAPTER 8

PRESIDENTIAL
LEADERSHIP,
PUBLIC OPINION,
AND THE
COMING OF
WORLD WAR II:
THE USS *GREER*
INCIDENT,
SEPTEMBER 4,
1941

It is clear to all Americans that the time has come when the Americas themselves must now be defended. A continuation of attacks in our own waters, or in waters that could be used for further and greater attacks on us, will inevitably weaken our American ability to repel Hitlerism.

Do not let us be hair-splitters. Let us not ask ourselves whether the Americas should begin to defend themselves after the first attack, or the fifth attack, or the tenth attack, or the twentieth attack.

The time for active defense is now.

Do not let us split hairs. Let us not say, "We will only defend ourselves if the torpedo succeeds in getting home, or if the crew and the passengers are drowned."

This is the time for prevention of attack.

If submarines or raiders attack in distant waters, they can attack equally well within sight of our own shores. Their very presence in any waters which America deems vital to its defense constitutes an attack.

In the waters which we deem necessary for our defense, American naval vessels and American planes will no longer wait until Axis submarines lurking under the water, or Axis raiders on the surface of the sea, strike their deadly blow—first.

Upon our naval and air patrol—now operating in large number over a vast expanse of the Atlantic Ocean—falls the duty of maintaining the American policy of freedom of the seas—now. That means, very simply, very clearly, that our patrolling vessels and planes will protect all merchant ships—not only American ships but ships of any flag—engaged in commerce in our defensive waters. They will protect them from submarines; they will protect them from surface raiders. . . .

My obligation as president is historic; it is clear. Yes, it is inescapable.

It is no act of war on our part when we decide to protect the seas that are vital to American defense. The aggression is not ours. Ours is solely defense.

But let this warning be clear. From now on, if German or Italian vessels of war enter the waters, the protection of which is necessary for American defense, they do so at their own peril.

The orders which I have given as commander in chief of the United States Army and Navy are to carry out that policy—at once.

The sole responsibility rests upon Germany. There will be no shooting unless Germany continues to seek it.

That is my obvious duty in this crisis. That is the clear right of this sovereign nation. This is the only step possible, if we would keep tight the wall of defense which we are pledged to maintain around this Western Hemisphere.

I have no illusions about the gravity of this step. I have not taken it hurriedly or lightly. It is the result of months and months of constant thought and anxiety and prayer. In the protection of your nation and mine it cannot be avoided.

The American people have faced other grave crises in their history—with American courage, with American resolution. They will do no less today.

They know the actualities of the attacks upon us. They know the necessities of a bold defense against these attacks. They know that the times call for clear heads and fearless hearts.

And with that inner strength that comes to a free people conscious of their duty, conscious of the righteousness of what they do, they will—with divine help and guidance—stand their ground against this latest assault upon their democracy, their sovereignty, and their freedom.

Source 21 from *New York Times*, September 16, 1941.

21. Excerpts from Speech by Secretary of the Navy Frank Knox to the American Legion Convention, September 15, 1941.

. . . A German submarine encountered an American destroyer engaged in carrying mail to our outpost on Iceland. The encounter came in broad daylight and the American destroyer carried identification marks which left no possible room for doubt as to its nationality.

At close range the submarine discharged three torpedoes aimed at the American destroyer. The Greer evaded them and promptly attacked the submarine with depth charges. After the second depth-charge attack all contact with the submarine was lost by the destroyer.

Immediately upon receipt of this news, the Navy Department gave the public every fact in its possession, based upon the dispatch direct from the commander of the American destroyer. The German Government countered by saying that the American destroyer had fired the first shot.

The whole issue is far too broad to make the question of who fired first of great importance. I allude to it chiefly because it offered a chance for that curious organization known as "the America First Committee"[15] to tell the American public that, in its judgment, it was more likely the German U-boat commander was telling the truth than the American naval officer who commanded the Greer.

15. Formed in September 1940, the America First Committee was a group that sought to mobilize American public opinion against intervention in the war. At its peak, there were over 800,000 members.

CHAPTER 8

PRESIDENTIAL
LEADERSHIP,
PUBLIC OPINION,
AND THE
COMING OF
WORLD WAR II:
THE USS *GREER*
INCIDENT,
SEPTEMBER 4,
1941

That is an important fact for the American public to digest: that we have in our midst an organization of American citizens who, on a question of veracity, declared publicly that they prefer to accept the word of a piratical murderer of women and children on the high seas, engaged in a type of warfare denounced by every civilized nation in the world, rather than accept the word of an American commander of an American warship. . . .

Source 22 from Leland M. Goodrich, ed., *Documents on American Foreign Relations* (Boston: World Peace Foundation, 1942), Vol. IV, pp. 95–99.

22. Statement of Admiral Harold R. Stark to the Senate Naval Affairs Committee, Undated (Committee Sent the Request for a Statement to Stark on September 5, 1941).

On September 4, 1941, at 08:40 G. C. T., the U.S.S. *Greer*, while en route to Iceland with United States mail and passengers and some freight, was informed by a British plane of the presence of a submerged submarine, distance about 10 miles directly ahead.

This British plane continued in the vicinity of the submarine until 10:52 when she departed. Prior to her departure, at 10:32, she dropped four depth charges in the vicinity of the submarine.

Acting on the information from the British plane the *Greer* proceeded to search for the submarine and at 09:20 she located the submarine directly ahead by her underwater sound equipment. The *Greer* proceeded then to trail the submarine and broadcasted the submarine's position. This action taken by the *Greer* was in accordance with her orders, that is, to give out information but not to attack.

The *Greer* maintained this contact until about 12:48. During this period (3 hours 28 minutes) the *Greer* maneuvered so as to keep the submarine ahead.

At 12:40 the submarine changed course and closed the *Greer*.

The disturbance of the surface and the change in color of the water marking the passage of the submarine was clearly distinguished by the *Greer*.

At 12:48 an impulse bubble (indicating the discharge of a torpedo by the submarine) was sighted close aboard the *Greer*.

At 12:49 a torpedo track was sighted crossing the wake of the ship from starboard to port, distant about 100 yards astern.

At 12:56 the *Greer* attacked the submarine with a pattern of eight depth charges.

At 12:58 a second torpedo track was sighted on the starboard bow of the *Greer,* distant about 500 yards. The *Greer* avoided this torpedo.

At this time the *Greer* lost sound contact with the submarine.

At 13:00 the *Greer* started searching for the submarine and at 15:12 in latitude 62–43 N., longitude 27–22 W., the *Greer* made underwater contact with a submarine. The *Greer* attacked immediately with depth charges.

In neither of the *Greer*'s attacks did she observe any results which would indicate that the attacks on the submarine had been effective.

The *Greer* continued search until 18:40, at which time she again proceeded toward her destination, Iceland.

From the above it is clearly evident that the *Greer,* though continuously in contact with the submarine for 3 hours 28 minutes, did not attack the submarine although the *Greer* herself was exposed to attack.

At no time did the *Greer* sight the submarine's periscope.

The weather was good.

The commander-in-chief of the Atlantic Fleet corroborates the above report in detail and further states that the action taken by the *Greer* was correct in every particular in accordance with her existing orders.

H. R. Stark

Questions Addressed to the Secretary of the Navy, by the Chairman of the Senate Naval Affairs Committee, and Proposed Answers Thereto, in Connection with the "Greer" Incident

QUESTION 1. Did the incident take place in an area declared to be blockaded by the German Government?

ANSWER. The *Greer* incident took place in an area approximately 175 miles southwest of Iceland, and directly in the path of communication between American ports and Iceland. This area was within the zone of operations announced by the German Government on March 26, 1941, as a zone within which vessels entering exposed themselves "to the danger of destruction."

QUESTION 2. Did the *Greer* have orders from the Department to proceed through this area?

ANSWER. The *Greer* had orders from the commander-in-chief of the Atlantic Fleet to proceed through the area. The Navy Department had full knowledge of this.

QUESTION 3. Were any other ships in company with, or in sight of, the *Greer* just before or at any time during the encounter? If so, (*a*) what were the names and nationality of these vessels, and (*b*) did any of these ships take part in the encounter either directly or indirectly?

CHAPTER 8

PRESIDENTIAL
LEADERSHIP,
PUBLIC OPINION,
AND THE
COMING OF
WORLD WAR II:
THE USS *GREER*
INCIDENT,
SEPTEMBER 4,
1941

ANSWER. A British destroyer was in sight about 5 miles distant from the *Greer* when the *Greer* made a depth bomb attack at 15:12. This British destroyer had arrived on the scene at 14:15 and had asked the *Greer* if she (the *Greer*) desired to conduct a coordinated search for the submarine. To this question, the *Greer* replied "No." The British destroyer stood through the area and disappeared to the southward.

QUESTION 4. Were any airplanes in sight of, or in communication with, the *Greer* just before or during the encounter? If so, (*a*) what were the nationality of these planes, and (*b*) did any of these planes furnish any information to the *Greer* or take part either directly or indirectly in the encounter?

ANSWER. Yes. At 08:40, a British plane approached the U.S.S. *Greer* and signaled that a submarine had submerged about 10 miles directly ahead of the *Greer*. The plane furnished no further assistance to the *Greer*. At 10:32, this plane dropped four depth charges in the vicinity of the submarine and, at 10:52, the plane departed from the area. It should be particularly noted that this plane left the area at 10:52 and did not return, and that the *Greer* fired no guns or torpedoes or dropped any depth charges until 12:56—some 8 minutes after the submarine fired a torpedo at the *Greer*—or, in other words, over 2 hours after the British plane had left the scene.

QUESTION 5. Was the commanding officer of the *Greer* informed that a submarine was operating in this vicinity before his vessel was attacked or before the submarine or her periscope was seen? If so, when and from whom did he receive this information?

ANSWER. Yes. See answer to preceding question. The periscope of the submarine was not seen at any time by the *Greer*.

QUESTION 6. If he had information from an outside source that there was a submarine in the vicinity, (*a*) did he change his course and speed and start a search for the submarine; (*b*) how long did he search for the submarine before he was fired upon; and (*c*) did other vessels or planes assist in this search?

ANSWER. As soon as information was received by the *Greer* from the British plane that a submarine was directly ahead of her, the *Greer* increased speed, started zigzagging, and commenced a search for the submarine. Five minutes after the search began, namely, at 09:20, the *Greer* located the submarine by her underwater sound equipment; she held this contact until 12:48, namely, 3 hours 28 minutes before the submarine made her attack. No assistance by either planes or ships was given to the *Greer* during this period.

QUESTION 7. If he first learned of the presence of the submarine from his submarine detection device or from sighting it, (*a*) did he change his course to search for or head for the submarine; or (*b*) would he have been out of range of the submarine's torpedoes if he had continued on his course?

ANSWER. The first part of this question is answered by the answer to the preceding question. As to the second part of this question, the answer is problematical. No person can predict what the submarine's course would have been. The answer, therefore, might be "Yes" or it might be "No."

QUESTION 8. How many torpedoes were fired at the *Greer* and at what intervals were they fired? How long was it after the submarine was sighted or first heard that the first torpedoes were fired? How near did the torpedoes come to hitting the ship?

ANSWER. Two torpedoes were fired at the *Greer*. The firing of the first one was indicated by the sighting of the impulse bubble at 12:48, just 3 hours and 28 minutes after the *Greer* first detected the submarine by means of her sound equipment. At 12:49 the wake of this torpedo was observed about 100 yards astern. At 12:58 the wake of a second torpedo was observed 500 yards distant on the starboard bow. The *Greer* avoided it, the torpedo passing about 300 yards clear of the ship.

QUESTION 9. How many depth charges were dropped by the *Greer* and at what intervals?

ANSWER. U.S.S. *Greer* dropped 8 depth charges, commencing at 12:56; 11 depth charges were dropped, commencing at 15:12. All these depth charges were dropped after the first torpedo had been fired at the *Greer*.

QUESTION 10. Has anything been seen or heard from this submarine since the last depth charges were dropped by the *Greer*?

ANSWER. Not by the U.S.S. *Greer*, nor has the Department any word.

[*The remainder of the questions concerned the deck log of the* Greer *(which Stark refused to make public) and whether the German embassy had issued any official explanation of the incident (it had not).*]

CHAPTER 8

PRESIDENTIAL
LEADERSHIP,
PUBLIC OPINION,
AND THE
COMING OF
WORLD WAR II:
THE USS *GREER*
INCIDENT,
SEPTEMBER 4,
1941

Source 23 from *Congressional Record—Senate,* 77th Cong., 1st sess., pp. 8283–8284.

23. Excerpt from Speech by Senator Robert A. Taft (R, Ohio), October 28, 1941.

Mr. President the whole approach of the administration today seems to be one of war. I think it is fair to say—at least, the impression given from the newspapers is—that the administration welcomes every incident which may possibly lead to war. Those incidents are not reported in the usual way. They are announced by the President at a press conference. They are sent out to the whole world as something by which, on the whole, the government is delighted. The story of the *Greer* was told by the President, it seems to me, in such a way as deliberately to incite more feeling than was justified by the actual event which occurred. He said, for instance: "Our destroyer at the time was in waters which the government of the United States had declared to be waters of self-defense, surrounding outposts of American protection in the Atlantic. The United States destroyer, when attacked, was proceeding on a legitimate mission."

As a matter of fact, the facts which came out much later before a committee, when the public had forgotten the *Greer,* show that it was in the neighborhood of a submarine of which it was told by a British destroyer which was also there; that after it had located the submarine a British plane came and dropped four depth bombs; and that the *Greer* then turned off its course and chased the submarine for three hours and twenty minutes, zigzagging in the way that a vessel would zigzag if it were going to attack a submarine. Whether or not the submarine was justified in finally shooting a torpedo, whether or not it thought this was a joint British-American attack, certainly the President's report of the incident was made in such a way as deliberately to incite the American people. No man who sincerely desired peace would have failed to state the actual circumstances. . . .

Mr. President, I may say that convoying was proposed last spring, but there was so much opposition to convoys that authority to convoy never was specifically presented to Congress. Apparently without such presentation we now have the United States engaging in convoying. But the point I wanted to make is that the whole intention of the administration, every indication that a reasonable man can draw from its acts, is that it intends to go into war; and certainly, if we pass this resolution, and the administration has such an intention, we are going very shortly to become involved in war.

There is no argument made today that, after all, we are already at war, and therefore we should not hesitate to go on and vote authority to conduct war. The power to declare war rests solely in the United States Congress. If the President can declare or create an undeclared naval war beyond our power to act upon, the Constitution might just as well be abolished. The Constitution deliberately gave to the representatives of the people the power to declare war, to pass on the question of war and peace, because that was something which kings had always done, which they had done against the interests of the people themselves, and which the founders of the Constitution thought the people ought to determine. It is true there have been one or two acts of war; but if Congress will refuse to repeal the Neutrality Act, I do not believe those acts of war can be continued. . . .

QUESTIONS TO CONSIDER

Almost immediately you will see that you will have to rearrange the evidence *twice:* once to answer the first question (What actually happened on September 4, 1941?) and a second time to answer the second question (What was the relationship between President Roosevelt's actions and American public opinion?). Although at first you may feel that rearranging the evidence twice will be too time-consuming, in fact it should save you a great amount of time, principally because several pieces of evidence may be set aside when answering either of the two questions (for example, Sources 1 through 11 are of no use in answering the first question).

To determine what actually happened in the *Greer* incident, Sources 12 through 23 all have a bearing. And yet a number of these accounts are at serious variance with one another. Lieutenant T. H. Copeman, who composed the *Greer's* deck log, and the author of U-652's report obviously were the two sources closest to the incident itself. Do those two accounts (Sources 12 and 13) vary in any sig-

nificant way? Are there any reasons that they should not be judged the most believable accounts? Since he was the only other source presented to you who actually saw the *Greer's* deck log, does Admiral Stark's account (Source 22) differ in any important way with the deck log itself? How do the three German sources (Sources 16 through 18) corroborate or fail to corroborate the two eyewitness accounts (Sources 16 and 17, obviously, by inference, since these two sources were written long before the incident itself)?

The *New York Times*'s account of the incident (Sources 14 and 15) contain some significant errors. What are those errors? Why do you think this was so? What were the *Times*'s sources?

The accounts by President Roosevelt (Sources 19 and 20) and by Secretary of the Navy Frank Knox (Source 21) also appear to contain some important inaccuracies. What are they? Do you think that FDR and Knox were misinformed? Did they know what actually had occurred? If they did, what

CHAPTER 8

PRESIDENTIAL
LEADERSHIP,
PUBLIC OPINION,
AND THE
COMING OF
WORLD WAR II:
THE USS *GREER*
INCIDENT,
SEPTEMBER 4,
1941

possible motivation might they have had for not being truthful?

Taft (Source 23) was a fierce Republican opponent of the president. Moreover, he was against American intervention in the war in Europe. What point does Taft make regarding the *Greer* incident? With what does he charge Roosevelt? How believable are those charges?

After examining and analyzing each source (especially as to any motivation behind each source's account), you should be able to answer the first question: What actually happened in the *Greer* incident?

In order to answer the second question, you will have to make use of Dr. George Gallup's polling data (Sources 1 through 11). You are looking for any changes or shifts in public opinion. For example, Gallup's poll taken April 10–15, 1941 (Source 2), revealed that 50 percent of those surveyed did not think the U.S. Navy should guard ships carrying war materiel to Britain. Yet by the time that question was next asked (on August 21–26, Source 6), fully 52 percent thought that the U.S. Navy should do so—and only 39 percent opposed. How might Roosevelt have interpreted that shift?

You will have to establish whether any significant events took place from one polling date to another. Consult your textbook as well as the Background section of this chapter, and ask your instructor to help you fill in the gaps. For example, the massive German bombing of England in 1940 clearly had an effect on American public opinion. Fill in the important events between the Gallup polls. Pay special attention to any speeches or actions of President Roosevelt. After doing this, can you establish whether Roosevelt was shaping public opinion (therefore ahead of it), was waiting for shifts in public opinion before taking action, or both—sometimes leading and sometimes following? How were his remarks about the *Greer* incident (Sources 19 and 20) perhaps intended to shape public opinion? Or did the polls (especially Sources 4 through 6) allow the president to detect an important shift in public opinion that would make his policy shift announced in the September 11 fireside chat acceptable to Americans? See Source 7, a poll taken after the fireside chat. Was Roosevelt shaping public opinion, following it, or both?

EPILOGUE

President Roosevelt's policy shift of September 11, 1941 (escorting convoys of Lend-Lease goods and shooting on sight German submarines), clearly put the United States on a collision course with the Third Reich. It was only a matter of time before a U.S. naval vessel would be hit by a U-boat torpedo. On October 16–17, the USS *Kearny,* speeding to the aid of a convoy that was under attack, dropped depth charges into the water and almost immediately was hit by a German torpedo. The *Kearny* limped to port under escort. Then, on the night of October 30–31, the USS *Reuben*

James was sunk by a torpedo while escorting a convoy west of Iceland, with a loss of 115 American sailors. Americans were outraged, and public opinion decidedly shifted against Germany. Congress amended the Neutrality Act to allow American ships to take Lend-Lease supplies to Britain. Clearly the United States had abandoned its neutral posture. And yet, because the vote in the House of Representatives to extend the draft had passed by only one vote and because Hitler wanted no diversions from his life-and-death struggle against the Soviet Union,[15] no actual declaration of war came from either side. Nevertheless, a shooting war had begun in the Atlantic.

And yet as Americans concentrated their attention on the nation's slipping into war in Europe, it was United States–Japanese relations that ultimately brought the United States into World War II. Relations between the two countries had been testy since the National Origins Act of 1929 almost completely banned the immigration of all Asians, a move that Japan considered a racial slap in the face. When Japan invaded Manchuria in September 1931, the United States refused to recognize Japan's conquests or its puppet government in Manchuria and sided with China against Japan. On September 27, 1940, Japan signed the Tripartite Pact with Germany and Italy, promising that if the United States joined Great Britain in the Atlantic war, then Japan would attack the United States in the Pacific, whereas if the United States declared war on Japan, then Germany and Italy would declare war on the United States. Relations went from bad to worse as the United States, increasingly committed to China as well as to blocking Japanese expansion, moved to freeze all Japanese assets in the United States, cut off petroleum exports to Japan, and ultimately clamp a total trade embargo on Japan. On December 7, 1941, Japanese dive bombers and torpedo planes attacked Pearl Harbor in Hawaii. On December 8, Congress declared war on Japan, and on December 11 the German Reichstag declared war on the "half Judaized and the other half Negrified" American people. After nearly two years of slipping precariously toward conflict, the United States at last was a combatant in World War II.

One of Franklin Roosevelt's biographers, James MacGregor Burns, described him as a lion and a fox. British prime minister Winston Churchill and many historians have concluded that Roosevelt had made up his mind to enter the war in Europe as early as January 1941, when the British and American military staffs held secret talks in Washington on a "broad design for the joint defense of the Atlantic Ocean" and on preparations for joint convoys of Lend-Lease goods.[17] Yet Roosevelt did not believe that the American public would support a war against Germany in January 1941. Instead, he would have to wait for public opinion to shift—or he would have to shape that opinion. The *Greer* incident

---

16. After signing the Non-Aggression Pact with Stalin, on June 22, 1941, Hitler attacked the Soviet Union in what was known as Operation Barbarossa.

17. Winston S. Churchill, *The Grand Alliance,* Vol. III of *The Second World War* (Boston: Houghton Mifflin Co., 1950), pp. 137–138.

CHAPTER 8

PRESIDENTIAL
LEADERSHIP,
PUBLIC OPINION,
AND THE
COMING OF
WORLD WAR II:
THE USS *GREER*
INCIDENT,
SEPTEMBER 4,
1941

may have been a pivotal event on the road to war.

U-652 escaped the *Greer*'s depth charges and went on to sink two British destroyers on March 20 and 26, 1942. The submarine was severely damaged by an air attack in the Aegean Sea in June 1942 and was sunk by U-81 after the crew had been recovered.

The USS *Greer* served throughout the war and was decommissioned on July 19, 1945. The destroyer was sold for scrap to the Boston Metal Salvage Company of Baltimore, Maryland, on November 30, 1945.

CHAPTER 9

SEPARATE BUT EQUAL?
AFRICAN AMERICAN EDUCATIONAL
OPPORTUNITIES AND THE
BROWN DECISION

↶ THE PROBLEM ↷

In the mid-1890s, Homer Plessy took his seat in a passenger coach on a Louisiana train. Plessy's racial heritage was seven-eighths Caucasian and one-eighth African American, and the railroad compartment in which he was sitting was reserved for whites. Asked to vacate his seat and move to the compartment reserved for blacks, Plessy refused and was arrested. He had violated an 1890 Louisiana law that required separate railroad accommodations for African Americans and for whites. People who broke the law by sitting in the wrong compartment or coach were fined twenty-five dollars or, if they could not pay, had to serve twenty days in jail. Plessy sued, and the case eventually reached the U.S. Supreme Court on appeal.

The majority opinion in *Plessy v. Ferguson* was that the Louisiana law was constitutional.[1] Because it provided for "separate but equal" accommodations, the law had not violated any rights guaranteed by the Fourteenth Amendment. In other words, states could legally segregate blacks and whites as long as they provided "separate but equal" facilities for African Americans. In an impassioned dissent, Justice John Marshall Harlan disagreed. "Our Constitution is color-blind," he argued, "and neither knows nor tolerates classes among citizens." But Harlan's opinion was not sup-

1. Seven justices agreed with the majority opinion, one abstained, and one (Harlan) dissented.

CHAPTER 9

SEPARATE
BUT EQUAL?
AFRICAN
AMERICAN
EDUCATIONAL
OPPORTUNITIES
AND THE
BROWN DECISION

ported by other judges or by the general public.

In fact, for almost sixty years *Plessy v. Ferguson* provided a powerful basis for other judicial decisions upholding segregation laws. Finally, in *Brown v. Board of Education of Topeka* (1954), the U.S. Supreme Court unanimously declared that separate but equal schools were unconstitutional. Why did the Court reverse itself after so many years? In this chapter, you will be asked to identify some of the major arguments that finally caused the Supreme Court to change its thinking.

 BACKGROUND

In the aftermath of the Civil War, much of the South was in economic and political chaos. Struggles between President Andrew Johnson and the Radical Republicans over who should control Reconstruction meant delay and confusion in readmitting the former Confederate states to the Union and providing economic relief where it was most needed. After nearly removing President Johnson from office, however, the Radicals were able to implement their plans in Congress.

Perhaps no other question of the Reconstruction era was more troublesome and divisive than that of the role of the newly freed slaves. Three amendments to the U.S. Constitution were intended to settle the legal questions: the Thirteenth Amendment that freed the slaves, the Fourteenth Amendment that defined citizenship and extended the protection of the Bill of Rights to citizens of the separate states, and the Fifteenth Amendment that gave African American men the vote. Would the freed slaves have full political rights? Should they be given land to farm? Could they be protected against discrimination and violence? Although African Americans briefly enjoyed some political rights and protection, by the late nineteenth century all these questions had been answered negatively. The South had returned to white political control, the Ku Klux Klan and other vigilante groups had limited African American opportunities, and the sharecropping, tenant farming, and crop lien systems had impoverished poor whites and blacks alike. Furthermore, the Union army had withdrawn, and the federal Civil Rights Act of 1875 had been declared unconstitutional. As ordinary people in the North and West turned their attention to their own problems, African Americans in the South were left to fend for themselves.

In 1900, approximately 7 million of the nation's 10 million African Americans lived in the rural South, although more and more younger African Americans were leaving the grinding poverty of the farms and moving to nearby cities and towns seeking better opportunities. The Black Codes of the Reconstruction era had evolved into Jim Crow laws that segregated everything from schools and parks to hospitals and cemeteries, while lynching took the lives of seventy-five to one hundred African American men each year. The trickle of African Americans moving North was accelerated by World War I; almost half a million southern blacks moved to northern cities such as Chicago, Cleveland, and Philadelphia to obtain jobs during the war.

By 1920, there were a million and a half African Americans in northern cities. Although rarely segregated by law and permitted to vote, nevertheless they usually faced pervasive discrimination in their search for housing and jobs. Membership in the National Association for the Advancement of Colored People (NAACP) grew steadily as a new black middle class increasingly identified with the civil rights program of W. E. B. Du Bois rather than the accommodationist message of Booker T. Washington.

In the 1920s, a section of New York City called Harlem became the center for a ferment of African American cultural creativity, the Harlem Renaissance. Poets, novelists, artists, actors, dancers, and musicians all explored ways to express their African American experience. Well-to-do whites often supported such efforts and patronized Harlem night spots such as the Cotton Club. Harlem was also badly overcrowded, with decaying housing, epidemic disease, widespread unemployment, and a rising crime rate. The Harlem Renaissance had little meaning for many poor blacks who had recently emigrated from the South. For these newcomers, Jamaican-born Marcus Garvey and his Universal Negro Improvement Association seemed to offer a more practical alternative. Glorifying black cultural

roots and sponsoring cooperative business ventures, Garvey also called on African Americans to return to Africa to found a new nation.

Garvey was convicted of fraud, imprisoned, and finally deported in the late 1920s, and the Harlem Renaissance was submerged by the stock market crash of 1929 and the ensuing depression. Both urban and rural blacks suffered extreme hardships during the Great Depression. New Deal urban relief programs were administered locally, and generally African Americans were among the last to receive aid. In the rural South, the New Deal agricultural policies had the unintended result of causing the eviction of sharecroppers and tenant farmers. Violence against African Americans also increased during the depression.

Not until the 1940s did the situation of African Americans begin to improve. In many ways, World War II was a turning point. From the beginning, black leaders declared a "Double V" campaign: a fight against fascism abroad and a fight against racism at home. The NAACP, with a half million members by the end of the war, was joined by the newly formed Congress of Racial Equality (CORE). While the NAACP pursued a strategy of boycotts and legal challenges, CORE began to experiment with nonviolent protests against racial discrimination during the 1940s. Full war production opened up new economic opportunities, nearly a million more African Americans continued the exodus from the South to northern cities, and almost a million blacks served in the armed forces. In spite of some serious race

CHAPTER 9

SEPARATE
BUT EQUAL?
AFRICAN
AMERICAN
EDUCATIONAL
OPPORTUNITIES
AND THE
BROWN DECISION

riots during 1943, African Americans entered the postwar era with rising expectations of equality.

Nowhere were these demands for equality more insistent or pressing than in education. For more than a decade, NAACP lawyers had been involved in cases testing the validity of state segregation laws. By the early 1950s, the Supreme Court had begun strictly scrutinizing separate but equal education to determine whether it really was equal. In 1938, the Court heard a case where a young African American college graduate and Missourian, Lloyd Gaines, had been denied entry into the University of Missouri law school because he was black.[2] There was no black law school in Missouri, so the state had offered to pay his tuition to any law school in a neighboring state that would accept him. Gaines had been denied equal protection of the laws, the Supreme Court ruled, because Missouri had not provided the same opportunities to black students as it had to white students. Ten years later, a similar case, involving a young woman, Ada Sipuel, who was refused admission to the law school of the University of Oklahoma because of her race, was decided the same way.[3]

In two cases decided in 1950, the Supreme Court expanded the understanding of separate but equal. A black graduate student, George McLaurin, had been admitted to the University of Oklahoma, but was forced to sit at special tables in the cafeteria and in the library and to sit in a separate row in his classes. This was *not* equal treatment, the Court declared.[4] In the second case, *Sweatt v. Painter,* a black student was denied admission to the University of Texas law school.[5] The state then built two new law schools for African Americans. When the Supreme Court justices compared the faculties, curricula, and libraries of the black and white schools, however, they found substantial inequalities. The opinion went even further, noting that intangible factors such as alumni networks, traditions, and prestige were also superior at the University of Texas Law School. Finally, the Court noted that no student could really learn to practice law at a school that was isolated from 85 percent of the population of the state.

All of these cases involved graduate or professional training and were decided on the question of the *equality* of the facilities. The plaintiffs won these cases because their educational facilities or opportunities were unequal to those provided for whites. In each case, then, *Plessy v. Ferguson* and the doctrine of separate but equal still formed the basis for the decision. Furthermore, the Supreme Court had clearly stated its reluctance to decide any broad constitutional issues, preferring instead to focus on specific questions raised by specific cases. "We have frequently reiterated that this Court will decide constitutional questions only when necessary to the disposition of the case at hand," wrote Chief Justice Fred Vinson in *Sweatt v. Painter* (1950), "and that such deci-

2. *Missouri ex rel. Gaines v. Canada,* 305 U.S. 337 (1938).
3. *Sipuel v. Board of Regents of the University of Oklahoma,* 332 U.S. 631 (1948).

4. *McLaurin v. Oklahoma State Regents,* 339 U.S. 637 (1950).
5. *Sweatt v. Painter,* 339 U.S. 629 (1950).

sions will be drawn as narrowly as possible."

In spite of the cautious stance of the Supreme Court, significant trends and events during the late 1940s and early 1950s were creating a climate more supportive of African American civil rights. The Nazi Holocaust that killed 6 million Jews and the cold war confrontations with the Soviet Union made Americans more aware of the democratic ideals of the United States. In his widely read book, *The America Dilemma,* sociologist Gunnar Myrdal had pointed out America's shortcomings with regard to race relations, and many whites began to feel guilty about the typical treatment of African Americans in the United States. An outpouring of social science literature also focused on inequality and its effects. Popularized through paperback books, middle-class magazines, and television, much of this research seems relatively unsophisticated by our standards today, although it was pioneering in its time period. For example, Professor Kenneth Clark of City College of New York did research to determine the effects of racial segregation on young African American children. After giving the children identical pink dolls or brown dolls (or pictures of the two sets of dolls), Clark asked the children which dolls were "nice," which dolls were "bad," and which doll the child would rather play with. The majority of the African American children preferred the white doll, identifying the white doll as "nice" and the brown doll as "bad." Such research not only was widely publicized but was also used in court cases by the NAACP to demonstrate the negative psychological effects of segregated schooling on African American children.

Finally, the personnel of the Supreme Court itself had begun to change. Five justices were still serving who had been appointed by President Franklin D. Roosevelt between 1937 and 1941, and President Truman had appointed four new justices between 1945 and 1949. After the Court had started to consider the *Brown* case, the relatively conservative chief justice, Fred Vinson, died suddenly from a heart attack at age sixty-three, and President Eisenhower appointed the more liberal Earl Warren, a former governor of California, to replace Vinson as chief justice.

In 1951, Topeka, Kansas, was a pleasant city of approximately 100,000 residents, 7,500 of whom were African American. The state capital, Topeka, had a city college, a good public library, several city parks, a major psychiatric research institute, and more than 100 churches. It was also segregated. Jim Crow laws and local customs prevented blacks from using white hotels, restaurants, movies, and the municipal swimming pool, and the elementary schools were segregated.

Oliver Brown was a thirty-two-year-old World War II veteran, union member, welder, and assistant pastor of his church. Not a militant, he was not even a member of the NAACP. The Browns lived in a racially mixed neighborhood near a railroad yard, and their oldest daughter, Linda, had to walk about six blocks through the tracks to get to her school bus stop. A white elementary school was located only seven blocks in the other direction from her house, but it refused to accept her because she was an African

CHAPTER 9

SEPARATE
BUT EQUAL?
AFRICAN
AMERICAN
EDUCATIONAL
OPPORTUNITIES
AND THE
BROWN DECISION

American. Brown reported this to the local NAACP and became the first plaintiff in the suit against the Board of Education of Topeka.

In spite of assistance from the national NAACP and the presentation of nationally known social science experts who testified about the negative effects of segregated education, Brown and the other plaintiffs lost the case. The school facilities and other measurable educational factors at the white and black elementary schools were roughly equal, the Kansas court said, referring to the precedent set by the *Plessy* case in 1896. Thus, the segregated schools were legal. However, the Kansas District Court also attached several "Findings of Fact" to its opinion, including one that directly reflected the impact of the social science evidence the NAACP had introduced. "Segregation . . . has a detrimental effect upon the colored children," wrote the judge, and he concluded that legal segregation created a sense of inferiority that tended "to retard the educational and mental development of Negro children and to deprive them of some of the benefits they would receive in a racially integrated school system."

By the fall of 1952, five cases challenging the constitutionality of racially segregated schools had been appealed to the U.S. Supreme Court. In addition to Kansas, South Carolina, Virginia, Delaware, and the District of Columbia plaintiffs all argued that although the educational facilities for whites and African Americans were equal (or were in the process of being equalized), racial segregation itself was unconstitutional because it violated the equal protection clause of the Fourteenth Amendment.[6] The five cases were argued together late in 1952, and the next spring, the Court asked for a reargument in the fall term of 1953. The first part of the decision was not announced until May 1954. *Brown I,* as it came to be called, declared that racially segregated education was indeed unconstitutional. The Court then called for another reargument, this time to determine how the desegregation decision should be implemented. In May 1955, after unusually long oral arguments, the Court announced in *Brown II* that there would be a flexible timetable for desegregation, which would be overseen by the federal district courts.

What persuaded the U.S. Supreme Court to reverse its thinking after upholding the constitutionality of segregation since *Plessy v. Ferguson* in 1896? What were some of the major arguments that changed the justices' opinions?

⌒ THE METHOD ⌒

Whenever possible, courts make decisions based on *precedents:* similar cases that other courts have already decided that lay out a direction for new decisions to follow. As we have seen, *Plessy v. Ferguson* (1896), the case that upheld racial segregation if

6. Because Washington, D.C., was not a state, this case was argued on the basis of the Fifth Amendment.

separate but equal facilities were provided, was just such a precedent. For the next sixty years, the courts had simply decided whether the racially segregated facilities were equal and never considered the effects of segregation itself. But in *Brown v. the Board of Education of Topeka, Kansas,* and the four other cases argued at the same time, everyone agreed that the facilities were basically equal or were being equalized. The question now was whether segregation itself violated the Constitution.

Cases are argued before the U.S. Supreme Court in two stages. First, lawyers for both sides submit written arguments called *briefs*. These briefs discuss the factual background of the case and, more important, develop a legal, constitutional argument supporting the decision that they believe the Court should make. In *Brown* and the other cases, the defendants basically argued that segregated education was not unconstitutional because equal facilities had been provided, and the plaintiffs insisted, based on social science research, that racial segregation itself caused inequality in education.

With permission, organizations and individuals who are not directly involved in the case may also file briefs explaining their interest and stating their opinions about the case. Seven of these *amicus curiae* (friend of the court) briefs were filed in the initial phase of the *Brown* school segregation cases, *Brown I,* and they reflect important changes in public opinion about African Americans and equality. Eventually some two dozen *amicus* briefs were filed, including those that the U.S. Supreme Court invited for *Brown*

II from the attorneys general of all the southern states that permitted or required segregated educational facilities.

In the second stage, oral argument, lawyers speak for a limited time to clarify points in their briefs and to answer any questions the justices might have. At the time of the *Brown* case, Robert Carter and Thurgood Marshall were lawyers for the NAACP's Legal Defense and Educational Fund. Carter later became general counsel for the NAACP, and Thurgood Marshall served as a U.S. circuit court judge and then as solicitor general of the United States. He was appointed to the U.S. Supreme Court in 1967. The defense attorneys were either hired by the school system being sued or provided by the attorney general's office of that particular state. In both cases, they were paid by taxpayers' money. John W. Davis represented the defendants in the South Carolina case, *Briggs v. Elliot,* which the U.S. Supreme Court considered along with *Brown* and the three other school cases. Widely admired by other attorneys, Davis had served as a U.S. congressman, U.S. solicitor general, ambassador to Great Britain, and president of the American Bar Association. In 1922, he had declined a nomination to the U.S. Supreme Court, and in 1924 he had run unsuccessfully for president of the United States.

Finally, after considerable discussion among themselves, the justices reach a decision. Since a Supreme Court decision affects so many people's lives either directly or indirectly, it usually contains a carefully worded explanation of the Court's reasoning. Justices who do not agree with the de-

CHAPTER 9

SEPARATE
BUT EQUAL?
AFRICAN
AMERICAN
EDUCATIONAL
OPPORTUNITIES
AND THE
BROWN DECISION

cision may write a dissent, but the decision in the *Brown* case was unanimous. In this chapter, you will read the relevant section of the Fourteenth Amendment, identify the arguments used in the early *amicus curiae* briefs and the oral exchanges between the lawyers and the Court, and study excerpts from the *Brown I* decision to explain why the Supreme Court decided that racially segregated education was unconstitutional.

 THE EVIDENCE

Source 1 from U.S. Constitution, Fourteenth Amendment.

1. First Section of the Fourteenth Amendment to the Constitution.

All persons born or naturalized in the United States, and subject to the jurisdiction thereof, are citizens of the United States and of the State wherein they reside. No State shall make or enforce any law which shall abridge the privileges or immunities of citizens of the United States; nor shall any State deprive any person of life, liberty, or property, without due process of law; nor deny to any person within its jurisdiction the equal protection of the laws.

Source 2 from the *amicus curiae* briefs for *Brown v. Board of Education of Topeka, Kansas,* 347 U.S. 483 (1954).

2. Excerpts from the *Amicus Curiae* Briefs, 1952.

AMERICAN VETERANS COMMITTEE, INC. (AVC)

The American Veterans Committee (AVC) is a nationwide organization of veterans who served honorably in the Armed Forces of the United States during World Wars I and II, and the Korean conflict. We are associated to promote the democratic principles for which we fought, including the elimination of racial discrimination. Most of us served overseas. There was no "community pattern" of racial discrimination and segregation when the chips were down and there was only the mud, the foxholes, and the dangers of the ocean and of mortal battle in the fight to preserve our Nation's democratic ideals. We believe that the segregation here involved is of the same cloth as the racism against which we fought in World War II, and that its continuance is detrimental to our national welfare, both at home and abroad.

AMERICAN JEWISH CONGRESS

The American Jewish Congress is an organization committed to the principle that the destinies of all Americans are indissolubly linked and that any act which unjustly injures one group necessarily injures all. . . .

Believing as we do that Jewish interests are inseparable from the interests of justice, the American Jewish Congress cannot remain impassive or disinterested when persecution, discrimination or humiliation is inflicted upon any human being because of his race, religion, color, national origin or ancestry. Through the thousands of years of our tragic history we have learned one lesson well: the persecution at any time of any minority portends the shape and intensity of persecution of all minorities. . . .

CONGRESS OF INDUSTRIAL ORGANIZATIONS (CIO)

. . . The CIO is an organization dedicated to the maintenance and extension of our democratic rights and civil liberties and therefore has a deep interest in the elimination of segregation and discrimination from every phase of American life.

The CIO's interest is also direct and personal. The CIO . . . is endeavoring to practice non-segregation and non-discrimination in the everyday functioning of union affairs. Repeatedly in the past this endeavor has been obstructed by statutes, ordinances, and regulations which require segregation in public dining places, public meeting halls, toilet facilities, etc. These laws attempt to require CIO unions to maintain "equal but separate" facilities in their own semi-public buildings, despite the avowed desire of the membership to avoid segregation in any form. . . .

AMERICAN FEDERATION OF TEACHERS

In a broad sense, the consequence [of segregation] is a denial of the highest ends of education, both to the dominant and minority groups. In an atmosphere of inequality, it is no more feasible to teach the principles of our American way to the white children than to the Negroes. The apparent insincerity of such teaching is as destructive to the moral sense of the majority as to the sense of justice of the minority. . . .

[247]

CHAPTER 9

SEPARATE
BUT EQUAL?
AFRICAN
AMERICAN
EDUCATIONAL
OPPORTUNITIES
AND THE
BROWN DECISION

For if justice is relative and depends on race or color how can we teach that ours is a government of laws and not of men? And if justice is relative and considers race and color then a different flag waves over a colored school and the pledge to the flag must mean different things. The one nation is really not one nation but at least two, it is found to be divisible, and liberty, like justice, has two meanings. . . .

FEDERATION OF CITIZENS' ASSOCIATIONS OF [WASHINGTON,] D.C.

The undersigned submit this brief because our organizations represent groups of Americans in the Washington community and throughout the nation of many creeds and many races who are deeply committed to the preservation and extension of the democratic way of life and who reject as inimical to the welfare and progress of our country artificial barriers to the free and natural association of peoples, based on racial or creedal differences. We believe this to be of especial importance in the Nation's capital. We are united in the belief that every step taken to make such differences irrelevant in law, as they are in fact, will tend to cure one of our democracy's conspicuous failures to practice the ideals we proclaim to the world, and to bring us closer to that peace and harmony with other peoples throughout the world for which we all strive.

ATTORNEY GENERAL OF THE UNITED STATES

This contention [*about the unconstitutionality of segregation*] raises questions of the first importance in our society. For racial discriminations imposed by law, or having the sanction or support of government, inevitably tend to undermine the foundations of a society dedicated to freedom, justice, and equality. The proposition that all men are created equal is not mere rhetoric. It implies a rule of law—an indispensable condition to a civilized society—under which all men stand equal and alike in the rights and opportunities secured to them by their government. . . . The color of a man's skin—like his religious beliefs, or his political attachments, or the country from which he or his ancestors came to the United States—does not diminish or alter his legal status or constitutional rights. . . .

It is in the context of the present world struggle between freedom and tyranny that the problem of racial discrimination must be viewed. The United States is trying to prove to the people of the world, of every nationality, race, and color, that a free democracy is the most civilized and most secure form of government yet devised by man. We must set an example for others by showing firm determination to remove existing flaws in our democracy.

Source 3 from *Oral Arguments of the Supreme Court of the U.S.* (Frederick, Md. University Publications, 1984).

3. Excerpts from the Oral Arguments.

BROWN, 1952

MR. CARTER. We have one fundamental contention which we will seek to develop in the course of this argument, and that contention is that no state has any authority under the equal protection clause of the Fourteenth Amendment to use race as a factor in affording educational opportunities among its citizens. . . .

JUSTICE MINTON. Mr. Carter, I do not know whether I have followed you on all the facts on this. Was there a finding that the only basis of classification was race or color?

MR. CARTER. It was admitted—the appellees admitted in their answer—that the only reason that they would not permit Negro children to attend the eighteen white schools was because they were Negroes.

JUSTICE MINTON. Then we accept on this record that the only showing is that the classification here was solely on race and color?

MR. CARTER. Yes, sir. I think the state itself concedes this is so in its brief.

BRIGGS v. ELLIOTT, 1952

MR. MARSHALL. I want to point out that our position is not that we are denied equality in these cases [because of inferior physical facilities.]. . . . We are saying that there is a denial of equal protection of the laws. . . .

So pursuing that line, we produced expert witnesses. . . .

Witnesses testified that segregation deterred the development of the personalities of these children. Two witnesses testified that it deprives them of equal status in the school community, that it destroys their self-respect. Two other witnesses testified that it denies them full

CHAPTER 9

SEPARATE
BUT EQUAL?
AFRICAN
AMERICAN
EDUCATIONAL
OPPORTUNITIES
AND THE
BROWN DECISION

opportunity for democratic social development. Another witness said that it stamps him with a badge of inferiority.

The summation of that testimony is that the Negro children have road blocks put up in their minds as a result of this segregation, so that the amount of education that they take in is much less than other students take in. . . .

MR. DAVIS. If the Court please, when the Court arose on yesterday, I was reciting the progress that had been made in the public school system in South Carolina, and with particular reference to the improvement of the facilities, equipment curricular, and opportunities accorded to the colored students. . . .

Now what are we told here that has made all that body of activity and learning [all the state legislatures that passed segregation laws and all the court decisions upholding segregation] of no consequence? Says counsel for the plaintiffs . . . we have the uncontradicted testimony of expert witnesses that segregation is hurtful, and in their opinion hurtful to the children of both races, both colored and white. These witnesses severally described themselves as professors, associate professors, assistant professors, and one describes herself as a lecturer and advisor on curricular. I am not sure exactly what that means.

I did not impugn the sincerity of these learned gentlemen and lady. I am quite sure that they believe that they are expressing valid opinions on their subject. But there are two things notable about them. Not a one of them is under any official duty in the premises whatever; not a one of them has had to consider the welfare of the people for whom they are legislating or whose rights they were called on to adjudicate. And only one of them professes to have the slightest knowledge of conditions in the states where separate schools are now being maintained. Only one of them professes any knowledge of the conditions within the seventeen segregating states.

Rebuttal

MR. MARSHALL. May it please the Court, so far as the appellants are concerned in this case, at this point it seems to me that the significant factor running through all these arguments up to this point is that for some reason, which is still unexplained, Negroes are taken out of the mainstream of American life in these states.

There is nothing involved in this case other than race and color, and I do not need to go into the background of the statutes or anything else. I just read the statutes, and they say, "White and colored."

While we are talking about the feeling of the people in South Carolina, I think we must once again emphasize that under our form of government, these individual rights of minority people are not to be left to even the most mature judgement of the majority of the people, and that the only testing ground as to whether or not individual rights are concerned is in this Court.

BRIGGS v. ELLIOTT REARGUMENT, 1953

MR. DAVIS. Let me say this for the State of South Carolina. It does not come here as Thad Stevens[7] would have wished in sack cloth and ashes. It believes that its legislation is not offensive to the Constitution of the United States.

It is confident of its good faith and intention to produce equality for all of its children of whatever race or color. It is convinced that the happiness, the progress and the welfare of these children is best promoted in segregated schools. . . .

I am reminded—and I hope it won't be treated as a reflection on anybody—of Aesop's fable of the dog and the meat: The dog, with a fine piece of meat in his mouth, crossed a bridge and saw the shadow in the stream and plunged for it and lost both substance and shadow.

Here is equal education, not promised, not prophesied, but present. Shall it be thrown away on some fancied question of racial prestige?

MR. MARSHALL. It gets me . . . to one of the points that runs throughout the argument . . . on the other side, and that is that they deny that there is any race prejudice involved in these cases. They deny that there is any intention to discriminate.

But throughout the brief and throughout the argument they not only recognize that there is a race problem involved, but they emphasize that that is the whole problem. And for the life of me, you can't read the debates [about the passage of the Fourteenth Amendment], even the sections they rely on, without an understanding that the Fourteenth Amendment took away from the states the power to use race.

As I understand their position, their only justification for this [race] being a reasonable classification is, one, that they got together and decided that it is best for the races to be separated and, two, that it has existed for over a century. . . .

7. Thaddeus Stevens (1792–1868) was a lifelong abolitionist and leader of the Radical Republicans.

CHAPTER 9

SEPARATE
BUT EQUAL?
AFRICAN
AMERICAN
EDUCATIONAL
OPPORTUNITIES
AND THE
BROWN DECISION

Those same kids in Virginia and South Carolina—and I have seen them do it—they play in the streets together, they play on their farms together, they go down the road together, they separate to go to school, they come out of school and play ball together. They have to be separated in school.

There is some magic to it. You can have them voting together, you can have them not restricted because of law in the houses they live in. You can have them going to the same state university and the same college, but if they go to elementary and high school, the world will fall apart. And it is the same argument that has been made to this Court over and over again. . . .

Source 4 from *Brown v. Board of Education of Topeka, Kansas, et al.* (1954).

4. Excerpts from the *Brown I* Decision.

[*Chief Justice Warren began by noting that all the cases had a common argument: that segregated public schools were not "equal," could not be made "equal," and thus denied African Americans the equal protection of the laws. He then briefly reviewed the inconclusive nature of information about the intent of the framers of the Fourteenth Amendment, the separate but equal doctrine established by the* Plessy *case, and the subsequent cases involving racially segregated education that had been before the Supreme Court. He concluded that the Court must focus on "the effect of segregation itself on public education."*]

In approaching this problem, we cannot turn the clock back to 1868 when the Amendment was adopted, or even to 1896 when *Plessy v. Ferguson* was written. We must consider public education in the light of its full development and its present place in American life throughout the Nation. Only in this way can it be determined if segregation in public schools deprives these plaintiffs of the equal protection of the laws.

Today, education is perhaps the most important function of state and local governments. Compulsory school attendance laws and the great expenditures for education both demonstrate our recognition of the importance of education to our democratic society. It is required in the performance of our most basic public responsibilities, even service in the armed forces. It is the very foundation of good citizenship. Today it is a principal instrument in awakening the child to cultural values, in preparing him for later professional training, and in helping him to adjust normally to his environment. In these days, it is doubtful that any child may reasonably be expected to succeed in life if he is denied the opportunity of an education. Such an opportunity, where the state has undertaken to provide it, is a right which must be available to all on equal terms.

We come then to the question presented: Does segregation of children in public schools solely on the basis of race, even though the physical facilities and other "tangible" factors may be equal, deprive the children of the minority group of equal educational opportunities? We believe that it does.

[*Warren reviewed the findings of the Court and social science literature that segregation resulted in feelings of inferiority and hindered the development of African American children.*]

We conclude that in the field of public education the doctrine of "separate but equal" has no place. Separate educational facilities are inherently unequal. . . .

[*Noting the variety of local conditions and wide applicability of the desegregation decision, Warren asked the plaintiffs, their opponents, the attorney general of the United States, and the attorneys general of the states that would be affected to appear again before the Court in reargument, stating how they believed the Court's desegregation decision should be put into effect.*]

 QUESTIONS TO CONSIDER

The Fourteenth Amendment was added to the U.S. Constitution after the Civil War. The first section (Source 1) was intended to protect the newly freed slaves against the actions of the states, in the same way that the Bill of Rights protects U.S. citizens against the actions of the central government. What are some of the "privileges and immunities" of the Bill of Rights? What do you think is meant by "due process of law"? By "equal protection of the laws"?

The *amicus* briefs (Source 2) provide important clues to changing public opinion about racial discrimination. What are the specific, major arguments of the groups representing veterans, American Jews, labor unions of the CIO, unionized teachers, and Washington, D.C., citizens' organizations? Why does the U.S. attorney general argue against segregation?

The excerpts from the oral arguments (Source 3) are from the first hearing of *Brown* and the four other cases in 1952, and the reargument ordered by the Court in 1953. Remember that Robert Carter and Thurgood Marshall were the NAACP lawyers for the plaintiffs, and John W. Davis was one of the lawyers for the defense.

What was the fundamental argument Carter established in the *Brown* case? Why was it important? What was Marshall's major argument about the effects of racially segregated education? How did Davis respond? On what

CHAPTER 9

SEPARATE
BUT EQUAL?
AFRICAN
AMERICAN
EDUCATIONAL
OPPORTUNITIES
AND THE
BROWN DECISION

bases did Davis reject the findings of the NAACP's expert witnesses? What are the two major points of Marshall's rebuttal?

In the reargument, Davis used a story about a dog with some meat to make his point. What exactly *was* his point? How does Marshall summarize his opponents' defense of segregation? What is the point of his story about African American and white children?

Finally, analyze the arguments put forth by Chief Justice Earl Warren in *Brown I* (Source 4). What does he mean when he writes, "We cannot turn the clock back"? Why does the Court believe that education is so important?

Now you are ready to summarize. What were the major arguments that persuaded the Supreme Court to overturn the doctrine of separate but equal that had been established by *Plessy v. Ferguson*?

EPILOGUE

In less controversial cases, once the U.S. Supreme Court has announced a decision, all those affected by it comply voluntarily. Progress in desegregating the school systems, however, was slow and uneven. In some areas of the South that had practiced legal segregation, change came fairly easily and peacefully. In other areas, widespread public hostility escalated into mob violence. Some systems, such as the Prince Edward County, Virginia, school district that was part of the original Supreme Court suits, simply abolished the public schools rather than desegregate. Ten years after the *Brown* decision, only about 10 percent of African American students in southern states were attending desegregated schools.

By the late 1960s, the federal government and U.S. court system had established new guidelines and timetables that accelerated desegregation in southern schools. Using the *Brown* decision as a precedent, the Supreme Court had also ordered the desegrega-

tion of public beaches, golf courses, and other recreational facilities throughout the South. By the 1970s, African American civil rights groups began to focus their attention on northern cities, where racially separate housing patterns had resulted in all-black and all-white neighborhood schools, but court-ordered busing of students in order to integrate education in these cities created hostility and often accelerated "white flight" to the suburbs. For example, by the early 1970s after riots, real estate "block busting," and busing, Detroit, Michigan, had so few remaining white residents that all its public schools were predominantly African American.

Although the *Brown* decision did not bring about complete and immediate desegregation of all schools, its significance should not be underrated. Segregation laws based on race were struck down, and for the newly expanding African American middle class, *Brown* was a milestone, a case that established new ideals for public education. Looking back, African American leaders have said that they were greatly encouraged in their struggle for further civil rights by the decision. Clearly the decision also created opportunities for political organizations based on racial hatred that opposed the African American freedom marches and voter registration drives of the 1960s. Yet the television and newspaper coverage of racial confrontations such as those in Birmingham, Alabama, also galvanized public opinion outside the South in support of such far-reaching civil rights legislation as the Civil Rights Act of 1964 and the Voting Rights Act of 1965. Today, more than forty years after the *Brown* decision, Americans are still striving to achieve equal educational opportunities for all.

CHAPTER 10

A GENERATION IN WAR AND TURMOIL: THE AGONY OF VIETNAM

∽ THE PROBLEM ∽

When the middle-class readers of *Time* magazine went to their mailboxes in January 1967, they were eager to find out who the widely read newsmagazine had chosen as "Man of the Year." To their surprise, they discovered that the "Inheritors"—the whole generation of young people under twenty-five years of age—had been selected as the major newsmakers of the previous year. *Time*'s publisher justified the selection of an entire generation by noting that, in contrast to the previous "silent generation," young people of the late 1960s were dominating history with their distinctive lifestyles, music, and beliefs about the future of the United States.

Those who wrote to the editor about this issue ranged from a writer who thought the selection was a long-overdue honor to one who called it an "outrageous choice," from a correspondent who described contemporary young people as "one of our best generations" to one who believed the choice of a generation was "eloquent nonsense." Furthermore, many writers were frightened or worried about their children, and some middle-aged correspondents insisted that they themselves belonged to the "put-upon" or "beaten" generation.

There is no doubt that there was a generation gap in the late 1960s, a kind of sharp break between the new generation of young people comprising nearly half the population and their parents. The first segment of the "baby-boom" generation came to adulthood during the mid- to late 1960s,[1] a time marked by the high

1. Although the birthrate began to climb during World War II (from 19.4 births per 1,000 in 1940 to 24.5 in 1945), the term *baby boom* generally is used to describe the increase in the birthrate between 1946 and the early 1960s.

point of the civil rights movement, the rise of a spirit of rebellion on college campuses, and serious divisions in America over the United States' participation in the Vietnam War. For most baby boomers, white and black alike, the war was the issue that concerned them most immediately, for this was the generation that would be called on to fight or to watch friends, spouses, or lovers called to military service.

Your task in this chapter is to identify and interview at least one member of the baby-boom generation (prefer- ably born between 1946 and 1956)[2] about his or her experiences during the Vietnam War era. Then, using your interview, along with those of your classmates and those provided in the Evidence section of this chapter, determine the ways in which the baby-boom generation reacted to the Vietnam War. On what issues did baby boomers agree? On what issues did they disagree? Finally, how can a study of birth cohorts (groups of people of the same generation) help historians to understand a particular era in the past?

 ## BACKGROUND

The year 1945 was the beginning of the longest sustained economic boom in American history. Interrupted only a few times by brief recessions, the boom lasted from 1945 to 1973. And although there were still pockets of severe poverty in America's deteriorating inner cities and in some rural areas such as Appalachia, most Americans had good cause to be optimistic about their economic situations.

The pent-up demand of the depression and war years broke like a tidal wave that swept nearly every economic indicator upward. Veterans returning from World War II rapidly made the transition to the civilian work force or used the GI Bill to become better educated and, as a result, secure better jobs than they had held before the war. Between 1950 and 1960, real wages increased by 20 percent, and disposable family income rose by a staggering 49 percent. The number of registered automobiles more than doubled between 1945 and 1955, and the American automobile industry was virtually unchallenged by foreign competition. At the same time, new home construction soared, as 13 million new homes were built in the 1950s alone—85 percent of them in the new and mushrooming suburbs.[3]

New homes were financed by new types of long-term mortgage loans that required only a small down payment (5 to 10 percent) and low monthly payments (averaging $56 per month for a tract house in the suburbs). And these new homes required furniture and appliances, which led to sharp upturns in these industries. Between 1945 and 1950, the amount

2. A person born during the late 1950s and early 1960s would technically be considered a baby boomer but would probably have been too young to remember enough to make an interview useful.
3. There were 114,000 housing starts in 1944. In 1950, housing starts had climbed to 1,692,000.

CHAPTER 10

A GENERATION
IN WAR AND
TURMOIL: THE
AGONY OF
VIETNAM

spent on household furnishings and appliances increased 240 percent, and most of these items were bought "on time" (installments).[4] Perhaps the most coveted appliance was a television set, a product that had been almost nonexistent before the war. In 1950 alone, 7.4 million television sets were sold in the United States, and architects began designing homes with a "family room," a euphemism for a room where television was watched.

This new postwar lifestyle could best be seen in America's burgeoning suburbs. Populated to a large extent by new members of the nation's mushrooming middle class, suburbanites (as they were called) for the most part were better educated, wealthier, and more optimistic than their parents had been. Most men commuted by train, bus, or automobile back to the center city to work, while their wives remained in the suburbs, having children and raising them. It was in these suburbs that a large percentage of baby boomers were born.

Sociologist William H. Whyte called America's postwar suburbs the "new melting pot," a term that referred to the expectation that new middle-class suburbanites should leave their various class and ethnic characteristics behind in the cities they had abandoned and become homogeneous. Men were expected to work their way up the corporate ladder, tend their carefully manicured lawns, become accom-

plished barbecue chefs, and serve their suburban communities as Boy Scout leaders or Little League coaches. For their part, women were expected to make favorable impressions on their husband's bosses (to aid their husbands in their climb up the corporate ladder), provide transportation for the children to accepted after-school activities (scouts, athletics, music and dance lessons), and make a happy home for the family's breadwinner. Above all, the goal was to fit in with their suburban neighbors. Thus suburbanites would applaud the 1956 musical *My Fair Lady,* which was based on the premise that working-class flower seller Eliza Doolittle would be accepted by "polite society" as soon as she learned to speak properly.

The desire for homogeneity (or conformity) would have a less beneficial side as well. The cold war and the McCarthy era meant that the demand for homogeneity could be enforced by the threat of job loss and ostracism. In addition, many suburban women had met their husbands in college and hence had had at least some college education.[5] But the expectation that they be primarily wives and mothers often meant that they were discouraged from using their education in other ways. As a result, one survey of suburban women revealed that 11 percent of them felt that they experienced a "great deal of emotional distur-

4. Between 1946 and 1956, short-term consumer credit rose from $8.4 billion to almost $45 billion, most of it to finance automobiles and home furnishings. The boom in credit card purchases ("plastic money") did not occur until the 1960s.

5. One midwestern women's college boasted that "a high proportion of our graduates marry successfully," as if that was the chief reason for women to go to college in the first place. Indeed, in many cases it was. See Elaine Tyler May, *Homeward Bound: American Families in the Cold War Era* (New York: Basic Books, 1988), p. 83.

bance." At the same time, men were expected to be good corporate citizens and good team players at work. It was rumored that IBM employees began each day by gathering together, facing the home office, and singing the praises of IBM and its executive vice president C. A. Kirk (to the tune of "Carry Me Back to Old Virginny"):

> Ever we praise our able leaders,
> And our progressive C. A. Kirk is one of them,
> He is endowed with the will to go forward,
> He'll always work in the cause of IBM.

Finally, homogeneity meant that suburbanites would have to purchase new cars, furniture, television sets, and so on to be like their neighbors (it was called "keeping up with the Joneses"), even though monthly payments already were stretching a family's income pretty thin.

There was an underside to the so-called affluent society. Indeed, many Americans did not share in its benefits at all. As middle-class whites fled to the suburbs, conditions in the cities deteriorated. Increasingly populated by the poor—African Americans, Latin American immigrants, the elderly, and unskilled white immigrants—urban areas struggled to finance essential city services such as police and fire protection. Moreover, poverty and its victims could be found in rural areas, as Michael Harrington pointed out in his classic study *The Other America,* published in 1962. Small farmers, tenants, sharecroppers, and migrant workers not only were poor but often lacked any access to even basic educa-

tional opportunities and health care facilities.

Young people who lacked the money or who were not brought up with the expectation of earning a college degree tended to continue in more traditional life patterns. They completed their education with high school or before, although others attended a local vocationally oriented community college or trade school for a year or two. They often married younger than their college counterparts, sought stable jobs, and aspired to own their own homes. In other words, they rarely rejected the values of their parents' generation.

The baby boomers began leaving the suburbs for college in the early 1960s. Once away from home and in a college environment, many of these students began questioning their parents' values, especially those concerned with materialism, conformity, sexual mores and traditional sex roles, corporate structure and power, and the kind of patriotism that could support the growing conflict in Vietnam. In one sense, they were seeking the same thing that their parents had sought: fulfillment. Yet to the baby boomers, their parents had chased false gods and a false kind of fulfillment. Increasingly alienated by impersonal university policies and by the actions of authority figures such as college administrators, political leaders, and police officers, many students turned to new forms of religion, music, and dress and to the use of drugs to set themselves apart from the older generation. The term *generation gap* could be heard across the American landscape as bewildered, hurt, and an-

CHAPTER 10

A GENERATION
IN WAR AND
TURMOIL: THE
AGONY OF
VIETNAM

gry parents confronted their children, who (in the parents' view) had "gotten everything." Nor could the children seem to communicate to their confused parents how bankrupt they believed their parents' lives and values actually were. In the midst of this generational crisis, the Vietnam War was becoming a major conflict.

The Japanese defeat of Western colonial powers, particularly Britain and France, in the early days of World War II had encouraged nationalist movements[6] in both Africa and Asia. The final surrender of Japan in 1945 left an almost total power vacuum in Southeast Asia. As Britain struggled with postwar economic dislocation and, within India, the independence movement, both the United States and the Soviet Union moved into this vacuum, hoping to influence the course of events in Asia.

Vietnam had long been a part of the French colonial empire in Southeast Asia and was known in the West as French Indochina. At the beginning of World War II, the Japanese had driven the French from the area. Under the leadership of Vietnamese nationalist (and communist) Ho Chi Minh, the Vietnamese had cooperated with American intelligence agents and fought a guerrilla-style war against the Japanese. When the Japanese were finally driven from Vietnam in 1945, Ho Chi Minh declared Vietnam independent.

The Western nations, however, did not recognize this declaration. At the end of World War II, France wanted to reestablish Vietnam as a French col-

6. Those in nationalist movements seek independence for their countries.

ony. But seriously weakened by war, France could not reassert itself in Vietnam without assistance. At this point, the United States, eager to gain France as a postwar ally and member of the North Atlantic Treaty Organization, and viewing European problems as being more immediate than problems in Asia, chose to help the French reenter Vietnam as colonial masters. From 1945 to 1954, the United States gave more than $2 billion in financial aid to France so that it could regain its former colony. U.S. aid was contingent upon the eventual development of self-government in French Indochina.

Ho Chi Minh and other Vietnamese felt that they had been betrayed. They believed that in return for fighting against the Japanese in World War II, they would earn their independence. Many Vietnamese viewed the reentry of France, with the United States' assistance, as a broken promise. Almost immediately, war broke out between the French and their Westernized Vietnamese allies and the forces of Ho Chi Minh. In the cold war atmosphere of the late 1940s and early 1950s, the United States gave massive aid to the French, who, it was maintained, were fighting against monolithic communism.

The fall of Dien Bien Phu in 1954 spelled the end of French power in Vietnam. The U.S. secretary of state, John Foster Dulles, tried hard to convince Britain and other Western allies of the need for "united action" in Southeast Asia and to avoid any use of American ground troops (as President Truman had authorized earlier in Korea). The allies were not persuaded, however. Rather than let the area fall to the communists, President Eisenhower and his secretary of state eventually allowed the temporary division of Vietnam into two sections: South Vietnam, ruled by Westernized Vietnamese formerly loyal to the French, and North Vietnam, governed by the communist Ho Chi Minh.

Free and open elections to unify the country were to be held in 1956. However, the elections were never held because American policymakers feared that Ho Chi Minh would easily defeat the unpopular but pro–United States Ngo Dinh Diem, the United States' choice to lead South Vietnam. From 1955 to 1960, the United States supported Diem with more than $1 billion of aid as civil war between the South Vietnamese and the Northern Vietminh (later called the Vietcong) raged across the countryside and in the villages.

President Kennedy did little to improve the situation. Facing his own cold war problems, among them the building of the Berlin Wall and the Bay of Pigs invasion,[7] Kennedy simply poured more money and more "military advisers" (close to seventeen thousand by 1963) into the troubled country. Finally, in the face of tremendous Vietnamese pressure, the United States turned against Diem, and in 1963 South Vietnamese generals, encouraged by the Central Intelligence Agency, overthrew the corrupt and repressive Diem regime. Diem was assassinated in the fall of 1963, shortly before Kennedy's assassination.

Lyndon Johnson, the Texas Democrat who had succeeded Kennedy in 1963 and won election as president in 1964, was an old New Dealer[8] who wished to extend social and economic programs to needy Americans. The "tragedy" of Lyndon Johnson, as the official White House historian, Eric Goldman, saw it, was that the president was increasingly drawn into the Vietnam War. Actually, President Johnson and millions of other Americans still perceived Vietnam as a major test of the United States' willingness to resist the spread of communism.

Under Johnson, the war escalated rapidly. In 1964 the Vietcong controlled almost half of South Vietnam, and Johnson obtained sweeping powers from Congress[9] to conduct the war as he wished. Bombing of North Vietnam and Laos was increased, refugees were moved to "pacification" camps, entire villages believed to be unfriendly were destroyed, chemical defoliants were sprayed on forests to eliminate Vietcong hiding places, and troops increased until by 1968 about 500,000 American men and women were serving in Vietnam.

As the war effort increased, so did the doubts. In the mid-1960s, the chair of the Senate Foreign Relations Com-

7. The Berlin Wall was a barricade created to separate East Berlin (communist) from West Berlin. The Bay of Pigs invasion was a United States–sponsored invasion of Cuba in April 1961 that failed. The American role was widely criticized.

8. Johnson served in Congress during the 1930s and was a strong supporter of New Deal programs.
9. The Tonkin Gulf Resolution gave Johnson the power to "take all necessary measures to repel any armed attack against the forces of the United States and to prevent further aggression."

CHAPTER 10

A GENERATION
IN WAR AND
TURMOIL: THE
AGONY OF
VIETNAM

mittee, J. William Fulbright, raised important questions about whether the Vietnam War was serving our national interest. Several members of the administration and foreign policy experts (including George Kennan, author of the original containment policy) maintained that escalation of the war could not be justified. Television news coverage of the destruction and carnage, along with reports of atrocities such as the My Lai massacre,[10] disillusioned more and more Americans. Yet Johnson continued the bombing, called for more ground troops, and offered peace terms that were completely unacceptable to the North Vietnamese.

Not until the Tet offensive—a coordinated North Vietnamese strike across all of South Vietnam in January 1968, in which the communists captured every provincial capital and even entered Saigon (the capital of South Vietnam)—did President Johnson change his mind. Two months later, Johnson appeared on national television and announced to a surprised nation that he had ordered an end to most of the bombing, asked North Vietnam to start real peace negotiations, and withdrawn his name from the 1968 presidential race. Although we now know that the Tet offensive was a setback for Ho Chi Minh, in the United States it was seen as a major setback for the West, evidence that the optimistic press releases about our imminent victory simply were not true.

As the United States' role in the Vietnam War increased, the government turned increasingly to the conscription of men for military service (the draft). Early in the war, all college men up to age twenty-six could get automatic deferments, which allowed them to remain in school while noncollege men (disproportionately poor and black) were drafted and sent to Vietnam. As the demand for men increased, however, such deferments became somewhat more difficult to obtain. College students had to maintain good grades, graduate student deferments were ended, and draft boards increasingly were unsympathetic to pleas for conscientious objector status.[11] Even so, the vast majority of college students who did not want to go to Vietnam were able to avoid doing so, principally by using one of the countless loopholes in the system (ROTC [Reserve Officers' Training Corps] duty, purposely failing physical examinations, getting family members to pull strings, obtaining conscientious objector status, and so on). Only 12 percent of the college graduates between 1964 and 1973 served in Vietnam (21 percent of high school graduates and an even higher percentage of high school dropouts served).

As the arbitrary and unfair nature of the draft became increasingly evident, President Richard Nixon finally replaced General Lewis Hershey (who had headed the Selective Service System since 1948) and instituted a new system of conscription: a lottery. In

10. This incident occurred in March 1968, when American soldiers destroyed a Vietnamese village and killed many of the inhabitants, including women and children.

11. Conscientious objectors are those whose religious beliefs are opposed to military service (such as the Society of Friends, or Quakers).

this system, draft-age men were assigned numbers and were drafted in order from lowest to highest number until the draft quota was filled. With this action, the very real threat of the draft spread to those who had previously felt relatively safe. Already divided, an entire generation had to come face to face with the Vietnam War.

THE METHOD

Historians often wish they could ask specific questions of the participants in a historical event—questions that are not answered in surviving diaries, letters, and other documents. Furthermore, many people, especially the poor, uneducated, and members of minority groups, did not leave written records and thus often are overlooked by historians.

But when historians are dealing with the comparatively recent past, they do have an opportunity to ask questions by using a technique called oral history. Oral history—interviewing famous and not-so-famous people about their lives and the events they observed or participated in—can greatly enrich knowledge of the past. It can help the historian capture the "spirit of an age" as seen through the eyes of average citizens, and it often bridges the gap between impersonal forces (wars, epidemics, depressions) and personal and individual responses to them. Furthermore, oral history allows the unique to emerge from the total picture: the conscientious objector who would not serve in the army, the woman who did not marry and devote herself to raising a family, and so forth.

Oral history is both fascinating and challenging. It seems easy to do, but it is really rather difficult to do well. There is always the danger that the student may "lead" the interview by imposing his or her ideas on the subject. Equally possible is that the student may be led away from the subject by the person being interviewed.

Still other problems sometimes arise: The student may miss the subtleties in what is being said or may assume that an exceptional person is representative of many people. Some older people like to tell only the "smiling side" of their personal history— that is, they prefer to talk about the good things that happen to them, not the bad things. Others actually forget what happened or are influenced by reading or television. Some older people cannot resist sending a message to younger people by recounting how hard it was in the past, how few luxuries they had when they were young, how far they had to walk to school, and so forth. Yet oral history, when used carefully and judiciously along with other sources, is an invaluable tool that helps one re-create a sense of our past.

Recently, much attention has been paid—and rightly so—to protecting the rights and privacy of human subjects. For this reason, the federal government requires that the interviewee

CHAPTER 10

A GENERATION
IN WAR AND
TURMOIL: THE
AGONY OF
VIETNAM

consent to the interview and be fully aware of how the interview is to be used. The interviewer must explain the purpose of the interview, and the person being interviewed must sign a release form (for samples, see Sources 1 through 3). Although these requirements are intended to apply mostly to psychologists and sociologists, historians who use oral history are included as well.

When you identify and interview an individual of the baby-boom generation, you will be speaking with a member of a *birth cohort*. A birth cohort comprises those people born within a few years of one another who form a historical generation. Members of a birth cohort experience the same events—wars, depressions, assassinations, as well as personal experiences such as marriage and childbearing—at approximately the same age and often have similar reactions to them. Sociologist Glen Elder showed that a group of people who were relatively deprived as young children during the Great Depression grew up and later made remarkably similar decisions about marriage, children, and jobs. Others have used this kind of analysis to provide insights into British writers of the post–World War I era and to explain why the Nazi party appealed to a great many young Germans.

Yet even within a birth cohort, people may respond quite differently to the same event(s). *Frame of reference* refers to an individual's *personal background,* which may influence that person's beliefs, responses, and actions. For example, interviews conducted with Americans who lived during the Great Depression of the 1930s reveal that men and women often coped differently with unemployment, that blacks and whites differed in their perceptions of how hard the times were, and that those living in rural areas had remarkably different experiences from city dwellers.

In this chapter, all the interviewees belong to the generation that came of age during the Vietnam War. Thus, as you analyze their frames of reference, age will not give you any clues. However, other factors, such as gender, race, socioeconomic class, family background, values, region, and experiences, may be quite important in determining the interviewees' frames of reference and understanding their responses to the Vietnam War. When a group of people share the same general frame of reference, they are a generational subset who tend to respond similarly to events. In other words, it may be possible to form tentative generalizations from the interviewees about how others with the same general frames of reference thought about and responded to the Vietnam War. To assist you in conducting your own interview of a member of the baby-boom generation (or birth cohort), we have included some instructions for interviewers and a suggested interview plan.

Instructions for Interviewers

1. Establish the date, time, and place of the interview well in advance. You may wish to call and remind the interviewee a few days before your appointment.

2. Clearly state the purpose of the interview *at the beginning*. In other words, explain why the class is doing this project.

3. Prepare for the interview by carefully reading background information about the 1960s and by writing down and arranging the questions you will be asking to guide the interview.

4. It is usually a good idea to keep most of your major questions broad and general so the interviewee will not simply answer with a word or two ("How did you spend your leisure time?"). Specific questions such as, "How much did it cost to go to the movies?" are useful for obtaining more details.

5. Avoid "loaded" questions, such as, "Everyone hated President Lyndon Johnson, didn't they?" Instead, keep your questions neutral: "What did you think about President Lyndon Johnson and his Vietnam strategy?"

6. If any of your questions involve controversial matters, it is better to ask them toward the end of the interview, when the interviewee is more comfortable with you.

7. Always be courteous, and be sure to give the person enough time to think, remember, and answer. Never argue, even if he or she says something with which you strongly disagree. Remember that the purpose of the interview is to find out what *that person* thinks, not what you think.

8. Always take notes, even if you are tape-recording the interview. Notes will help clarify unclear portions of the tape and will be essential if the recorder malfunctions or the tape is accidentally erased.

9. Many who use oral history believe that the release forms should be signed at the beginning of the interview; others insist that this often inhibits the person who is to be interviewed and therefore should not be done until the end of the session. Although students who are using the material only for a class exercise are not always held strictly to the federal requirements, it is still better to obtain a signed release. Without such a release, the tape cannot be heard and used by anyone else (or deposited in an oral history collection), and the information the tape contains cannot be published or made known outside the classroom.

10. Try to write up the results of your interview as soon as possible after completing it. Even in rough form, these notes will help you capture the sense of what was said as well as the actual information that was presented.

A Suggested Interview Plan

Remember that the person you have chosen to interview is a *person,* with feelings, sensitivities, and emotions. If you intend to tape-record the interview, ask permission first. If you believe that a tape recorder will inhibit the person you have selected, leave it at home and rely on your ability to take notes.

CHAPTER 10

A GENERATION
IN WAR AND
TURMOIL: THE
AGONY OF
VIETNAM

The following suggestions may help you get started. People usually remember the personal aspects of their lives more vividly than they remember national or international events. That is a great advantage in this exercise because what you are attempting to find out is how this person lived during the 1960s. Begin by getting the following important data on the interviewee:

1. Name
2. Age in 1968
3. Race, sex
4. Where the person lived in the 1960s and what the area was like then
5. Family background (what the interviewee's parents did for a living; number of brothers and sisters; whether the interviewee considered himself or herself rich, middle class, or poor)
6. Educational background

Then move on to the aspects of the person's life that will flesh out your picture of the 1960s and early 1970s.

1. Was the person in college at any time? What was college life like during the period?
2. If the person was not in college, what did he or she do for a living? Did he or she live at home or away from home?
3. How did the person spend his or her leisure time? If unmarried, did the person go out on dates? What was dating like? Did he or she go to the movies (if so, which ones)? Did he or she watch much television (if so, which shows)?

These questions should give you a fairly good idea of how the person lived during the period. Now move on to connect the interviewee with the Vietnam War.

1. Did the person know anyone who volunteered or was drafted and sent to Vietnam? How did the interviewee feel about that? Did the person lose any relatives or friends in Vietnam? What was his or her reaction to that?
2. (Male) Was the person himself eligible for the draft? Did he volunteer for the service or was he drafted? Was he sent to Vietnam? If so, what were some memorable Vietnam experiences? What did the person's family think of his going to Vietnam? (Female) If you intend to interview a female who went to Vietnam as a nurse, alter the above questions.
3. Was the person a Vietnam War protester? If so, what was that experience like? If not, did the person know any Vietnam War protesters? What did the person think of them?
4. Did the person know anyone who tried to avoid going to Vietnam? What did the person think of that?

Finally, review the national events and people of the Vietnam era and develop some questions to ask your interviewee about these events and people. As you can see, you have guided the interview through three stages, from personal information and background to the interviewee's reactions to a widening sphere of experiences and events.

↬ **THE EVIDENCE** ↬

Sources 1 and 2 from Collum Davis, Kathryn Back, and Kay MacLean, *Oral History: From Tape to Type* (Chicago: American Library Association, 1977), pp. 14, 15.

1. Sample Unconditional Release for an Oral Interview.

<u>Tri-County Historical Society</u>

For and in consideration of the participation by <u>Tri-County Historical Society</u> in any programs involving the dissemination of tape-recorded memories and oral history material for publication, copyright, and other uses, I hereby release all right, title, or interest in and to all of my tape-recorded memoirs to <u>Tri-County Historical Society</u> and declare that they may be used without any restriction whatsoever and may be copyrighted and published by the said <u>Society,</u> which may also assign said copyright and publication rights to serious research scholars.

In addition to the rights and authority given to you under the preceding paragraph, I hereby authorize you to edit, publish, sell and/or license the use of my oral history memoir in any other manner which the <u>Society</u> considers to be desirable and I waive any claim to any payments which may be received as a consequence thereof by the <u>Society.</u>

PLACE   <u>Indianapolis,</u>
             <u>Indiana</u>
DATE   <u>July 14, 1975</u>

<u>   Harold S. Johnson   </u>
(Interviewee)

<u>   Jane Rogers   </u>
(for <u>Tri-County Historical Society</u>)

CHAPTER 10

A GENERATION
IN WAR AND
TURMOIL: THE
AGONY OF
VIETNAM

2. Sample Conditional Release for an Oral Interview.

Tri-County Historical Society

I hereby release all right, title, or interest in and to all or any part of my tape-recorded memoirs to   Tri-County Historical Society,   subject to the following stipulations:

That my memoirs are to be *closed* until five years following my death.

PLACE   Indianapolis,

Indiana

DATE   July 14, 1975

Harold S. Johnson
(Interviewee)

Jane Rogers
(for   Tri-County Historical Society   )

Source 3 from the University of Tennessee.

3. Form Developed by a Large U.S. History Survey Class at the University of Tennessee, Knoxville, 1984.

This form is to state that I have been interviewed by _____ on
(Interviewer)
_____ on my recollections of the Vietnam War era. I understand that
(date)
this interview will be used in a class project at the University of Tennessee, and that the results will be saved for future historians.

Signature

Date

Sources 4 through 10 are from interviews conducted by the authors. Photographs were supplied by the interviewees.

4. Photograph of John and His Family. Left to Right: John's Father, John, John's Mother, and John's Brother.

John

[*John was born in 1951. His father was a well-to-do and prominent physician, and John grew up in a midwestern town that had a major university. He graduated from high school in 1969 and enrolled in a four-year private college. John dropped out of college in 1971 and returned home to live with his parents. He found work in the community and associated with students at the nearby university.*]

My earliest memory of Vietnam must have been when I was in the seventh grade [1962–1963] and I saw things in print and in *Life* magazine. But I really don't remember much about Vietnam until my senior year in high school [1968–1969].

I came from a repressive private school to college. College was a fun place to hang out, a place where you went after high school. It was just expected of you to go.

CHAPTER 10

A GENERATION
IN WAR AND
TURMOIL: THE
AGONY OF
VIETNAM

At college there was a good deal of apprehension and fear about Vietnam—people were scared of the draft. To keep your college deferments, you had to keep your grades up. But coming from an admittedly well-to-do family, I somehow assumed I didn't have to worry about it too much. I suppose I was outraged to find out that it *could* happen to me.

No, I was outraged that it could happen to *anyone*. I knew who was going to get deferments and who weren't going to get them. And even today my feelings are still ambiguous. On one hand I felt, "You guys were so dumb to get caught in that machine." On the other, and more importantly, it was wrong that *anyone* had to go.

Why? Because Vietnam was a bad war. To me, we were protecting business interests. We were fighting on George III's side, on the wrong side of an anticolonial rebellion. The domino theory didn't impress me at all.[12]

I had decided that I would not go to Vietnam. But I wasn't really worried for myself until Nixon instituted the lottery. I was contemplating going to Canada when my older brother got a CO.[13] I tried the same thing, the old Methodist altar boy gambit, but I was turned down. I was really ticked when I was refused CO status. I thought, "Who are you to tell me who is a pacifist?"

My father was conservative and my mother liberal. Neither one intervened or tried to pressure me. I suppose they thought, "We've done the best we could." By this time I had long hair and a beard. My dad had a hard time.

The antiwar movement was an intellectual awakening of American youth. Young people were concentrated on college campuses, where their maturing intellects had sympathetic sounding boards. Vietnam was part of that awakening. So was drugs. It was part of the protest. You had to be a part of it. Young people were waking up as they got away from home and saw the world around them and were forced to think for themselves.

I remember an argument I had with my father. I told him Ho Chi Minh was a nationalist before he was a Communist, and that this war wasn't really against communism at all. It's true that the Russians were also the bad guys in Vietnam, what with their aid and support of the North Vietnamese, but they had no business there either. When people tried to compare Vietnam to World War II, I just said that no Vietnamese had ever bombed Pearl Harbor.

The draft lottery certainly put me potentially at risk. But I drew a high number, so I knew that it was unlikely that I'd ever be drafted. And yet, I

12. The domino theory, embraced by Presidents Eisenhower, Kennedy, and Johnson, held that if one nation fell to the communists, the result would be a toppling of other nations, like dominoes.
13. CO stands for conscientious objector.

wasn't concerned just for myself. For example, I was aware, at least intellectually, that blacks and poor people were the cannon fodder in Vietnam. But I insisted that *no one,* rich or poor, had to go to fight this war.

Actually I didn't think much about the Vietnamese people themselves. The image was of a kid who could take candy from you one day and hand you a grenade the next. What in hell were we doing in that kind of situation?

Nor did I ever actually know anyone who went to Vietnam. I suppose that, to some extent, I bought the "damn baby napalmers" image. But I never had a confrontation with a veteran of Vietnam. What would I think of him? I don't know. What would he think of me?

Kent State was a real shock to me. I was in college at the time, and I thought, "They were students, just like me." It seemed as if fascism was growing in America.

I was part of the protest movement. After Kent State, we shut down the campus, then marched to a downtown park where we held a rally. In another demonstration, later, I got a good whiff of tear gas. I was dating a girl who collapsed because of the gas. I recall a state policeman coming at us with a club. I yelled at him, telling him what had happened. Suddenly he said, "Here, hold this!" and gave me his club while he helped my date to her feet.

But there were other cops who weren't so nice. I went to the counter-inaugural in Washington in June 1973. You could see the rage on the cops' faces when we were yelling, "One, two, three, four, we don't want your f——ing war!" It was an awakening for me to see that much emotion on the subject coming from the other side. I know that I wasn't very open to other opinions. But the other side *really* was closed.

By '72 their whole machine was falling apart. A guy who gave us a ride to the counter-inaugural was a Vietnam vet. He was going there too, to protest against the war. In fact, he was hiding a friend of his who was AWOL,[14] who simply hid rather than go to Vietnam.

Then Watergate made it all worthwhile—we really had those f——ers scared. I think Watergate showed the rest of the country exactly what kind of "Law and Order" Nixon and his cronies were after!

I have no regrets about what I did. I condemn them all—Kennedy, Johnson, Nixon—for Vietnam. They all had a hand in it. And the war was wrong, in every way imaginable. While I feel some guilt that others went and were killed, and I didn't, in retrospect I feel much guiltier that I wasn't a helluva lot more active. Other than that, I wouldn't change a thing. I can still get angry about it.

14. AWOL is an acronym for "absent without leave."

CHAPTER 10

A GENERATION
IN WAR AND
TURMOIL: THE
AGONY OF
VIETNAM

How will I explain all that to my sons? I have no guilt in terms of "duty towards country." The *real* duty was to fight *against* the whole thing. I'll tell my sons that, and tell them that I did what I did so that no one has to go.

[*John chose not to return to college. He learned a craft, which he practices today. He married a woman who shared his views ("I wouldn't have known anyone on the other side, the way the country was divided"), had two children, and shared the responsibilities of child care. John and his wife are now divorced.*]

5. Photograph of Mike in Vietnam.

Mike

[*Mike was born in 1948. His family owned a farm in western Tennessee, and Mike grew up in a rural environment. He graduated from high school in 1966 and enrolled in a community college not far from his home. After two quarters of poor grades, Mike left the community college and joined the United States Marine Corps in April 1967. He served two tours in Vietnam, the first in 1967–1969 and the second in 1970–1971.*]

I flunked out of college my first year. I was away from home and found out a lot about wine, women and song but not about much else. In 1967 the old system of the draft was still in effect, so I knew that eventually I'd be rotated up and drafted—it was only a matter of time before they got me.

My father served with Stilwell in Burma and my uncle was career military. I grew up on a diet of John Wayne flics. I thought serving in the military was what was expected of me. The Marines had some good options—you could go in for two years and take your chances on the *possibility* of not going to Vietnam. I chose the two-year option. I thought what we were doing in Vietnam was a noble cause. My mother was against the war and we argued a lot about it. I told her that if the French hadn't helped us in the American Revolution, then we wouldn't have won. I sincerely believed that.

I took my six weeks of basic training at Parris Island [South Carolina]. It was sheer hell—I've never been treated like that in my life. Our bus arrived at Parris Island around midnight, and we were processed and sent to our barracks. We had just gotten to sleep when a drill instructor threw a thirty-two gallon garbage can down the center of the barracks and started overturning the metal bunks. We were all over the floor and he was screaming at us. It was that way for six weeks—no one ever talked to us, they shouted. And all our drill instructors geared our basic training to Vietnam. They were always screaming at us, "You're going to go to Vietnam and you're gonna f—— up and you're gonna die."

Most of the people in basic training with me were draftees. My recruiter apologized to me for having to go through boot camp with draftees. But most of the guys I was with were pretty much like me. Oh, there were a few s—— birds, but not many. We never talked about Vietnam—there was no opportunity.

There were a lot of blacks in the Corps and I went through basic training with some. But I don't remember any racial tension until later. There were only two colors in the Marine Corps: light green and dark green. My parents drove down to Parris Island to watch me graduate from basic training, and they brought a black woman with them. She was from Memphis and was the wife of one of the men who graduated with me.

CHAPTER 10

A GENERATION
IN WAR AND
TURMOIL: THE
AGONY OF
VIETNAM

After basic training I spent thirteen weeks in basic infantry training at Camp Lejeune [North Carolina]. Lejeune is the armpit of the world. And the harassment didn't let up—we were still called "scumbag" and "hairbag" and "whale——." I made PFC [private first class] at Lejeune. I was an 03-11 [infantry rifleman].

From Lejeune [after twenty days' home leave] I went to Camp Pendleton [California] for four-week staging. It was at Pendleton where we adjusted our training at Parris Island and Lejeune to the situation in Vietnam. I got to Vietnam right after Christmas 1967.

It was about this time that I became aware of antiwar protests. But as far as I was concerned they were a small minority of malcontents. They were the *protected,* were deferred or had a daddy on the draft board. I thought, "These people are disloyal—they're selling us down the drain."

We were not prepared to deal with the Vietnamese people at all. The only two things we were told was don't give kids cigarettes and don't pat 'em on the heads. We had no cultural training, knew nothing of the social structure or anything. For instance, we were never told that the Catholic minority controlled Vietnam and they got out of the whole thing—we did their fighting for them, while they stayed out or went to Paris or something. We had a Catholic chaplain who told us that it was our *duty* to go out and kill the Cong,[15] that they stood against Christianity. Then he probably went and drank sherry with the top cats in Vietnam. As for the majority of Vietnamese, they were as different from us as night and day. To be honest, I still hate the Vietnamese SOBs.

The South Vietnamese Army was a mixed bag. There were some good units and some bad ones. Most of them were bad. If we were fighting alongside South Vietnam units, we had orders that if we were overrun by Charley[16] that we should shoot the South Vietnamese first—otherwise we were told they'd turn on us.

I can't tell you when I began to change my mind about the war. Maybe it was a kind of maturation process—you can only see so much death and suffering until you begin to wonder what in hell is going on. You can only live like a nonhuman so long.

I came out of country[17] in January of 1969 and was discharged not too long after that. I came home and found the country split over the war. I thought, "Maybe there *was* something to this antiwar business after all." Maybe these guys protesting in the streets weren't wrong.

15. "Cong" was short for the Vietcong, also known as the VC.
16. "Charley" was a euphemism for the Vietcong.
17. "Country" meant Vietnam.

But when I got back home, I was a stranger to my friends. They didn't want to get close to me. I could feel it. It was strange, like the only friends I had were in the Marine Corps. So I re-upped[18] in the Marines and went back to Vietnam with a helicopter squadron.

Kent State happened when I was back in Vietnam. They covered it in *Stars and Stripes*.[19] I guess that was a big turning point for me. Some of the other Marines said, "Hooray! Maybe we should kill more of them!" That was it for me. Those people at Kent State were killed for exercising the same rights we were fighting for for the Vietnamese. But I was in the minority— most of the Marines I knew approved of the shootings at Kent State.

Meanwhile I was flying helicopters into Cambodia every day. I used pot to keep all that stuff out of my mind. Pot grew wild in Vietnam, as wild as the hair on your ass. The Army units would pick it and send it back. The first time I was in Vietnam nobody I knew was using. The second time there was lots of pot. It had a red tinge, so it was easy to spot.

But I couldn't keep the doubts out of my mind. I guess I was terribly angry. I felt betrayed. I would have voted for Lyndon Johnson—when he said we should be there, I believed him. The man could walk on water as far as I was concerned. I would've voted for Nixon in '68, the only time I ever voted Republican in my life. I believed him when he said we'd come home with honor. So I'd been betrayed twice, and Kent State and all that was rattling around in my head.

I couldn't work it out. I was an E5 [sergeant], but got busted for fighting and then again for telling off an officer. I was really angry.

It was worse when I got home. I came back into the Los Angeles airport and was spit on and called a baby killer and a mother raper. I really felt like I was torn between two worlds. I guess I was. I was smoking pot.

I went back to school. I hung around mostly with veterans. We spoke the same language, and there was no danger of being insulted or ridiculed. We'd been damn good, but nobody knew it. I voted for McGovern in '72—he said we'd get out no matter what. Some of us refused to stand up one time when the national anthem was played.

What should we have done? Either not gotten involved at all or go in with the whole machine. With a different attitude and tactics, we could have *won*. But really we were fighting for just a minority of the Vietnamese, the westernized Catholics who controlled the cities but never owned the back-country. No, I take that back. There was no way in hell we could have won that damned war and won anything worth winning.

18. "Re-upped" means reenlisted.
19. *Stars and Stripes* is a newspaper written and published by the armed forces for service personnel.

CHAPTER 10

A GENERATION
IN WAR AND
TURMOIL: THE
AGONY OF
VIETNAM

I went to Washington for the dedication of the Vietnam Veterans Memorial. We never got much of a welcome home or parades. The dedication was a homecoming for me. It was the first time I got the whole thing out of my system. I cried, and I'm not ashamed. And I wasn't alone.

I looked for the names of my friends. I couldn't look at a name without myself reflected back in it [the wall].

One of the reasons I went back to school was to understand that war and myself. I've read a lot about it and watched a lot of TV devoted to it. I was at Khe Sanh and nobody could tell about that who wasn't there. There were six thousand of us. Walter Cronkite said we were there for seventy-two days. I kept a diary—it was longer than that. I'm still reading and studying Vietnam, trying to figure it all out.

[*Mike returned to college, repeated the courses he had failed, and transferred to a four-year institution. By all accounts, he was a fine student. Mike is now employed as a park ranger. He is married, and he and his wife have a child. He is considered a valuable, respected, and popular member of his community. He rarely speaks of his time in the service.*]

6. Photograph of MM, Boot Camp Graduation.

MM[20]

[*MM was born in 1947 and grew up in a midsize southern city. He graduated from high school in 1965. A standout in high school football, he could not get an athletic scholarship to college because of low grades. As a result, he joined the United States Army two months after graduating from high school to take advantage of the educational benefits he would get upon his discharge. He began his basic training in early September 1965.*]

I went into the service to be a soldier. I was really gung ho. I did my basic training at Fort Gordon [Georgia], my AIT [advanced infantry training] at

20. Since MM's first name also is Mike, his initials are used to avoid confusion.

CHAPTER 10

A GENERATION
IN WAR AND
TURMOIL: THE
AGONY OF
VIETNAM

Ford Ord [California], and Ranger school and Airborne at Fort Benning [Georgia].

All of this was during the civil rights movement. I was told that, being black, I had a war to fight at home, not in Vietnam. That got me uptight, because that wasn't what I wanted to do—I'd done some of that in high school.[21] I had one mission accomplished, and was looking for another.

A lot of guys I went into the service with didn't want to go to Nam—they were afraid. Some went AWOL. One guy jumped off the ship between Honolulu and Nam and drowned. Another guy shot himself, trying to get a stateside wound. He accidentally hit an artery and died. Most of us thought they were cowards.

I arrived in Nam on January 12, 1966. I was three days shy of being eighteen years old. I was young, gung ho, and mean as a snake. I was with the Twenty-fifth Infantry as a machine gunner and rifleman. We went out on search and destroy missions.

I did two tours in Vietnam, at my own request. You could make rank[22] faster in Nam and the money was better. I won two silver stars and three bronze stars. For my first silver star, I knocked out two enemy machine guns that had two of our platoons pinned down. They were drawing heavy casualties. The event is still in my mind. Two of the bronze stars I put in my best friend's body bag. I told him I did it for him.

I had a friend who died in my arms, and I guess I freaked a little bit. I got busted[23] seven times. They [the army] didn't like the way I started taking enemy scalps and wearing them on my pistol belt. I kept remembering my friend.

I didn't notice much racial conflict in Nam. In combat, everybody seemed to be OK. I fought beside this [white] guy for eleven months; we drank out of the same canteen. When I got home, I called this guy's house. His mother said, "We don't allow our son to associate with niggers." In Vietnam, I didn't run into much of that.

The Vietnamese hated us. My first day in Vietnam, Westmoreland[24] told us that underneath every Vietnamese was an American. I thought, "What drug is he on?" But they hated us. When we weren't on the scene, the enemy would punish them for associating with us. They would call out to us, "G.I. Number Ten."[25] They were caught between a rock and a hard place.

---

21. MM participated in sit-ins to integrate the city's lunch counters and movie theaters.
22. Earn promotions.
23. Demoted.
24. General William Westmoreland, American commander in Vietnam.
25. "Number Ten" meant bad; no good.

We could have won the war several times. The Geneva Convention[26] wouldn't let us, and the enemy had the home court advantage. To win, it would have taken hard soldiering, but we could have done it. America is a weak country because we want to be everybody's friend. We went in there as friends. We gave food and stuff to the Vietnamese and we found it in the hands of the enemy. We just weren't tough enough.

I got out of the Army in 1970. I was thinking about making the Army a career, and was going to re-enlist. But when they wanted me to go back for a third tour in Vietnam, I got out. Hell, everybody told me I was crazy for doing two.

[*MM used his GI Bill benefits to obtain three years of higher education: two years at two four-year colleges and one in a business school. According to him, however, jobs have been "few and far between." He describes himself as "restless" and reports that automobile backfires still frighten him. He has been married and divorced twice.*]

7. Photograph of Eugene (Second from Right) Marching.

26. The Geneva Convention refers to international agreements for the conduct of war and the treatment of prisoners. The agreements began to be drawn up in the 1860s.

[279]

CHAPTER 10

A GENERATION
IN WAR AND
TURMOIL: THE
AGONY OF
VIETNAM

Eugene

[Eugene was born in 1948 in a large city on the West Coast. He graduated from high school in June 1967 and was drafted in August. Initially rejected because of a hernia, he had surgery to correct that problem and then enlisted in the Marine Corps.]

It was pretty clear from basic training on, no ifs, ands, or buts, that we were going to Vietnam. The DIs[27] were all Vietnam vets, so we were told what to expect when we got there. They'd tell us what to do and all we had to do was do it.

I got to Vietnam in June of 1968. Over there, the majority of blacks stuck together because they had to. In the field was a different story, but in the rear you really caught it. Blacks would catch hell in the rear—fights and things like that. When we went to the movies with Navy guys, they put us in the worst seats. Sometimes they just wanted to start a fight. My whole time in Vietnam I knew only two black NCOs[28] and none above that.

We were overrun three times. You could tell when we were going to get hit when the Vietnamese in our camp (who cleaned up hooches) disappeared. Usually Charley had informants inside our base, and a lot of info slipped out. They were fully aware of our actions and weapons.

When we were in the rear, we cleaned our equipment, wrote letters home, went to movies, and thought a lot about what we'd do when we got out. I had training in high school as an auto mechanic, and I wanted to start my own business.

You had to watch out for the rookies until they got a feel for what was going on. We told one new L.T.,[29] "Don't polish your brass out here or you'll tip us off for sure." He paid us no mind and Charley knocked out him and our radio man one night.

You could get anything over there you wanted [drugs]. Marijuana grew wild in the bush. Vietnamese kids would come up to you with a plastic sandwich bag of twenty-five [marijuana] cigarettes for five dollars. It was dangerous, but we smoked in the bush as well as out. At the O.P.s,[30] everybody knew when the officer would come around and check. We'd pass the word: "Here comes the Man." That's why a lot of guys who came back were so strung out on drugs. And opium—the mamasans[31] had purple teeth because of it.

27. Drill instructors.
28. Noncommissioned officers; sergeants.
29. Lieutenant.
30. Outposts.
31. Old Vietnamese women.

We could have won the war anytime we wanted to. We could have wiped that place off the map. There was a lot of talk that that's what we should have done. But we didn't because of American companies who had rubber and oil interests in Vietnam, and no telling what else. To them, Vietnam was a money-making thing. We were fighting over there to protect those businesses.

It was frustrating. The Army and Marines were ordered to take Hill 881 and we did, but it was costly. A couple of weeks later we just up and left and gave it back.

When I got out [in January 1970], I was a E5.[32] I couldn't find a job. So I talked to an Air Force recruiter. I got a release from the Marines[33] and joined the Air Force. I rigged parachutes and came out in 1975.

I stayed in L.A.[34] until 1977. Then I became a long-distance truck driver. I was doing pretty good when I got messed up in an accident. My truck jackknifed on ice in Pennsylvania and I hit the concrete barrier.

[*Eugene has not worked regularly since the accident. A lawsuit against the trucking company is pending. He is divorced.*]

32. Sergeant.
33. Eugene had four years of reserve obligation.
34. Los Angeles, California.

CHAPTER 10

A GENERATION
IN WAR AND
TURMOIL: THE
AGONY OF
VIETNAM

8. Photograph of Helen at an Army Hospital in Phu Bai, South Vietnam.

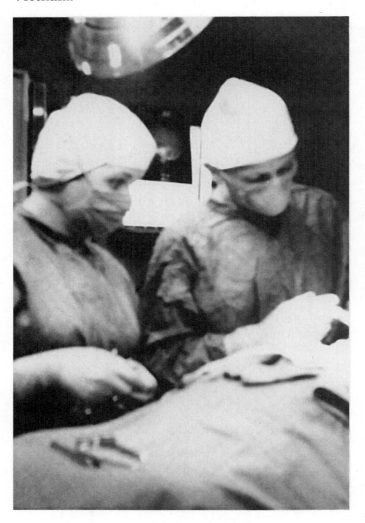

Helen

[*Helen was born in 1942 in Cleveland, Ohio, and grew up there. Since grade school, she had wanted to be a nurse. After graduation from high school, she spent three years in nurses' training to become a registered nurse. She worked for three years in the operating rooms of a major medical facility in Cleveland. In 1966, she joined the United States Navy.*]

I joined the Navy in 1966 and reported to Newport, Rhode Island, for basic training. Our classes consisted of military protocol, military history, and physical education. There was only a passing reference made to our medical assignments and what was expected of us.

I was assigned to the Great Lakes Naval Hospital [outside Chicago]. Although I had been trained and had experience as an operating room surgical nurse, at first I was assigned to the orthopedic wards. It was there that I got my first exposure to mass casualties [from Vietnam]. Depending on the extent of their injuries, we would see patients at Great Lakes about seven to ten days after them being wounded in Vietnam.

I became attached to some of the boys—they were young, scared and badly injured. I remember a Negro who in tears asked for his leg to be taken off—he couldn't stand the smell of it anymore and had been to surgery once too often for the removal of dead tissue. He was in constant pain.

On the wards, we always kept nightlights on. If someone darkened a ward by accident, it produced a sense of terror in the patients. Many were disoriented, and a lot had nightmares.

When I made the decision to go to Vietnam, I volunteered in 1968 and requested duty aboard a hospital ship. It was necessary to extend my time on active duty in order to go. I felt I had a skill that was needed and it was something I felt I personally had to do. I didn't necessarily agree with our policy on being there, but that wasn't the point.

The median age of our troops in Vietnam was nineteen years old. It was like treating our kid brothers. I would have done as much for my own brothers. I know this sounds idealistic, but that's the way I felt then.

The troops got six weeks of staging, preparing them for duty in Vietnam. Most of the nurses were given no preparation, no orientation as to what to expect when you go into a war zone. No one said, "These are the things you'll see," or "These are the things you'll be expected to do."

I was assigned to the U.S.S. *Sanctuary,* which was stationed outside of Da Nang harbor. The *Sanctuary* was a front-line treatment facility. Casualties were picked up in the field combat areas and then brought by Medevac choppers to the ship. During our heaviest months, we logged over seven hundred patient admissions per month. That was at the height of the Tet offensive in January through March, 1968. I had just gotten to Vietnam.

It was terribly intense. There was nothing to shelter you, no one to hold your hand when mass casualties came in. If you had time to think, you'd have thought, "My God, how am I to get through this?" We dealt with multiple amputations, head injuries, and total body trauma. Sometimes injuries were received from our own people caught in crossfires. When all

CHAPTER 10

A GENERATION
IN WAR AND
TURMOIL: THE
AGONY OF
VIETNAM

hell breaks loose at night in the jungle, a nineteen-year-old boy under ambush will fire at anything that moves.

How do you insulate yourself against all this? We relaxed when we could, and we put a lot of stock in friendships (the corpsmen were like our kid brothers). We played pranks and sometimes took the launch ashore to Da Nang. Occasionally we were invited to a party ashore and a helicopter came out for the nurses. The men wanted American women at their parties.

There were some people who had the idea that the only reason women were in the service was to be prostitutes or to get a man. Coming back from Vietnam, I was seated next to a male officer on the plane who said to me, "Boy, I bet you had a great time in Vietnam." I had my seat changed. When I got home and was still in uniform I was once mistaken for a police officer.

On the *Sanctuary,* we had Vietnamese patients too. But our guys were distrustful of them, especially children who had been observed planting mines (probably in exchange for a handful of rice). The Vietnamese were often placed under armed guard. I have friends who were nurses in country who harbor a real hatred for the Vietnamese.

I heard a story of a Vietnamese child running up to a chopper that was evacuating casualties and tossing a grenade into it. Everyone on board was killed in a split second; both crew and casualties, because they paused to help a child they thought needed them. A soldier I knew said, "If they're in the fire zone, they get killed." War really takes you to the lowest level of human dignity. It makes you barbaric.

After Vietnam, I was stationed at the Naval Academy in Annapolis to finish out my duty. There I dealt basically with college students—measles and sports injuries. It was a hard adjustment to make.

In Vietnam, nurses had a great deal of autonomy, and we often had to do things nurses normally aren't allowed to do. You couldn't do those things stateside. Doctors saw it as an encroachment on their areas of practice. I'd been a year under extreme surgical conditions in Vietnam, and then in Annapolis someone would ask me, "Are you sure you know how to start an IV?"[35] It was hard to tame yourself down. Also, in the civilian setting, mediocrity was tolerated. I heard people say, "That's not my job." Nobody would have said that in Vietnam. There, the rules were put aside and everybody did what they could. When we got back to the states, there was no one to wind us down, deprogram us, tell us that Vietnam was an abnormal situation. . . . It was as if no one cared, we were just expected to cope and go on with our lives. . . .

I guess the hardest thing about nursing in Vietnam was the different priorities. Back home, if we got multiple-trauma cases from, say, an auto-

35. Intravenous mechanism.

mobile accident, we always treated the most seriously injured first. In Vietnam, it was often the reverse. I remember working on one soldier who was not badly wounded, and he kept screaming for us to help his buddy, who was seriously wounded. I couldn't tell him that his buddy didn't have a good chance to survive, and so we were passing him by. That was difficult for a lot of us, went against all we'd been trained to do. It's difficult to support someone in the act of dying when you're trained to do all you can to save a life. Even today, I have trouble with patients who need amputations or who have facial injuries.

It is most important to realize that there is a great cost to waging war. Many men are living out their lives in veterans' hospitals as paraplegics or quadriplegics, who in World War II or Korea would not have survived. Most Americans will never see these people—they are hidden away from us. But they are alive.

Maybe the worst part of the war for many of these boys was coming home. The seriously wounded were sent to a military hospital closest to their own homes. Our orthopedic ward at Great Lakes Naval Hospital had forty beds, and it was like taking care of forty kid brothers. They joked around and were supportive of each other. But quite a few of them got "Dear John"[36] letters while they were there. Young wives and girlfriends sometimes couldn't deal with these injuries, and parents sometimes had trouble coping too. All these people were "casualties of war," but I believe that these men especially need our caring and concern today, just as much as they did twenty years ago.

[*On her discharge from the United States Navy in August 1969, Helen returned to nursing. She married in 1972. She and her husband, an engineering physicist, have two children. Helen returned to school and received her B.S. degree in nursing. She is now a coordinator of cardiac surgery and often speaks and writes of her Vietnam experience. She also actively participates in a local veterans' organization. Recently, her daughter offered her mother's services to speak on Vietnam to a high school history class, but she was rebuffed by the teacher, who said, "Who wants to hear about that? We lost that war!" Both Helen and her daughter (who is proud of what her mother did) were offended.*]

36. A "Dear John" letter is one that breaks off a relationship.

CHAPTER 10

A GENERATION
IN WAR AND
TURMOIL: THE
AGONY OF
VIETNAM

9. Photograph of Nick (on Right) with Some Buddies in Vietnam.

Nick

[*Nick was born in 1946 in a midsize southern city. Both his parents were skilled factory workers. Nick graduated from high school in 1964 and wanted to work for the fire department, but he was too young for the civil service. He got a job at the local utility company and got married in 1966. Nick was drafted in 1967. He served with the First Cavalry Division.*]

I suppose I could have gotten a deferment, but I didn't know they were available. My wife was pretty scared when I got drafted, but neither of us ever imagined that I would shirk my duty.

I did my boot camp at Fort Benning [Georgia]. About 80 percent of the people in boot camp with me were draftees. A number of the draftees were black. I had worked with blacks before the Army, had many black friends, and never saw any racial problems. We were then sent to Fort Polk, Louisiana, for advanced infantry training. They had built simulated Vietnamese villages that were very similar to what we later encountered in Vietnam. Overall, we were trained pretty well, but we were still pretty scared.

I arrived in Vietnam on December 12, 1967, and was assigned to go out on "search and destroy" missions. Even though I was prepared mentally, I was still very frightened. I was wounded once when we got ambushed while we were setting up an ambush of our own. Another time I got hit with some shrapnel from a 60 mm mortar. That was at 3:00 A.M. and the medics didn't arrive until 7:30.

I'm not proud of everything I did in Vietnam, but I won't run away from it either. You got so hard at seeing friends killed and things like that. We desecrated their dead, just as they did ours. We used to put our unit's shoulder patches on the VC dead (we nailed 'em on) to get credit for it.

I didn't like the Vietnamese themselves. Most of the civilians were VC sympathizers, and the South Vietnamese army just wouldn't fight. I was in some kind of culture shock. Here we were, trying to help these people, and some of them were living in grass huts. Once I asked myself, "What am I doing here?"

The highest rank I made was sergeant, but I was demoted when I caught a guy in my unit asleep on guard duty and busted him with a shotgun. I was demoted for damaging the shotgun, government property.

I got back to the States in December 1968. There were some protesters at the Seattle airport, but they just marched with signs and didn't harass us at all. Over time, I lost my hostility to the antiwar protesters, although at the time I despised them. Except for Jane Fonda[37] (who went too far), I have no bad feelings for them at all. I have a friend who threatened to run his daughter off because she had a Jane Fonda workout tape.

I'm no hero and didn't do anything special. But college students today need to know that the people who fought in that war are no less important than people who fought in World War I, World War II, or Korea.

---

37. Movie star and antiwar activist Jane Fonda organized shipments of food and medical supplies to North Vietnam and traveled to Vietnam during the war.

CHAPTER 10

A GENERATION
IN WAR AND
TURMOIL: THE
AGONY OF
VIETNAM

[Nick returned to his position with the utility company. He and his wife have two sons, born in 1969 and 1972. He never talked about Vietnam and wanted to throw his medals out, but his wife made him keep them. When his sons started asking questions, he told them about Vietnam. They convinced him to bring his medals out and display them. Since returning from Vietnam, he has never voted "and never will. . . . I have no use for politicians at all." He is now enjoying retirement.]

10. Photograph of Robyn as a College Student.

Robyn

[Robyn was born in 1955 and raised in a Wisconsin farming town of around fifteen hundred people. Her father owned a small construction business and, like many other men in town, had proudly served in World War II. Her mother was a high school teacher. Robyn has three sisters and three brothers, none of whom served in Vietnam.]

I remember starting to watch the war on television when I was about ten. I asked my mother, "How come they're killing each other?" She said that America was the land of freedom and that we were in Vietnam to help make the people free. As a teacher, though, she always encouraged us to think for ourselves and find our own answers.

The guys in town started going away [to Vietnam], and, in a town that size, everybody knows. When my ninth-grade algebra teacher suddenly disappeared, no adults would talk about it. Later, we found out that he had received CO status. In my town, that wasn't much different from being a Communist. The peer pressure was tremendous.

I have always believed the United States is the greatest country in the world, but it's not perfect. The more I heard about the war, the more I realized something was wrong. Although only in high school, I felt obligated to let the government know that I thought it was in the wrong. And yet at no time while I was protesting the war was I *ever* against the guys fighting it. My quarrel was with how the government was running the war.

I recall one of my first "protests." I was in the high school band and we were playing "The Star-Spangled Banner" at a basketball game. Although I stood and played with the rest of the band, I turned my back to the flag. When I came home that night, my father hit me for being disrespectful. So much for the right to free speech we were fighting to protect.

When I left for college in 1973, one brother had just gotten a medical deferral, and another would soon be registering for the draft. The war was becoming more and more personal. I skipped classes to attend rallies and antiwar events, and I wrote lots of letters to politicians. When the POW-MIA bracelets[38] came out, I helped sell them. There were quite a few heated discussions with some protesters who thought that wearing a bracelet (my guy is still MIA) was contrary to the cause. In those days, I tended to "discuss" things in decibels.

My second year of college ended with me skipping classes to watch the televised returns of our POWs. I would have loved to hug each one, so this was my way of saying "Welcome home" and to bear witness. I cried the whole time—for them, for their families, and for all the agony we'd all gone through during the war. Then I dropped out of school and just "vegetated" for a year. My idealistic perceptions of humanity had been severely challenged, and I was drained.

After Vietnam, I got involved in some projects that were targets to help Vietnam vets. One of my best and proudest experiences will always be my

38. Bracelets were worn to show that Prisoners of War and Missing in Action were remembered by the public; they also were intended to urge government action in returning these soldiers.

CHAPTER 10

A GENERATION
IN WAR AND
TURMOIL: THE
AGONY OF
VIETNAM

work at the Vietnam Veterans Memorial in Washington, D.C. I worked at the wall as a volunteer every week for almost ten years. Unlike past memorials, this one doesn't honor the war. It's the Vietnam *Veterans* Memorial, not War Memorial, and it honors those who fought it.

I have seen firsthand its healing effects on vets and their families. And on me. At the wall, the former protester and the Vietnam veteran share something in common—our great sadness for those who were lost and those who haven't yet returned. Vietnam vets also don't seem to have the glorified view of war that older vets do.

The government's lack of support for Vietnam vets (during and after the war) might be part of the reason. If more people were aware of the other side of war, the side the vets saw, they'd have a lot more incentive to work things out. Instead of seeing war as an alternative solution, people would finally realize that war is simply the result of our failure to find a solution.

[*Robyn returned to college and eventually graduated from law school. She worked in Washington, D.C., for a nonprofit education organization and as a government relations consultant. Robyn now works at a public and government relations firm. She continues to work with Vietnam veterans and, in particular, on the POW-MIA issue.*]

 QUESTIONS TO CONSIDER

The interviews in this chapter were conducted between 1985 and 1992. As you read through the seven interviews, try to get a sense of the tone and general meaning of each one. Then try to establish the respective frames of reference for each interviewee by comparing and contrasting their backgrounds. From which socioeconomic class does each person come? From what region of the country? What do you know about their parents and friends? What did they think was expected of them? Why?

After high school, all the interviewees' experiences diverged greatly. Eventually, Mike, MM, Eugene, and Helen enlisted in the armed services.

What reason did each person give (if any) for enlisting? How different were their reasons? For his part, Nick was drafted. What was his reaction to being drafted?

Both John and Robyn became involved in antiwar protests, but for very different reasons. Why did each become involved? Would John and Robyn have agreed on why the war should have been opposed?

Return to the five veterans. What were their feelings about the Vietnamese people? What did they believe were the reasons for American involvement in the war? What were their reactions to events of the times—the draft, antiwar protests, Kent State, race relations in the armed services, what they actually did in Vietnam? What did each one think about the situation of returning veterans? Some of the interviewees seem to have made the adjustment to civilian life better than others. Can you think of why that might have been so? Finally, what do you think each person (veterans and civilians alike) learned from his or her personal experiences during the Vietnam War era?

Now look at the photographs carefully. Are they posed or unposed? For whom might they have been intended? What image of each person is projected? How does each person help to create that image?

The majority of the interviewees have never met one another. Do you think they could meet and talk about the Vietnam era today? What might such a conversation be like?

∞ EPILOGUE ∞

In the spring of 1971, fifteen thousand antiwar demonstrators disrupted daily activities in the nation's capital by blocking the streets with trash, automobiles, and their own bodies. Twelve thousand were arrested, but the protest movement across the country continued. In June, the Pentagon Papers, a secret 1967 government study of the Vietnam War, was published in installments by the *New York Times*. The Pentagon Papers revealed that government spokespersons had lied to the American public about several important events, particularly about the Gulf of Tonkin incident.

As part of his reelection campaign in 1972, President Nixon traveled first to China and then to the Soviet Union and accelerated the removal of American troops from Vietnam. "Peace," his adviser Henry Kissinger announced, "is at hand." Withdrawal was slow and painful and created a new group of refugees—those Vietnamese who had supported the Americans in South Vi-

etnam. Nixon became mired in the Watergate scandal and resigned from office in 1974 under the threat of impeachment. The North Vietnamese entered Saigon in the spring of 1975 and began a "pacification" campaign of their own in neighboring Cambodia. Nixon's successors, Gerald Ford and Jimmy Carter, offered amnesty plans that a relatively small number of draft violators used. Many who were reported Missing in Action (MIA) in Vietnam were never found, either dead or alive. The draft was replaced by a new concept, the all-volunteer army.

The Vietnam veterans who never had their homecoming parades and had been alternately ignored and maligned finally got their memorial. A stark, simple, shiny black granite wall engraved with the names of 58,000 war dead, the monument is located on the mall near the Lincoln Memorial in Washington, D.C. The idea came from Jan Scruggs (the son of a milkman), a Vietnam veteran who was wounded and decorated for bravery when he

CHAPTER 10

A GENERATION
IN WAR AND
TURMOIL: THE
AGONY OF
VIETNAM

was nineteen years old. The winning design was submitted by twenty-year-old Maya Lin, an undergraduate architecture student at Yale University. A representational statue designed by thirty-eight-year-old Frederick Hart, a former antiwar protester, stands near the wall of names. All one hundred United States senators cosponsored the gift of public land, and the money to build the memorial was raised entirely through 650,000 individual public contributions. Not everyone was pleased by the memorial, and some old emotional wounds were reopened. Yet more than 150,000 people attended the dedication cere- monies on Veterans Day 1982, and the Vietnam veterans paraded down Constitution Avenue. Millions of Americans have already viewed the monument, now one of Washington's most visited memorials.

As for the baby boomers, many have children old enough to have served in Operation Desert Storm. Many have put their Vietnam-era experiences behind them as they pursue careers, enjoy middle age, and wait for grandchildren (a new birth cohort). For many, however, Vietnam is a chapter in American history that will never be closed.

CHAPTER 11

DEMOCRACY AND DIVERSITY:
AFFIRMATIVE ACTION IN CALIFORNIA

∽ THE PROBLEM ∽

On November 5, 1996, Californians who went to the polls for the presidential election were asked to vote on several other questions as well. The most controversial was Proposition 209, a proposal to ban all California state programs involving gender preference or race. If the proposal was approved, affirmative action in such areas as state university admissions, state jobs, and state contracts would end. There had been intense campaigning by both supporters and opponents of affirmative action, with both sides invoking ideals of equality and justice. Proposition 209 did pass, with 54 percent of the voters, or over 4.5 million people, approving it.

A coalition of California civil rights groups, joined by the U.S. Department of Justice with President Clinton's support, immediately filed a lawsuit, arguing that Proposition 209 was un-constitutional. As a result of the suit, a California federal district court issued an injunction preventing the implementation of Proposition 209 until the case could be tried and the constitutional question decided.

Is California's situation unique? Not at all, as contemporary observer and author Haynes Johnson has noted. California has always been a "mirror" for what is happening in America, "the pacesetter, the place where national cultural and political trends started."[1] In fact, during the 1990s, affirmative action programs everywhere began to encounter opposition.

What has happened? How has the meaning of equality changed over time? What are the arguments for and

1. Haynes Johnson, *Divided We Fall* (New York: Norton, 1994), p. 98.

[293]

CHAPTER 11

DEMOCRACY
AND DIVERSITY:
AFFIRMATIVE
ACTION IN
CALIFORNIA

against affirmative action? In this chapter, you will examine California as a test case to determine why affirmative action is so controversial today.

BACKGROUND

California became part of the United States as a result of the Mexican-American War (1846–1848). The Treaty of Guadalupe Hidalgo, which ended the war, ceded some two million square miles of Mexican land to the United States. In return, the United States paid Mexico $15 million and also assumed another $3.25 million of American citizens' claims against the Mexican government.

Gold had been discovered earlier, in 1842, by a Mexican rancher who lived about 35 miles north of Los Angeles, but it was a small strike that seemed to run out quickly. Not so the discovery of gold at Sutter's Mill in the Sierra Madre foothills in 1848. The resulting rush of miners and settlers populated California so rapidly that it skipped a territorial stage and became a state as part of the Compromise of 1850.

Rich also in natural resources such as lumber, fish, salt, borax, and range land, California continued to grow rapidly in the second half of the nineteenth century. Immigrants from Japan and China arrived by ship (until the Chinese Exclusion Act of 1882), while settlers from the eastern and midwestern United States arrived via the new transcontinental railroad. In spite of earthquakes and fires, droughts and floods, California was a magnet whose population doubled every twenty years until the mid-1920s, with one-third of the increase due to the birth rate and the remainder from immigration and in-migration from states. Ethnic tensions and violence against minority groups were common.

The early twentieth century also witnessed the growth of new sectors of California's economy, such as the birth of the Hollywood film industry, the development of the oil industry, the establishment of wineries, and the rise of the agribusinesses of the Central Valley. At the same time, Progressive reformers moved to restrain the political influence of railroads and big business and began efforts to conserve some of the natural beauty of the state, such as that of the Yosemite area. Ethnic tensions were still evident, however, as Chinese residents were confined to Chinatowns, and Japanese were denied access to property ownership and education. During the depression of the 1930s, Mexican Americans along with Mexican citizens were forcibly returned to Mexico. Even the displaced Okies and other Americans fleeing the dust bowl of the plains states were often barred from California towns and cities.

The two worst outbreaks of prejudiced behavior in California occurred during World War II. The forced relocation and internment of over 100,000 Japanese, two-thirds of whom were U.S. citizens, caused them enormous psychological and financial hardship. Although most returned to California after the war, only about 10 percent of their assets remained; the majority had to start all over again. The other instance, called the "zoot suit riots" because of the gangster-style clothes worn by some young Mexican Americans, took place in 1943, when about two hundred U.S. Navy sailors went on a rampage in East Los Angeles, attacking members of the neighborhood Hispanic gangs. The Los Angeles Police Department stood by and watched, maintaining that it was the job of the shore patrol and the military police to control the rioters. Only after a formal protest by the Mexican government did the riots finally end.

The cold war that followed World War II brought prosperity to large areas of California. Between the 1940s and the 1970s, the U.S. government poured $100 billion into defense-related industries such as aircraft and electronics. By the 1960s, the golden state was also known for its youth culture, which encompassed surfers, hippies, and a music scene as varied as the folksongs of Joan Baez, the surfer sound of the Beach Boys, and the hard rock of Jefferson Airplane. A decade later, California had established a well-regarded system of higher education: 8 state universities, 21 state colleges, and 100 junior or community colleges. During the 1960s, the U.S. government had promoted civil rights through a series of initiatives such as affirmative action, the Civil Rights Act of 1964, and the Voting Rights Act of 1965. California, with its increasingly diverse population, also struggled to provide its minority groups

and women with increased access to jobs, to government contracts, and to higher education.

But the sixties, a decade that seemed in some ways to hold out the promise of a better life for all, had a darker side, even in California. Militant Native Americans occupied Alcatraz Island in San Francisco Bay as a symbolic gesture of cultural and economic protest. Cesar Chavez, leader of the United Farm Workers, exposed the terrible living conditions and exploitation of the migrant agricultural workers whom he was trying to organize. The *bracero* (day laborer) program that had permitted "temporary" work by immigrant Mexicans ended in 1964, but illegal (or "undocumented") workers continued to pour across the border. At the same time, more public concern focused on the young people in the barrios who were deeply involved in gangs. The rock concerts, protest marches, and demonstrations of the sixties were increasingly marked by violence.

Preceded by smaller riots in eastern cities and followed by riots in other major cities, the Watts riot of 1965 in Los Angeles shocked many Americans with its violence and revealed poverty and despair in the midst of what had appeared to be prosperity and optimism. After an incident involving a drunk-driving arrest, African American rioters looted and burned buildings in that inner-city ghetto, where the population was ten times greater in 1965 than it had been in 1940. During the six days that the riot lasted, it spread to adjoining areas, and the National Guard was called out to help contain it. Thirty-four people were

CHAPTER 11

DEMOCRACY
AND DIVERSITY:
AFFIRMATIVE
ACTION IN
CALIFORNIA

killed; more than a thousand were injured; and $40 million worth of property was damaged or destroyed. In 1970, riots broke out in the Hispanic section of Los Angeles. Rioting occurred again in Los Angeles in 1992, after the acquittal of several white police officers who had been videotaped while brutally beating a black motorist.

During the 1970s, 1980s, and 1990s, California experienced major changes in its economy, population patterns, and politics. The economy, particularly the large sector dependent upon federal defense spending, plunged into a recession as cold war tensions decreased and American foreign policy changed. Blue-collar jobs contracted; low-paying jobs in the service sector expanded only slightly; and as technical and communications skills became more important for job seekers, access to good education became crucial.

Equally striking were changes in the population. After 1965, when the United States began to loosen immigration restrictions, the country experienced another "new" immigration: from Latin America, especially Mexico, and from Asia and the Pacific Islands. For example, between 1970 and 1983, over one million Hispanics, Asians, and other foreign-born people moved to the county of Los Angeles. Although African Americans are currently the largest minority group in the United States (about 12.5 percent of the population, according to the 1990 census), Hispanics and Asians and Pacific Islanders are the fastest-growing groups. In California, in 1990, the 7.6 million Hispanics were the largest minority group, followed by the 2.8 million Asian and Pacific Islanders and the 2.2 million African

Americans. It is estimated that in the year 2000, Hispanics will make up over 30 percent of California's population; Asians, 14 percent; and African Americans, just under 7 percent. Combined, these groups will compose 51 percent of the state's population. Because of immigration, California has grown so rapidly that Hispanics and Asians have often crowded into poorer inner-city areas such as Watts, where African Americans were already living. Conflicts have increased between the African Americans and some of the newer immigrants, such as Korean store owners, and even occur at times between earlier immigrants such as the Chinese and the newer arrivals. Since the late 1960s, politics has reflected the new ethnic and racial identities and awareness.

As the California economy worsened and the racial and ethnic composition of the state's population continued to change, the practice of affirmative action came under increasingly critical scrutiny, especially with regard to access to the better universities and colleges. As Professor Steven Cahn[2] has pointed out, two different kinds of affirmative action have developed during the past thirty-six years. In a 1961 executive order, President Kennedy called for *procedural* affirmative action to ensure that job applicants would not be discriminated against because of national origin, race, religion, or creed. By 1965, President Johnson had prohibited discrimination on the basis of gender and called for the development of affirmative action plans to promote full employment of women

2. Steven Cahn, "Two Concepts of Affirmative Action," *Academe*, January–February, 1997, pp. 14, 16.

and minorities. During President Nixon's administration in the 1970s, *preferential* affirmative action required goals and timetables to correct the "under-utilization"[3] of women and minorities. In some instances, separate lists of African Americans, Asian Americans, Hispanic Americans,[4] and Caucasian Americans have been used for job openings, promotions, and college admissions in a conscious effort to provide such diversity.

Thus, the intent of affirmative action has been to provide more nearly equal economic and educational opportunities for two very different categories of people who have previously suffered discrimination: members of racial and ethnic minority groups, and women. There is no doubt that affirmative action programs have offered women new options in the areas of employment and government contracts. However, women still do not earn as much as men with similar levels of education and experience, nor are women usually found in upper-management or administrative positions. Sexism, like racism, remains in many areas of American society and institutions. Nevertheless, gender is a category that includes females of all classes, races, and ethnic groups.

Although issues of gender and affirmative action are very important, this chapter focuses on affirmative action for members of racial and ethnic minority groups, and to a lesser extent, on some related socioeconomic issues. As we have seen, California already has a very diverse population and is the home of many different cultures. What happens in California also tends to reflect what is happening in the nation as a whole. On the basis of the 1990 census, population experts estimate that by the year 2020, Hispanics will make up 16 percent of the U.S. population; African Americans, 14 percent; and Asian Americans, 7 percent. By 2050, these groups, along with Native Americans, will be approximately 50 percent of the U.S. population. The problems in reconciling democracy and diversity, in providing equality and justice for all Americans, raise some very difficult and sensitive issues. Underlying these issues, of course, are our own attitudes about other races and cultures. How has the meaning of equality changed since 1776? What are the pros and cons of affirmative action? Why is affirmative action so controversial?

THE METHOD

One definition of racism is expecting certain kinds of thought patterns or behavior just because of a person's racial background. Or racism may mean treating a person differently merely because of his or her race. However it may be expressed, racism is still pre-

3. Under-utilization means that there are fewer people in an employment category—for example, African American history professors—than the number of African Americans receiving doctorates in history would lead you reasonably to expect.

4. Hispanics may be of any race.

CHAPTER 11

DEMOCRACY
AND DIVERSITY:
AFFIRMATIVE
ACTION IN
CALIFORNIA

sent in American society. Prejudice against members of ethnic minority groups, whether Hispanics, Asians, Pacific Islanders, or others, sometimes is blatant and direct, as in incidents involving name-calling on college campuses and even in corporate boardrooms. At other times it is subtle, absorbed almost unthinkingly from images in television, films, newspapers, books, and so forth. Unfortunately, as one professor of American history noted recently, discussing racial or ethnic issues in the classroom is very difficult, "like walking on eggshells."[5] Many white students are afraid that they will say something that will offend minority students; some politically conservative students believe that their ideas will be dismissed as "racist" without any discussion; some minority students either doubt that such discussions are worthwhile or fear that they will get angry with their classmates. Yet we *must* talk about race, ethnicity, equality, and justice because what makes American democracy work is not simply a representative system of government, but also what Americans think and believe as well as how they act in their daily lives.

In this chapter, you will be using some analytical skills that you learned in previous chapters and practicing the skills necessary for discussing sensitive issues. You will begin by analyzing how the American concept or ideal of equality has changed over time. (California's Proposition 209 illus-

5. Robbie Lieberman, "Walking on Eggshells? Teaching Recent U.S. History in the 1990s," *Organization of American Historians' Newsletter,* November 1995, p. 3.

trates the challenge to affirmative action.) Next, you will identify arguments for and against affirmative action in the 1990s. You will see those arguments in a variety of sources including speeches, articles, statistics, and opinion polls.

Describing historical changes in the meanings of words and listing pro-and-con arguments from historical evidence can be done by most students fairly easily and dispassionately. Inevitably, however, the evidence in this problem leads into the present and one's own value systems and judgments. These beliefs are very important to each of us and involve our convictions and emotions.

When we analyze a historical person's words or actions, we try to understand why that individual in that place or time might have spoken or acted a particular way. As you learned in the preceding chapter, frame of reference (unique, personal background), as well as the times in which one lives, can be very influential in forming value systems and judgments. In the same way, each of your classmates has developed attitudes and beliefs from a particular place, background, and time period. Recognizing that others around you may not share your beliefs, try to listen to others fully and respectfully, allowing them sufficient uninterrupted time to express their points of view. The goal of this kind of discussion is to hear and to understand—although not necessarily to share or to approve of—other people's ideas about diversity, equality, and justice.

The evidence is divided into three sections: (1) the changing meanings of equality (Sources 1–5); (2) the challenge to affirmative action in California (Source 6); and (3) arguments for and against affirmative action (Sources 8–15). Sources 1 through 3 are the classic statements of American ideals. In Source 4, Abraham Lincoln tries to explain his understanding of equality between whites and blacks on the eve of the Civil War. Over one hundred years later, President Lyndon Johnson describes what he thinks equality means (Source 5). Source 6 consists of Proposition 209, called by its supporters the California Civil Rights Initiative.

Source 7 consists of excerpts from a landmark decision of the U.S. Supreme Court, in the case of *Regents of the University of California v. Bakke.* Alan Bakke was an aerospace engineer who wanted to become a physician. He applied twice to the University of California medical school at Davis and was rejected both times. After discovering that the school had reserved for members of racial minorities sixteen of the one hundred admissions places, Bakke sued, claiming that there was now "reverse discrimination" because less-qualified members of minority groups were being admitted instead of better-qualified whites. Sources 8 through 11 present differing opinions about affirmative action from four prominent African Americans: Ward Connerly is a well-to-do land consultant, member of the Board of Regents of the University of California, and leader of the campaign to pass Proposition 209. Retired General Colin Powell commanded American forces during the Gulf War and was widely suggested as a potential vice-presidential candidate in 1996. Shelby Steele is a professor at San Jose State University, California, and Thomas Sowell is a nationally syndicated newspaper columnist and fellow at the Hoover Institution in Stanford, California.

Scholastic Aptitude Test (SAT) scores (see Source 12), along with high school grades, are used by nearly all colleges and universities to predict success in college. Responding to criticism of the SATs, the College Board has worked in recent years to reduce cultural or racial biases in the questions, although standardized test-taking itself may be culturally biased. Other factors, such as possessing athletic skills or being the child of an alumnus or of a generous donor to the school, may also be considered for admissions. However, SAT scores are still a major factor in determining most admissions to top colleges and universities. Source 12 is a chart presenting SAT scores by racial and ethnic group as well as by family income.

Finally, you will be reading a public opinion poll (Source 14) and excerpts from two speeches about affirmative action: Republican presidential candidate Bob Dole's speech in San Diego, California, in 1996 and President Bill Clinton's speech in the same city in 1997 (Sources 13 and 15).

CHAPTER 11
DEMOCRACY
AND DIVERSITY:
AFFIRMATIVE
ACTION IN
CALIFORNIA

∽ THE EVIDENCE ∽

THE CHANGING MEANINGS OF EQUALITY

1. Excerpt from the Declaration of Independence, 1776.

We hold these truths to be self-evident: That all men are created equal; that they are endowed by their Creator with certain unalienable rights; that among these are life, liberty, and the pursuit of happiness. . . .

2. The Motto of the United States.

E Pluribus Unum ("From many, one")

3. The Pledge of Allegiance, 1942.[6]

I pledge allegiance to the flag of the United States of America, and to the Republic for which it stands, one nation, under God, indivisible, with liberty and justice for all.

Source 4 quoted in Arthur Zilversmit, ed., *Lincoln on Black and White: A Documentary History* (Belmont, Calif.: Wadsworth, 1971), pp. 47–48.

4. Excerpts from Abraham Lincoln's Fourth Debate with Stephen A. Douglas, at Charleston, Illinois, 1858.

I have never hesitated to say, and I do not now hesitate to say, that I think, there is a physical difference between the white and black races which I believe will for ever forbid the two races living together on terms of social and political equality. And inasmuch as they cannot so live, while they do remain together there must be the position of superior and inferior, and I as much as any other man am in favor of having the superior position

6. Originally published in 1892 in a boys' magazine, the Pledge was reworded in the 1920s and became official in 1942. The words "under God" were added in 1954.

assigned to the white race. I say upon this occasion I do not perceive that because the white man is to have the superior position the negro should be denied everything. I do not understand that because I do not want a negro woman for a slave I must necessarily want her for a wife. . . . My understanding is that I can just let her alone. . . . I will add to this that I have never seen to my knowledge a man, woman or child who was in favor of producing a perfect equality, social and political, between negroes and white men.

Source 5 quoted in Lee Rainwater and William L. Yancey, eds., *The Moynihan Report and the Politics of Controversy* (Cambridge, Mass.: MIT Press, 1967), pp. 126–127.

5. Excerpts from President Lyndon Johnson's Speech at Howard University, 1965.

But freedom is not enough. You do not wipe away the scars of centuries by saying: Now you are free to go where you want, do as you desire, and choose the leaders you please.

You do not take a person who, for years, has been hobbled by chains and liberate him, bring him up to the starting line of a race and then say, "you are free to compete with all the others," and still justly believe that you have been completely fair.

Thus it is not enough just to open the gates of opportunity. All our citizens must have the ability to walk through those gates. . . .

To this end, equal opportunity is essential, but not enough. Men and women of all races are born with the same range of abilities. But ability is not just the product of birth. Ability is stretched or stunted by the family you live with, and the neighborhood you live in, by the school you go to and the poverty or the richness of your surroundings. It is the product of a hundred unseen forces playing upon the infant, the child, and the man. . . .

CHAPTER 11

DEMOCRACY
AND DIVERSITY:
AFFIRMATIVE
ACTION IN
CALIFORNIA

THE CHALLENGE TO AFFIRMATIVE ACTION

Source 6 from "Text of Proposition 209," *San Jose Mercury News*, September 20, 1996.

6. Excerpts from Proposition 209, the California Civil Rights Initiative, 1996.

a) The state shall not discriminate against, or grant preferential treatment to, any individual or group on the basis of race, sex, color, ethnicity, or national origin in the operation of public employment, public education, or public contracting. . . .

c) Nothing in this section shall be interpreted as prohibiting bona fide qualifications based on sex which are reasonably necessary to the normal operation of public employment, public education, or public contracting. . . .

e) Nothing in this section shall be interpreted as prohibiting action which must be taken to establish or maintain eligibility for any federal program, where ineligibility would result in a loss of federal funds to the state.

f) For the purposes of this section, *state* shall include, but not necessarily be limited to, the state itself, any city, county, city and county, public university system, including the University of California, community college district, school district, special district, or any other political subdivision or governmental instrumentality of or within the state. . . .

ARGUMENTS FOR AND AGAINST AFFIRMATIVE ACTION

Source 7 from *Regents of the University of California v. Bakke,* 438 U.S. 265 (1978).

7. Excerpts from *Regents of the University of California v. Bakke,* 1978.

If petitioner's [the University of California's] purpose is to assure within its student body some specified percentage of a particular group merely because of its race or ethnic origin, such a preferential purpose must be rejected. . . . Preferring members of any one group for no reason other than race or ethnic origin is discrimination for its own sake. This the Constitution forbids. . . .

Physicians serve a heterogeneous population. An otherwise qualified medical student with a particular background—whether it be ethnic, geographic, culturally advantaged or disadvantaged—may bring to a professional school of medicine experiences, outlook, and ideas that enrich the training of its student body and better equip its graduates to render with understanding their vital service to humanity.

Ethnic diversity, however, is only one element in a range of factors a university may properly consider in attaining the goal of a heterogeneous student body. . . .

Justice Lewis Powell

Source 8 quoted in *New York Times,* April 18, 1996, p. A1; April 29, 1996, p. A27.

8. Ward Connerly, 1996.

Nobody ever gave me any race or sex preferences when I came into the cold world 56 years ago, and I made it anyway—high school, college, my own big business, important friends. If I could make it, anybody can, because the playing field is a lot closer to level now. The truth is that preferences at this point are not just reverse discrimination, they're degrading to people who accept them. They've got to go.

The greatest harm caused by lowering the admission requirements for blacks is the personal damage done to students who are the "beneficiaries" of such policies. Do we not understand that these young men and women will soon be required to compete in a world that will not give them any concessions? . . .

People tend to perform at the level of competition. When the bar is raised, we will rise to the occasion. That is exactly what black students will do in a society that has equal standards for all.

Source 9 from Shelby Steele, *The Content of Our Character* (New York: Harper Perennial, 1990), pp. 94–96, 143–144.

9. Shelby Steele, 1990.

Black though I may be, it is impossible for me to sit in my single-family house with two cars in the driveway and a swing set in the backyard and *not* see the role class has played in my life. . . .

CHAPTER 11

DEMOCRACY
AND DIVERSITY:
AFFIRMATIVE
ACTION IN
CALIFORNIA

What became clear to me is that people like myself, my friend, and middle-class blacks in general are caught in a very specific double bind that keeps two equally powerful elements of our identity at odds with each other. The middle-class values by which we were raised—the work ethic, the importance of education, the value of property ownership, of respectability, of "getting ahead," of stable family life, of initiative, of self-reliance, et cetera—are, in themselves, raceless and even assimilationist. They urge us toward participation in the American mainstream, toward integration, toward a strong identification with the society, and toward the entire constellation of qualities that are implied in the word individualism. . . .

But the particular pattern of racial identification that emerged in the sixties and that still prevails today urges middle-class blacks (and all blacks) in the opposite direction. This pattern asks us to see ourselves as an embattled minority, and it urges an adversarial stance toward the mainstream and an emphasis on ethnic consciousness over individualism. It is organized around an implied separatism.

The opposing thrust of these two parts of our identity results in the double bind of middle-class blacks. There is no forward movement on either plane that does not constitute backward movement on the other. . . .

Most of the white students I talked with spoke as if from under a faint cloud of accusation. There was always a ring of defensiveness in their complaints about blacks. A white student I spoke to at UCLA told me: "Most white students on this campus think the black student leadership here is made up of oversensitive crybabies who spend all their time looking for things to kick up a ruckus about." A white student at Stanford said, "Blacks do nothing but complain and ask for sympathy when everyone really knows that they don't do well because they don't try. If they worked harder, they could do as well as everyone else."

That these students felt accused was most obvious in their compulsion to assure me that they were not racist. . . . I think it was the color of my skin itself that accused them.

. . . My skin not only accused them; it judged them. And this judgment was a sad gift of history that brought them to account whether they deserved such accountability or not. It said that wherever and whenever blacks were concerned, they had reason to feel guilt. And whether it was earned or unearned, I think it was guilt that set off the compulsion in these students to disclaim. I believe it is true that, in America, black people make white people feel guilty.

Source 10 quoted in *New York Times,* June 8, 1996, p. B8.

10. Colin Powell, 1996.

There are those who rail against affirmative action preferences, while living lives of preference, who do not understand that the progress achieved over the past generation must be continued if we wish to bless future generations. . . . We must fight misguided government efforts that seek to shut it all down. . . . When one black man graduates from college for every one hundred who go to jail, we still need affirmative action. When half of all African American men between 24 and 35 years of age are without full-time employment, we need affirmative action.

Source 11 quoted in *Knoxville News Sentinel,* July 12, 1997, p. A8.

11. Thomas Sowell, 1997.

Crucial facts have been left out in much of the hysteria about declining black enrollments at the University of California at Berkeley in the wake of the end of affirmative action policies there. . . .

During the decade of the 1980s, Berkeley's rapid increase in the number of black students on campus did not translate into comparable increases in the number of blacks actually graduating. . . .

Where group body count has been the overriding consideration, minority students who were perfectly capable of graduating from a good college have been artificially turned into failures by being admitted to high-pressure campuses where only students with exceptional academic backgrounds can survive. . . .

Despite much hysteria over the fact that there is only one black student entering Berkeley's law school this year [in 1997, after affirmative action admissions were discontinued], 15 were admitted—and 14 chose to go somewhere else. These other places included Harvard, Stanford, and the like, so don't shed tears over these students, either.

Not only have double standards produced needless educational failures among minority students, they have polarized the races by producing great resentments among white students. It has been a policy under which both groups have lost, though in different ways—and in which the country as a whole has lost. . . .

CHAPTER 11

DEMOCRACY
AND DIVERSITY:
AFFIRMATIVE
ACTION IN
CALIFORNIA

Source 12 from the College Entrance Examination Board. Cited in Dana Y. Takagi, *The Retreat from Race* (New Brunswick, N.J.: Rutgers University Press, 1992), p. 200.

12. SAT Scores by Race and Class, 1991.

Mean SAT Scores by Race and by Class, 1991

Income	Black		Asian		White	
	Verbal	Math	Verbal	Math	Verbal	Math
Less than $10,000	321	358	340	485	407	452
$10,000–$20,000	334	370	353	499	416	457
$20,000–$30,000	348	381	393	512	423	466
$30,000–$40,000	361	392	414	523	429	474
$40,000–$50,000	371	403	435	535	437	484
$50,000–$60,000	376	408	449	546	445	494
$60,000–$70,000	386	417	456	556	454	502
$70,000 or more	413	447	482	590	471	526

Source 13 quoted in *New York Times,* October 29, 1996, p. A21.

13. Excerpts from Presidential Candidate Bob Dole's Speech, San Diego, California, 1996.

Now we've reached another turning point, this time for quality and opportunity in America. And the California Civil Rights Initiative allows the voters of this state to endorse a great principle, the principle that racial distinctions have no place in our lives or in our laws. . . .

. . . We believe it's wrong to use quotas, set-asides[7] and other preferences that serve only to pit one American against another American, or group against group. . . .

It is true that many of us in the years following 1964—and I did—supported some race-conscious measures designed to speed the process of inclusion, a measure that was supposed to be transitional, transitional and temporary. But it didn't work. . . .

But this was a blind alley in the search for equal justice. . . . Programs that started as temporary and limited have become permanent and broad. . . .

7. A set-aside is a percentage of the contract or subcontracts on public projects that is reserved for minority businesses to bid on.

And I just want to end this on a positive note. We must bring quality education to every child in every community. And I believe the surest route to economic mobility for all Americans lies in the access to a good school. Letting parents choose the best school for their children is perhaps the most urgent civil rights issue of our time. . . .

And finally, we must bring a growing economy to every community. . . . Give people an opportunity to make it in the private sector. They don't need quotas and preferences.

Source 14 from Gallup Organization, "Black/White Relations," June 10, 1997. <http://gallup.com/poll/special race>.

14. Summary of Gallup Poll on Black-White Relations, June 10, 1997.

There are major differences in the perceptions of blacks and whites about the status of race relations in this country today. Whites are more positive than blacks on a variety of perceptual measures of how well blacks are faring in our society, and how they are treated in the local community. These gaps are in some instances smaller than they were in the 1960's, but have not narrowed in recent years.

Whites also tend to view themselves as having very little personal prejudice against blacks, but perceive that "other" whites in their area have much higher levels of prejudice against blacks. Blacks also ascribe to whites significantly higher levels of racial prejudice than whites give themselves. Blacks claim that they have little prejudice against whites. . . .

. . . There has thus been a significant decline in the past several decades in the number of whites who express overtly prejudicial sentiments.

Whites and blacks have distinctly different views on the role of the government—perhaps building off of their differential perceptions of the status of race relations in the U.S. today. Whites want the number of affirmative action programs to decrease or at the least stay the same, and feel that blacks should help themselves rather than relying on the government. Blacks hold the contrary views.

The average white American tends to live, work and send their child to school in environments which are mostly or all white. Blacks, on the other hand, have relatively high degrees of contact in these everyday settings with whites. Less than a majority of blacks live in mostly or all black neighborhoods, and only a fourth send their children to schools that are mostly or all black. Both blacks and whites, however, are very highly likely to worship only with members of their race.

CHAPTER 11

DEMOCRACY
AND DIVERSITY:
AFFIRMATIVE
ACTION IN
CALIFORNIA

Source 15 from "Remarks of the President at University of California at San Diego Commencement," June 14, 1997 (The White House, Office of the Press Secretary).

15. Excerpts from President Bill Clinton's Speech in San Diego, California, June 14, 1997.

To be sure, there is old, unfinished business between black and white Americans, but the classic American dilemma has now become many dilemmas of race and ethnicity. We see it in the tension between black and Hispanic customers and their Korean or Arab grocers; in a resurgent anti-Semitism even on some college campuses; in a hostility toward new immigrants from Asia to the Middle East to the former communist countries to Latin America and the Caribbean—even those whose hard work and strong families have brought them success in the American Way.

We see a disturbing tendency to wrongly attribute to entire groups, including the white majority, the objectionable conduct of a few members. If a black American commits a crime, condemn the act—but remember that most African Americans are hard-working, law-abiding citizens. If a Latino gang member deals drugs, condemn the act—but remember that the vast majority of Hispanics are responsible citizens who also deplore the scourge of drugs in our life. If white teenagers beat a young African American boy almost to death just because of his race, for God's sakes [sic] condemn the act—but remember the overwhelming majority of white people will find it just as hateful. If an Asian merchant discriminates against her customers of another minority group, call her on it—but remember, too, that many, many Asians have borne the burden of prejudice and do not want anyone else to feel it. . . .

In our efforts to extend economic and educational opportunity to all our citizens, we must consider the role of affirmative action. I know affirmative action has not been perfect in America—that's why two years ago we began an effort to fix the things that are wrong with it—but when used in the right way, it has worked.

It has given us a whole generation of professionals in fields that used to be exclusive clubs. . . . There are more African American, Latino and Asian American lawyers and judges, scientists and engineers, accountants and executives than ever before.

But the best example of successful affirmative action is our military. Our armed forces are diverse from top to bottom. . . . And, more important, no one questions that they are the best in the world. . . .

There are those who argue that scores on standardized tests should be the sole measure of qualification for admissions to colleges and universities.

But many would not apply the same standard to the children of alumni or those with athletic ability. . . .

I believe a student body that reflects the excellence and the diversity of the people we will live and work with has independent educational value. . . .

And beyond the educational value to you, it has a public interest because you will learn to live and work in the world you will live in better. When young people sit side by side with people of many different backgrounds, they do learn something that they can take out into the world. And they will be more effective citizens.

Many affirmative action students excel. They work hard, they go out and serve the communities that need them for their expertise and role model. If you close the door on them, we will weaken our greatest universities and it will be more difficult to build the society we need in the 21st century. . . .

Let me say, I know that the people of California voted to repeal affirmative action without any ill motive. The vast majority of them simply did it with a conviction that discrimination and isolation are no longer barriers to achievement. But consider the results. Minority enrollments in law school and other graduate programs are plummeting for the first time in decades. . . .

. . . To those who oppose affirmative action, I ask you to come up with an alternative. I would embrace it if I could find a better way. And to those of us who still support it, I say we should continue to stand for it, we should reach out to those who disagree or are uncertain and talk about the practical impact of these issues, and we should never be thought unwilling to work with those who disagree with us to find new ways to lift people up and bring people together. . . .

∽ QUESTIONS TO CONSIDER ∽

What do you think the word *equal* meant to the authors of the Declaration of Independence in 1776 (Source 1)? What groups of people were probably excluded, and why? Do you think it is possible to relate the United States motto "From many, one" (Source 2) to our diverse population? Should we try? Why or why not? What, if anything, should the government do to ensure "liberty and justice for all" (Source 3)? What are Lincoln's views on equality between whites and blacks (Source 4)? Why did he use the example of the African American woman? Do you think that he was viewed as a liberal or as a conservative in 1858? Why? President Johnson's speech (Source 5) was intended especially for African Americans but obviously has

CHAPTER 11

DEMOCRACY
AND DIVERSITY:
AFFIRMATIVE
ACTION IN
CALIFORNIA

implications for all Americans. Why did he say that "freedom is not enough"?

In this chapter, we have represented the challenge to affirmative action by California's Proposition 209, although Texas, Mississippi, and several other states have recently proposed similar measures. Why, do you think, did Proposition 209's supporters call it the California Civil Rights Initiative? Sections we have omitted explain that the law would not be retroactive, that the remedies would be the same as they currently were for discrimination cases, and that any section in conflict with a federal law could be dropped. What exactly would the law cover? What do you think section c means?

When Alan Bakke sued for admission to medical school, claiming that he was being discriminated against because he was white, the U.S. Supreme Court had to consider the constitutionality of "racially conscious" university admissions programs. Reread the excerpts from Justice Powell's opinion carefully. What is he saying about racial quotas? about the relationship between race and diversity? about the needs of society?

Sources 8, 9, 10, and 11 represent the beliefs of four middle-class or upper-class professional African American men. What major points does each make? On what issues do they disagree?

What is the relationship between SAT scores and income (Source 12)? If *only* SAT combined math and verbal scores were used, which group would have the most college admissions? the second-most? the fewest? Would giving preference to students from families whose income is below $10,000 and using combined SAT scores change these results? If so, how? What factors might account for these differences in the scores?

What major reasons does Bob Dole give for opposing affirmative action? What do you think are the most significant findings of the 1997 Gallup Poll on race relations? What major reasons does President Bill Clinton give for supporting affirmative action? What do *you* think about affirmative action? Finally, having studied all the evidence, can you describe how the meaning of *equality* has changed since the American Revolution? Why is affirmative action so controversial today?

EPILOGUE

One of the major reasons that we study American history is to understand how we, as a nation, reached where we are today. Although all Americans agree that a democracy like ours must provide equality and justice for all, we often disagree among ourselves about what these goals mean

and how we can best achieve them. Furthermore, the historical record of the relationships between the dominant white Euro-American society and Native Americans, African Americans, Hispanic Americans, and Asian Americans is filled with shocking examples of injustice and inequality.

There are no easy answers to the complex issues raised by this chapter. Yet a democracy is not simply a static form of representative government, but rather a dynamic, constantly changing political, economic, and social system based on shared, deeply held beliefs. In the twenty-first century, there is no doubt that the very concept of "minority groups" will be altered by changes in the composition of our population. What will not be altered is our commitment to achieving equality and justice for all.

TEXT CREDITS